Social Inequality

Development and Inequality in the Market Economy

The purpose of this series is to encourage and foster analytic and policy-oriented work on market-based reform in developing and post-socialist countries. Special attention will be devoted in the series to exploring the effects of free market policies on social inequality and sustainable growth and development.

Editor:
Andrés Solimano

Editorial Board:
Alice Amsden
François Bourguignon
William Easterly
Patricio Meller
Vito Tanzi
Lance Taylor

Titles in the Series:

Andrés Solimano, Editor. *Road Maps to Prosperity: Essays on Growth and Development*
Andrés Solimano, Editor. *Social Inequality: Values, Growth, and the State*

Social Inequality
Values, Growth, and the State

Andrés Solimano, Editor

Ann Arbor

THE UNIVERSITY OF MICHIGAN PRESS

Copyright © by the University of Michigan 1998
All rights reserved
Published in the United States of America by
The University of Michigan Press
Manufactured in the United States of America
Ⓢ Printed on acid-free paper

2001   2000   1999   1998   4   3   2   1

A CIP catalog record for this book is available from the British Library.

Library of Congress Cataloging-in-Publication Data

Social inequality : values, growth, and the state / Andrés Solimano.
        p.   cm. — (Development and inequality in the market economy)
    Includes bibliographical references and index.
    ISBN 0-472-10906-5 (cloth : alk. paper)
    1. Distributive justice. 2. Income distribution. 3. Wealth.
    I. Solimano, Andrés. II. Series.
    HB523.S63   1998
    339.2—dc21   98-20637
                                                                      CIP

Preface

This book initiates social inequality as a main thematic concern of the series Development and Inequality in the Market Economy, published by the University of Michigan Press. Economic development will be an incomplete process if it does not articulate, as a central concern, a strategy to deal with inequality of income, wealth, and, perhaps more important, opportunity among all members of society.

This volume takes a comprehensive view of social inequality by focusing on three dimensions: (1) inequality as a philosophical and economic issue that raises fundamental questions about human nature, economic systems, and social organization; (2) the interdependence of basic goals in the development strategy, such as economic growth, macroeconomic stability, improvement in living standards, and social inequality; and (3) the impact of policies aimed at reducing inequality and improving social conditions on the size and effectiveness of the state.

Most of the chapters in this volume were presented at a conference held in El Escorial, Spain, in July 1995. The El Escorial conferences sponsored by Universidad Complutense of Madrid have become a place of intellectual exchange on important contemporary issues, in a beautiful natural and historical setting. Professors Carlos Abad and Osvaldo Sunkel from the Spanish journal *Pensamiento Iberoamericano* have provided great support and enthusiasm in bringing scholars, international officials, and policymakers from the other side of the Atlantic to the El Escorial summer conferences. Previous conferences have also yielded publications by the University of Michigan Press.

I would also like to acknowledge the support provided by Pilar Brown at the Inter-American Development Bank and Gladys M. López at the World Bank, in the preparation of this book, which required substantial coordination with a group of contributors scattered around different places. The editing work provided by Kevin Rennells and Melissa Holcombe, along with the support of Ellen McCarthy, Economics Editor, all at the University of Michigan Press, is greatly appreciated.

Contents

CHAPTER 1

Introduction

Andrés Solimano

Social inequality, say of income and wealth, has been an ancient public concern among philosophers, economists, political thinkers, social movements, and policymakers, particularly since capitalism replaced older modes of production. The unprecedented potential for wealth creation, entrepreneurship, and innovation developed under capitalism has often come along with persistent income and wealth inequalities. In this vein, one view argues that capitalism, notwithstanding its economic dynamism and capacity to adapt and transform itself, is an inherently inequalizing system of economic organization that requires remedying public action to correct inequality. In contrast, an alternative view argues that capitalism succeeds precisely by rewarding, differentially, higher levels of risk taking, entrepreneurship, talent, and effort among market participants. In this context, observed inequalities reflect, mainly, differential economic performance among individuals in society. This debate about the causes and effects of inequality under capitalism has been strongly influenced by three currents of social and political thought: social democracy (and liberalism), Marxism, and libertarianism.

Social democracy recognizes the inequalizing tendencies of capitalism but admits that through state action inequality can be reduced so as to match the economic dynamism of capitalism with the demands for social justice from the less privileged in society. In contrast, Marxism sees a fundamental contradiction between the economic potential for resource mobilization and growth unleashed by capitalism and its inegalitarian character that will threaten the stability and eventually the very survival of the system. Accordingly, Marxism seeked the replacement of capitalism with a socialist regime as the ultimate cure for inequality. The libertarians, in turn, focus on the basic natural rights of the individual, whose fulfillment is best enhanced by the combination of a minimal state with a free-market economy. According to libertarian views, inequality of income and wealth is a natural consequence of a market society, and policies to reduce these disparities are bound to interfere with the process of wealth creation and eventually lead to a growing state that can reduce individual freedom.

In the last three decades political philosophy and philosophical economics have been developing a growing literature on distributive justice and social inequality oriented toward examining the ethical, economic, and political dimensions of inequality and justice. Moreover, these disciplines seek to derive criteria for designing economic and political institutions conducive to a "just society." This theme is highly complex, as it involves difficult questions regarding the nature of inequality, the role of individual rights, the common good, the conditions for a fair social contract, and the role of background conditions, relative to individual responsibility, in generating income and wealth inequality, among other issues.

Historically, the twentieth century has witnessed two main economic and political responses to the problem of social inequality and market-related instability: (1) the creation of the welfare state in advanced capitalist countries and its equivalent of the dirigiste state in developing countries; and (2) the instauration of socialism in Russia, Eastern Europe, and China during the first half of the twentieth century, and other countries (e.g., Cuba) later on, around the project of creating an egalitarian socialist society as an alternative to capitalism.

Nevertheless, the collapse of socialism in the East and the demise of state dirigisme in developing countries followed by the rise of free-market economics have relegated the issues of distributive justice and social inequality to a secondary place in the public debate.

The purpose of this volume is to argue for a thorough reexamination of social inequality from three different angles:

1. The ethical and philosophical dimensions of inequality and distributive justice
2. The effects (and interactions) of income and wealth inequality on other dimensions of economic performance such as the rate of economic growth, the level of saving and investment, and the degree of social stability
3. The effect of redistributive policies aimed to reduce inequality on the size of the state and the accountability of government actions

Inequality and Distributive Justice: Recent Literature in Philosophy and Economics

There are several strands of literature on this subject, coming from both economics and political philosophy, with recent attempts at synthesis under the heading of philosophical economics.

Utilitarianism (Bentham, Mill, Pareto) and welfare economics (Pigou,

Bergson, Samuelson) argue that a "just" (or "socially optimal") pattern of resource allocation is one that maximizes the sum of total utility across individuals in society irrespective of how these utilities are distributed among the members of society.

The *Theory of Justice,* by the philosopher John Rawls, published in 1971, was a major breakthrough in political philosophy in the search for criteria to define a just society. Rawls departs from utilitarianism and welfare economics in two key respects. First, the concept of utility is replaced by that of "primary goods," composed of commodities such as food, shelter, and clothing as well as an entitlement of basic civil and political rights concerning the rights to vote, to speech, to be elected for representation, and others. Second, Rawls's theory of justice focuses not on the maximization of total utility, as utilitarians did, but on the conditions for a fair social contract negotiated by the citizens (or their representatives) under an "original position" in which the "veil of ignorance" assures that the negotiators do not know their future place in society in terms of ownership of productive assets, talents, and social background. Under those conditions, the rational negotiator chooses a set of rules and institutions that maximize the amount of primary goods available to the worst off in society (the maximin principle and "justice as fairness") because, in the end, the negotiators may end up being the worst off in society after the veil of ignorance is lifted. Interestingly, Rawls's concept of justice is derived as the outcome of a social contract negotiated under conditions of uncertainty. In other words, society acts as an insurer through a given set of institutions embodied in the social contract.

Rawls's *Theory of Justice* was contested by a main exponent of the Libertarian School, Robert Nozick, who published, in 1974, his *Anarchy, State, and Utopia.* This book shifts the focus from the "social good" and the design of just institutions and a fair social contract to the individual and his personal political and economic rights to dispose of the fruits of individual efforts (self-ownership) and the legitimacy of private self-ownership of productive wealth as a superior arrangement to common ownership. Nozick's proposal is for a minimal state with no compulsory powers of taxation and redistribution.

In contrast to Rawls, in Nozick the justice of a given distribution of income and wealth in society depends on the historical evolution that led to that distribution, focusing mainly on procedural justice and the origin and assignment of property rights.

Another source of criticism of Rawls comes from Marxism. A main Marxist critique to Rawls is that in a capitalist society in which most of productive wealth is owned and managed by a small social class (the capitalists), they have a special advantage and influence in setting the rules of the game on how income and wealth are distributed. Moreover, Marxism argues that the basic institutions in society are far from being designed from a "veil of

TABLE 1.   Theories of Distributive Justice

Representative/School	Main Dimension
Utilitarians (liberals)	Maximize aggregate utility as a concept of the social good
Rawls (liberals–social democrats)	Fair social contract (maximin criteria and difference principle)
Nozick (libertarians)	Primacy of individual (self-ownership and minimal state)
Marxists	Distributive patterns shaped by class structure and capital ownership

ignorance" on the ownership of productive resources; quite the contrary, those institutions are oriented toward protecting existing patterns of resource ownership. (For a comparison of these theories of distributive justice, see table 1.)

Coming back to Rawls, his contribution gave a new impetus to the analysis of distributive justice and social inequality, particularly on what is the right dimension (or vector of variables) on which to focus. Amartya Sen, for example, argued for an emphasis on "capabilities" and "functionings" as a link between goods and welfare. The issue was further developed in the early 1980s by Robert Dworkin, who suggests that the right (set of) variables, or dimension(s), to focus on when evaluating the justice of distributive patterns is the access to resources and opportunities by individuals and not the level of welfare (utilitarians), primary goods (Rawls), or functionings and capabilities (Sen). An important innovation in Dworkin's work was to include among resources not only physical capital, land, money, and financial assets but also nontransferable or internal resources such as talent. In addition, Dworkin focused attention in the discussions on inequality on an important factor only implicit in Rawls and Sen, that is, the issue of individual responsibility. This is an important dimension with far-reaching implications. What really matters in evaluating the degree of justice of a given distribution is not the equalization of outcomes—say, welfare, income, or wealth—but the equalization of access to resources, or, in other words, the equality of opportunities. The emphasis on personal responsibility supports the idea that individuals are responsible for transforming resources and opportunities available to them into actual outcomes through hard work, invention, and risk taking. An individual's fortunes in life are not predetermined entirely by background conditions; personal initiatives and decisions also matter a great deal.

The neat distinction between resources, opportunities, and personal responsibility arising from Dworkin's work was qualified, and partially challenged, in the late 1980s and early 1990s by authors such as P. Arneson and G. A. Cohen. They contest the notion that resources and preferences can be considered truly independent dimensions. In fact, they argue, background variables and resources (family, social status, ownership of productive resources) influence the preferences of people, their attitudes toward risk, their ambitions, and their effort levels. The idea is certainly intuitive: the children of a poor peasant family in Haiti are unlikely to have the same entrepreneurial attitudes as do the children of a successful industrialist or banker in Manhattan. No wonder their chances for success in life are very different.

Summing up this debate, it can be said that conceptions of justice should focus mainly on the set of "morally arbitrary" factors (in philosophical terms) or "background-initial conditions" (in economic terms) that are often beyond individual control, but are of crucial importance for wealth generation and its distribution, and shape people's place in society. In turn, what people actually achieve in life (outcomes) depends, given a set of initial conditions, also on factors pertaining to the realm of personal responsibility. Thus, observed inequality constitutes a moral problem when it largely reflects the effect of "morally arbitrary" factors, for example, a society in which by design or default a majority of the population has limited access to opportunities for education and jobs could be deemed to be "unjust." Finally, an often neglected but relevant case that affects the justice of distributive patterns is the acquisition of wealth by illegal means, such as corruption or drug trafficking. This is becoming a widespread practice in some countries and often involves a very significant volume of resources concentrated upon a small number of people. This practice constitutes a serious moral, economic, and political problem, affects the legitimacy of basic institutions in society, and is a big source of social inequality.

Inequality, Growth, and Development

Let's move from the philosophical questions of distributive justice to the second main theme of this volume, the economic interactions between inequality, economic growth, and long-run development. Is income and wealth inequality the price to be paid for accelerated economic growth? Or, conversely, does inequality retard economic growth? How does inequality evolve during the course of economic development? These questions invite us to examine the issue of social inequality in terms of its effects on other dimensions of economic development.

Classical economists viewed output growth as a savings-driven process. In that context, if profit earners save in a greater proportion than wage recipients do, a pattern of income distribution more concentrated on capital (e.g., inegalitarian distribution) will increase national savings and accelerate the rate of economic growth. In these models, there is no independent investment function (all of what is saved is invested) and the savings rate drives the growth path. In this model, a more egalitarian pattern of income distribution (toward labor) involves a trade-off in terms of slower economic growth acting through a decline in national savings.

Conversely, neo-Keynesian and the endogenous growth theories view the process of economic growth mainly as an investment-driven process. In this context, countries with large personal income and wealth inequalities invite, through a political mechanism, higher taxation and redistributive policies that depress the profitability of capital, hampering investment and slowing down output growth. The corollary here is that inequality is bad for growth. Other channels have also been highlighted to show a negative correlation between personal income inequality and economic growth: inequality can lead to political instability and/or populist economic policies that are ultimately destabilizing and hamper private capital formation and economic growth. The new literature combines an investment-driven growth process with a political mechanism transmitting public preferences, or social pressures, into actual government policies. These policies, in turn, affect capital accumulation and growth. The causality goes from initial inequality to subsequent growth.

The relationship between development levels (proxied by the level of per capita income) and inequality (measured by Gini coefficients or the ratio between top and bottom income quintiles or deciles) postulated by Simon Kuznets has been subject to controversy and empirical testing for a long time. As is well known, the Kuznets hypothesis states the existence of a nonlinear relationship between per capita income and an index of income inequality, reflected in an inverted U-shape curve; income inequality worsens at the initial stages of development, characterized by low per capita income levels, improving thereafter as income per person rises. The Kuznets mechanisms focused on the shift from a surplus-labor agricultural sector paying subsistence wages to a modern industrial sector with higher wages during the initial stages of development. Later on, inequality declines due to a narrowing of wage differentials as the pool of labor surplus is exhausted and the skills profile of the work force gets upgraded through formal education and learning by doing during the course of development. The causality in Kuznets goes from development levels to inequality, and the sign of the relationship evolves over historical time during the process of economic development.

Other mechanisms for the switch from unequalizing to more equalizing development can be postulated as well; they involve a lower sociopolitical tolerance for inequality in societies with higher per capita incomes, which leads to income redistribution in exchange for greater social stability and support for the development process. This may require greater access to education, credit, and other resources for low-income groups in response to political demands for redistribution.

This volume seeks to reassess some of these relationships in light of recent analytical developments and empirical evidence. Also, special attention is devoted to some key transmission mechanisms, such as the relationship between inequality and savings and investment at macro- and microlevels, and then to output growth.

Responses to Inequality: The Scope and Limits of State Action

Historically, a chief factor behind the steady growth in the economic role of the state—particularly the formation of the welfare state—throughout the twentieth century has been the responsibility attached to the state in providing economic security to counteract adverse market-related outcomes like unemployment, absolute income deprivation, absence of income after retirement, and lack of access to universal health care and education. To finance the provision of those services by the state, the government has the "power to tax" higher income groups. Redistributing income is at the heart of the state's action.

Mounting criticism on the economic and social role of the state has developed since the 1970s, coinciding with the rise of conservative economics in the United States and the United Kingdom, the demise of state dirigisme in developing countries, and the collapse of socialism in Eastern Europe and Russia during the late 1980s and early 1990s.

The critique maintains that growing involvement of the state in the economy through taxation, regulation, and ultimately budget deficits reduces the private incentives to work, accumulate capital, and innovate, thwarting economic efficiency and reducing the potential for economic growth. Moreover, the income redistribution carried out by the state is allegedly dominated by special interest groups and lobbies and does not necessarily favor low-income and more vulnerable groups.

In spite of the relative validity of this critique, it is still unclear that a retreat of the role of the state, particularly in the social sectors—as opposed to its withdrawal as a producer through policies of privatization and deregulation—is either socially desirable or politically feasible.

A sensible approach is to ask for more effective social policies through a combination of state policies and broader social participation. For example, centralized state provision of social services such as education and health care can be replaced with decentralized management and provision of social services through local governments. Other reforms, which may include mixed systems in which the private sector supplies the services and the government subsidizes the demand through mechanisms such as voucher systems or others, can be envisaged to foster freer choice and competition in social sectors. Moreover, nongovernmental organizations are institutions different and autonomous from the state that can provide a vehicle for the voice and participation of the beneficiaries in the formulation and management of social policies.

Another dimension of the action of the state is of a more political nature. The issue raised here refers to the accountability of government. In fact, the problem is how to avoid situations in which the government, which has a mandate to design and implement social policies and redistribute income, either wastes resources or redirects them to other uses. The problem is largely political in a sense that highlights problems of enforcing popular mandates and often involves failures in the feedback enforcement mechanisms between elected officials and voters. The central issue becomes how to make more effective the control by the principal (voters, the people) over the agent (the government and the state) to implement certain agreed-upon policies and deliver results.

Outline of the Chapters

The volume is divided into three parts. Part I focuses on philosophical and methodological issues of inequality.

Chapter 2, by Andrés Solimano, surveys alternative theories of distributive justice: the utilitarians, welfare economics, the liberal theories of Rawls and Sen, neo-Marxist theory, and Nozick and Hayek as exponents of the libertarian school. The crucial distinction between "initial and background conditions," or "morally arbitrary" factors (initial wealth, talent, family background), and personal responsibility (effort and preferences) in determining distributive outcomes is assessed through alternative theories of justice. The chapter also discusses issues of self-ownership, self-realization and well-being, property relations, social contracts, and alternative concepts of equality. This chapter provides an analytical overview of the philosophical and economic foundations behind existing debates on inequality.

Chapter 3, by Stephen Marglin, discusses the methodological foundations of economics, critically assessing the emphasis given to scarcity, desire, and individualism in mainstream economic theory. Marglin's point is that the central problem in economics is not how to allocate scarce resources to unlimited ends—the scarcity problem—as in many economies the availability of resources is enough to cover much more than the basic needs of most families. From this perspective, distributional motivations, social status, and the pursuit of social differentiation become very important as driving forces behind the organization of economic activity, the accumulation of capital, and the potential for growth in market societies. Marglin calls for an "economics of community" that deemphasize rivalry, competition, and atomization and stresses the achievement of self-realization in economic and social life through enhanced community links.

Part II of the book is devoted to exploring the interactions between inequality, growth, and development. Chapter 4, by Andrés Solimano, examines the relationship between income distribution and growth from a macro perspective. The analysis focuses on how income distribution fits in a variety of macro and growth models, distinguishing between savings-driven (classical, Solow, neo-Marxist) and investment-driven (endogenous-growth, Keynesian, structuralist) growth models.

The analysis explores: (1) the "model closure" (e.g., what variables adjust) to attain macroeconomic balance, (2) the sociopolitical mechanisms of the models, and, (3) how causality links between (1) and (2) affect the sign and shape of the growth/inequality relationship. In addition, the chapter discusses the stability of the Kuznets curve in view of new empirical evidence on the relationship between inequality, per capita income, and growth. This chapter seeks to integrate alternative theories of growth and distribution, making explicit the economic and sociopolitical mechanisms of each view.

Chapter 5, by Nancy Birdsall, Thomas Pinckney, and Richard Sabot, discusses the relationship between inequality and growth from a microeconomic perspective. The chapter focuses on the microbehavior of low-income households regarding their savings and investment decisions and highlights the potentially high rates of return of projects undertaken by the poor when they have access to credit. After developing a theoretical model illustrated with country experiences, the authors favor a labor-intensive development strategy that provides access to finance to poor households holding potentially profitable investment projects as a mechanism to show that a more egalitarian pattern of income distribution can foster economic growth.

Chapter 6, by Klaus Schmidt-Hebbel and Luis Servén, reviews analytically and empirically the links between aggregate savings and income distribution from a macroeconomic perspective. The authors consider the impact of distribution on the savings behavior of different groups and examine the impact of this heterogeneity on aggregate savings. The chapter finds, for a large cross-section sample of countries, only weak evidence that increased income inequality goes along with higher national savings ratios once other standard determinants of savings are taken into account. Therefore, the chapter can be interpreted as lending little support to the notion that it is necessary to concentrate income distribution in favor of high-savings groups in order to raise national savings and accelerate economic growth.

Chapter 7, by Felipe Larraín B. and Rodrigo Vergara M., focuses on the empirical impact of personal income distribution on economic growth in a sample of 45 (developed and developing) countries, including countries in Latin America and East Asia. The analysis is conducted in the framework of the new growth theory and gives explicit consideration to the impact of income inequality on private investment and the rate of GDP growth. The authors find that, after controlling for other growth determinants, an increase in income inequality of 10 percentage points in the ratio of the income of the top quintile to the income of the bottom quintile results in per capita growth dropping by 0.9 percent per year. They also find a negative impact of income inequality on private investment, although inequality is found to affect growth through other channels as well. This study provides evidence that a more equitable income distribution brings a positive "bonus" in terms of extra investment and more rapid growth.

Chapter 8, by Oscar Altimir, explores the evolution of poverty and inequality in Latin America under the strategy of import substitution in the 1950s, 1960s, and 1970s and then market-based reform in the 1980s and 1990s, addressing the growth-distribution link and the relation between inequality, reform, and development. The chapter also attempts to distinguish between short-run fluctuations due to external shocks and macropolicies and long-run changes in policy regimes and "styles of development" in terms of their impact on income distribution.

Part III of the book deals both with the historical evolution of the state in response to demands for public action in face of economic insecurity, poverty, and income inequality and with issues of political accountability of government and economic efficiency of the state.

Chapter 9, by Vito Tanzi and Ludger Schuknecht, studies the tendency for steady growth in the size of government throughout the twentieth century in industrial countries. The authors document the rapid expansion of government as caused largely by expenditures normally associated with the welfare state. The dynamics in the growth of government associated with the redistributive role of the state reflects also complex influences of lobbying groups, organized sectors, bureaucrats, and a favorable attitude, at least until a couple of decades ago, toward an increasing role of government in the economy.

The authors call for scaling back the size of the state, especially in "big government industrial countries," provided that they already show favorable levels of social welfare, which would not be affected, according to the authors, by the reform of the state.

Chapter 10, by Adam Przeworski, explores conditions for an effective role of the state in the economy in which the "quality" of state intervention in the economy—say, justified for redistributive reasons—requires adequate mechanisms of political accountability by the citizens. The author evaluates alternative theories of the role of the state in the economy using the principal-agent approach and compares the neoliberal state, concerned with efficiency considerations, and the interventionist state, more focused on distributive objectives. The author stresses the idea of a double relation between the citizen and the state in which the state is empowered to pursue collective goals, such as distributive justice, security, and solidarity, but is subject to control by its citizens through an effective institutional and political system.

What Have We Learned?

Although definite conclusions are hard to derive in this subject, some of the main findings (and open questions) of this volume follow.

1. In the tradition of political philosophy, revitalized in the early 1970s by Rawls's *Theory of Justice,* the ultimate goal of the analysis of social inequality and distributive justice is in illuminating the choices of institutions that reflect a social contract that can be considered just and fair in a democratic society. Our examination of the modern literature on distributive justice shows the importance of the distinction between factors that are outside the control of the individual—say, background conditions or "morally arbitrary factors" (initial endowments of wealth, talent, race, or family status)—and elements of "personal responsibility" (attitudes toward risk, individual ambition, and work effort).

This distinction suggests that seeking "equality of opportunity" and fair and effective access to physical and human capital accumulation through equal access to education and credit, complemented by the rights of political participation and voice, is a more sensible concept than seeking "equality of outcomes." In fact, outcomes are more influenced by individual choices and actions, whereas opportunities are many times a "given" for most individuals.

2. The theoretical models and country experiences reviewed in this book suggest a complex relationship between income distribution and economic growth. In general, savings-driven growth models in which income distribution affects national savings imply a trade-off between a more egalitarian income distribution and the rate of economic growth. However, the cross-section macroevidence presented by Schmidt-Hebbel and Servén (chap. 6) in this volume suggests very weak positive effects of income inequality on national savings, lending little or no support to the equity-growth trade-off view operating through national savings. On the other hand, Birdsall, Pinckney, and Sabot (chap. 5) show, at the microlevel, evidence for a positive savings potential of low-income households entertaining productive investment projects. These two studies, one macro and the other micro, cast doubts on the long-held view that more equitable income distribution tends to depress national savings and output growth.

3. In investment-driven growth models, initial income inequality is expected to lead to depressed private investment through several channels such as (i) induced capital taxation to finance redistributive policies, (ii) inequality-led social instability, and (iii) the rise of macroeconomic populism under conditions of sharp social inequality. Larraín and Vergara, in chapter 7, find cross-country evidence of a negative effect of income inequality on private capital formation, although they find that inequality can negatively affect economic growth through other channels as well.

Altimir's analysis in chapter 8 illustrates, for Latin America, a considerable variation in the relationship between income distribution and economic growth, both over time and across countries. Moreover, he suggests that macroeconomic stabilization and adverse external shocks can initially deteriorate income distribution during the course of reform. Long-term policy reform has ambiguous effects on income distribution. His analysis, in a way, cautions against broad generalizations on the social impact of market reform, noting the importance of specific national characteristics in shaping that impact.

4. The historical analysis of a growing role of the state in the economy suggests that it is closely linked to the redistributive role of government. Tanzi and Schuknecht provide considerable evidence for this in industrialized countries throughout the twentieth century and argue in favor of serious disincentive effects of the welfare state on the decisions to work, save, and invest. An open question remains: to what degree does divesting the social role of the state contribute to higher savings, investment, and productivity growth in the economy? Could a state stripped of its responsibilities for social protection be socially desirable and politically feasible?

Reform of education, health care, and social security requires greater private and communitarian participation in the provision of social services. The precise mechanisms through which these new forms of delivery of social services are effective in avoiding the allegedly disincentive growth effects of the welfare state have to be investigated more fully.

5. The political effects of social inequality is a theme that appears repeatedly in this volume. New (and some old) growth and distribution models emphasize that the adverse effects of income and wealth inequality on economic growth is filtered by the political system. There is a "demand for redistribution" that often leads to higher taxation and business regulation by government. One specific political mechanism postulated in these models is the median-voter model, although other mechanisms such as worker-union activism, social conflict, and political polarization can be also relevant in transmitting social demands for income redistribution to the society at large and its institutions, including, of course, the state.

Another political dimension of inequality is raised by Przeworski in chapter 10 of this volume, which asks how we can make (redistributive) governments more accountable to the citizens that elect them in a democracy. Issues of effective enforcement of popular mandates and principal-agent dilemmas are important when government officials become autonomous and start pursuing their own agendas, failing to implement popular mandates, particularly social mandates seeking a more egalitarian distribution of income and wealth in society.

PART I

Basic Philosophical and Methodological Issues

CHAPTER 2

Alternative Theories of Distributive Justice and Social Inequality: Liberal, Socialist, and Libertarian Perspectives

Andrés Solimano

This chapter examines alternative views of the concept of distributive justice (or social equity) as an intellectual idea, a vision of society, and a guide to public policy. The chapter is, in a sense, an exploration of the interface between economics and philosophy. This is an expanding field, receiving recent contributions by both economists such as Amartya Sen and John Roemer and philosophers such as John Rawls, Robert Nozick, Ronald Dworkin, G. A. Cohen, and others.[1]

This chapter identifies three main views on distributive justice. One is the *liberal* perspective. In turn, within the liberal view two main approaches can be distinguished: (1) utilitarianism and modern welfare economics and (2) the theory of justice of John Rawls. A second main perspective is *socialist,* chiefly associated with Marxist theory in its different incarnations, both classical and "reconstructed." A third perspective, that of the *libertarians,* although it shares some principles with liberalism, is critical of the concepts of distributive justice and social equity, highlighting the central role of individual freedom, self-ownership, and a minimal state as the main building blocks of their vision of society.

Next, common questions and different answers of each view are discussed in an attempt to integrate the main issues. The chapter concludes with some implications of the preceding discussions for social reform.

Liberals I: Utilitarians and Welfare Economics

The main exponents of the utilitarian tradition are Adam Smith, Jeremy Bentham, John Stuart Mill, Francis Edgeworth, and Wilfredo Pareto, whose work was later incorporated in the formal framework of welfare economics by Arthur Pigou, Abraham Bergson, Paul Samuelson, and others. Methodologically, utilitarianism and neoclassical economics are individualistic and assume rational choice in the modern sense that individuals maximize utility, say, a well-defined order of preferences over a certain space of goods.[2] A central feature of utilitarianism and welfare economics is that it casts the problems of *social* choice in the same terms as *individual* choice; in the case of society, alternative states and policies are ordered and evaluated in terms of their contribution to the maximization of an economywide welfare function. Productive factors are paid according to their marginal productivities, so income distribution reflects personal abilities, effort, and endowments of productive resources. The theory is said to be concerned with social equity in the specific sense of including *all* individual utility functions, each carrying equal weight, in the construction of the social welfare function. So, in judging alternative social states, everybody matters and each person counts equally. What is sought is to maximize the total utility in society.[3] Interpersonal comparisons of utility are ruled out, and Pareto criteria are used to evaluate alternative social positions. This procedure, as we shall see with Rawls's theory of justice, is not innocuous for altering initial distributions of income and wealth.

The theory has been subject to several criticisms. Two of them are particularly important. The first is that a social preference ordering that satisfies certain basic conditions cannot be constructed (Arrow's impossibility theorem).[4] The second objection, and perhaps the most important from an ethical perspective, is that posing the problem of social choice in terms of maximization of a social welfare function may tolerate distributions of individual welfare that can be very unfair or regressive from a distributional perspective. The egalitarian critique of utilitarianism is that it cares only about *total* utility in society (the sum of individual utilities) and not how utility is *distributed* among its members.[5]

Liberals II: Rawls's Theory of Justice

An important alternative to utilitarianism (and welfare economics) in the liberal tradition is the theory of justice developed by John Rawls. In turn, this theory is strongly influenced by liberal political philosophers such as John Locke, Jean-Jacques Rousseau, and Immanuel Kant.[6]

Rawls seeks to develop a theory of justice that is unaffected by initial differences of wealth, social status, and talents, all traits considered to be "morally arbitrary" for Rawls, in the adoption of general principles for social justice embedded in a social contract (in practice, the social contract could be thought as a constitution or institutional design meant to define economic and social policies). Like the theory of the utilitarians, the theory of justice of Rawls rests on the assumption of rational choice in the sense that individuals will seek the consistent achievement of their preferences. However, Rawls stops there and does not make the utilitarian jump from individual to social preferences expressed in the welfare function, a procedure strongly rejected by him.[7]

Another important difference between Rawls's theory and utilitarianism is the substitution of "primary social goods" for the concept of utility. Primary social goods include (besides income and wealth) basic political rights: rights of voice, association, political participation, election to government office, and so on. Then the key problem for Rawls is how to choose a political-economic system that assures just access to the vector of primary social goods by individuals.

To ensure "fairness" in the result of a just social contract governing cooperation among individuals, Rawls creates the fiction of the "original position" of a rational individual negotiating the social contract that will set the principles of a just social order. That "original position" will be subject to a "veil of ignorance," which makes each individual negotiator ignorant of his or her endowment of wealth, talent, social connections, and other attributes that can bias negotiation in favor of or (against) him or her. In other words, the veil of ignorance seeks to avoid a situation in which the personal interests of the players, negotiators, or legislators affect their stances at the moment of designing the social contract. In that position, say, one under the veil of ignorance, and the original position, the rational choice of the individual negotiating the contract will embed two principles: the first requires equality in the assignment of basic rights (the liberty principle), and the second (the difference principle) holds that social and economic inequalities can be justified only if they provide the most benefits for the least advantaged members of society, compared with any alternative institutional arrangements that can be envisaged or designed. This second principle is intended to maximize the position of the least well-off individual or group, in a sort of "maximin" procedure. The liberty principle will dominate the difference principle should they both enter into conflict. The social contract incorporating these two principles will be fair since it was negotiated from a veil of ignorance in the original position that precludes contracts that will be beneficial or detrimental to specific groups or individuals. In addition, this contract minimizes the possibility of being the worst off once the endowments of wealth are revealed. Moreover, the liberty and difference principles seek to avoid justifying institutions on the grounds that the hardships of some people are offset by a greater good in the aggregate, as a utilitarian approach, resting on a social welfare function and adopting Pareto criteria, would do.

Interestingly, Rawls's theory combines rational choice (individualistic, self-interested negotiators of the social contract) with a moral concept of fairness, "justice as fairness" guaranteed by the assumption of the veil of ignorance.

One difference between the results of Rawls's theory of justice and welfare economics and utilitarianism becomes clear in comparing and evaluating alternative social positions. A situation is Pareto superior, more efficient, if someone is better off without worsening the situation of somebody else, irrespective of whether the better-off person is rich or poor. In contrast, in Rawls's theory it matters who is better off; in general, a given situation will be preferred over other relevant alternatives if it improves the situation of the poor or the least well off in society. Clearly, distributional concerns are brought up front in Rawls.

The theory of justice of Rawls has been subject to some criticism as well: the notion that many features that affect the access to primary goods are "morally arbitrary" leaves largely unconsidered the fact that individual efforts and the ability to exploit opportunities are "morally responsible" features. In fact, individual responsibility has become a key concept in modern theories of justice. A potential inconsistency of the metaphor of the negotiators of the social contract under the veil of ignorance is that, while they know their "morally responsible" features, they are ignorant of the "morally arbitrary" ones (see Roemer 1996, chap. 5).

Another criticism of Rawls, expressed by Sen, is that "primary goods" might not be the right variable to maximize. Sen argues that what matters for well-being is what he terms "functioning and capability," which lie between goods and welfare. In fact, goods enable people to function in various ways: say, to be mobile, healthy, and so on. Sen calls the set of functioning available to a person his or her capability; so he argues for equality of capabilities rather than equality of such outcomes as primary goods, utility, and welfare.

Most of these criticisms and a personal reexamination of *Theory of Justice* is carried out by Rawls himself in his more recent book, *Political Liberalism* (1993). The key modification introduced in this book is the replacement of the idea that in a democratic society all members hold a common view of the social good, a critical ingredient in negotiating a fair social contract, with the recognition that in a modern democracy there is a diversity of outlooks and "comprehensive moral doctrines" of the social good that threaten the stability of democracy and can impede achieving a social contract.

The solution to this potential impasse is provided by Rawls, who postulates an "overlapping consensus" across competing views of society on a common set, or core, of moral values. In addition, Rawls brings in the notion of "reasonable" people who abide by rules or norms, which allows social cooperation. These two concepts, overlapping consensus and reasonable behavior, permit, according to Rawls (1993), a more realistic characterization of a modern democracy that seeks to develop fair and just institutions.

Socialists: Classical and Reconstructed Marxism

Traditionally, the main analytical foundation of socialist analysis is Marxist theory. Marxism was intended to serve as a broad theory of the economy and society and its laws of historical change. Its analysis of capitalism was not explicitly cast in terms of a moral condemnation of social inequality, though this is an important underlying motivation behind Marxist theory, particularly in the political practice of social organizations influenced by Marxism.

"Classical" Marxism frames its critique of the social inequalities of capitalism in the theory of exploitation.[8] The theory of exploitation rests on the labor theory of value, which proposes that workers are the only source of value creation; therefore, exploitation is related to the fact that workers are paid less than the total value of output they create.

According to this theory, an unequal exchange develops between workers and capitalists: while the workers' only asset is labor (in flow terms, "labor power"), capitalists are in an advantageous position due to their ownership of the productive capital that allows them to organize production, set the rules of the game in the enterprise, and decide the distribution of the economic surplus. Thus, in Marxism, distributive outcomes and individual welfare are strongly influenced by property relationships regarding productive wealth. The theory goes further and proposes that ownership of productive wealth gives the capitalist class the dominant political power in society as a whole to preserve, through the state apparatus, favorable conditions for the stability, reproduction, and flourishing of the capitalist system.

It is apparent that classic Marxism differs substantially at the methodological level from liberal theory, either utilitarian or Rawlsian, in organizing the analysis around the concept of social classes rather than individual actions. In contrast to liberal theory, which assumes that individuals are free to enter into the social contract, following the mutual benefits of voluntary exchange, Marxist theory underscores the relative advantage of those who own and control productive wealth in setting the rules of the game regarding the distribution of the economic surplus and the content and shape of the basic institutions of society.

The labor theory of value, on which the Marxist theory of exploitation rests, has been criticized for analytical shortcomings in treating aggregation problems in the face of different types of skilled and unskilled labor and the treatment of past labor, besides other measurement issues. Moreover, and most importantly, the theory denies completely the role of the entrepreneur and other factors of production, besides labor, as sources of value in production. These conceptual problems, besides the failure of "real" or actual socialism, have led to a critique "from within" Marxism. This new critique attempts to recast Marxist theory in a modified framework, one that still stresses the fundamental inequalities of modern capitalism but abandons the theory of exploitation (and the labor theory of value) as its central foundation.[9]

Reconstructed Marxist theory expands and redefines the concept of productive resources using new contributions from liberal writers such as Dworkin and others.[10] In the expanded framework, resources can be either *external* to the individual (capital, land, real estate, or financial assets) or *internal* (talent, skills, attitude toward risk, ambition, etc.).

This redefinition poses significant problems for the traditional Marxist view that property relations are a central factor in shaping distributive patterns and social inequalities. In fact, it is not clear how property rights of internal resources, such as talent, which are inherently private and nontransferable, can be modified in the direction of a more egalitarian distribution of resources in society. In fact, now it would only make sense to focus on the property rights of *external* resources. Moreover, recognizing a wider range of productive resources that create value besides labor leads to recognizing entrepreneurship, talent, and risk taking as valid categories that deserve a share in the distribution of the economic surplus. The very concept of social class has to be redefined, as in classical Marxism social classes were determined by the ownership (or lack) of capital (e.g., capitalists vs. workers). In a context in which the vector of attributes of individuals is much broader than the ownership of capital, the concept of class would have to be redefined to include some common sharing among groups of individuals of attributes (such as race, talent, and family background) that will affect their ability to create wealth and generate income.

The implications for social reform aimed at a more egalitarian society need to be redefined in any meaningful Marxist conception of reform. Compensatory schemes for initial inequalities in the endowment of internal resources at the "birth lottery" can be as important as is the old Marxist prescription of redistributing physical property as a supposedly socially equalizing mechanism. Moreover, the recognition of complex agent-principal problems in state-owned enterprises (as well as private corporations) and the failure of Soviet socialism have led to a questioning, among neo-Marxist authors, of the validity of identifying public with state property.[11]

Critics of Social Justice: The Libertarians

Let us turn now to the critics of the very concept of distributive justice and egalitarian policies. Hayek, a main exponent of the libertarian school, admits that the concept of justice is valid at individual level, but he strongly rejects the concept of *social* justice.[12] His main argument is the following: while it makes sense to judge a certain outcome following an individual, deliberate, and conscious action as just or unjust, it becomes meaningless to extend this reasoning at the societal level, since outcomes cannot be attributed to deliberate societal actions (understanding society as different from government and other hierarchical organizations). In Hayek's vision, distributive outcomes are the result of a self-ordering or spontaneous process—"the market order"—and not the result of design by a central authority. For Hayek, a "social" outcome can be good or bad, but not just or unjust, for a normative judgment like this presumes attributing to *society* (a complex concept to define) deliberate actions.[13] Hayek (like Rawls), is clearly antiutilitarian in declaring as futile and inadmissible the attempt to define social preferences for the economy as a whole. Libertarians believe in the evolutionary, spontaneous creation of institutions and reject any attempt to design institutions that alter the allocative and distributive patterns emerging from a market order.

For Hayek, a crucial theme is the fundamentally dispersed character of information; in that sense, most individual actions have unforeseen outcomes and produce unintended results. Moreover, Hayek goes a step further and argues that there is no such thing as social behavior, say, a consistent relation between means and ends in a spontaneous order. For Hayek, the big mistake of utilitarianism is the extrapolation of individual behavior to social conduct.

In this perspective, libertarians become highly critical of both liberal and socialist attempts to pursue distributive justice and egalitarian policies. Quoting Hayek: "There is no need morally to justify specific distributions (of wealth or income) which have not been brought about deliberately, but are the outcomes of a game that is played because it improves the chances of all" (1976, 117).

For Hayek, a valid objective (for public policy) is establishing such rules of "just conduct" or "abstract rules of behavior" that allow every person to pursue their own ends. Beyond establishing rules, any other policies oriented toward judging or changing end results at the societal level are devoid of content.

For Robert Nozick (1974), another main exponent of the libertarian school, the fundamental principles for judging human actions are self-ownership and individual natural rights rather than concepts of the social good. The self-ownership hypothesis states that each person is the morally rightful owner of him- or herself. Moreover, this hypothesis says that it is morally valid for a person to use resources of the outside world for his or her own benefit to the extent that this does no harm to others. The minimal role of the state follows in that involuntary appropriation by the state, through taxes, of the fruits of work and wealth owned by the individual is unjust. For Nozick, "justice in acquisition" refers to the extent to which the appropriation of unowned natural resources makes no one else worse off compared with the situation in which the resources remained unowned.[14] As Roemer (1996) points out, Nozick provides a justification for inequality under capitalism, maintaining that the distribution of resources under this economic system is not unjust, a priori, to the extent that private ownership and operation of productive assets is a superior arrangement to the situation of unowned resources.

The criticisms of Nozick's theory of justice focus on the counterfactual of his "justice in acquisition." For Nozick, the alternative to private ownership is no ownership; some authors argue that another alternative is common ownership of natural resources.[15]

For Nozick, each individual owns the fruits of his or her actions (income, social position, status, accumulated wealth). In this perspective, redistributive policies that compulsorily transfer resources or income between individuals violate the basic principle of self-ownership of the fruits of individual effort and productive wealth privately owned. For libertarians, the right to dispose of and command initial resources such as inherited wealth falls in the realm of individual rights and actions.

Before finishing this discussion of the libertarians, the question arises of how Nozick's approach relates to that of Hayek. Both emphasize individual rights to own the fruits of individual effort and the yields of assets as a main justification for the "minimal state," although Hayek also emphasizes the threat of a larger state to individual freedom and other political rights of the individual.

Another distinction is that Hayek openly rejects any notion of distributive justice and challenges the very concept of society (as different from a "market order"); Nozick, in contrast, is more open in admitting the issue of justice under capitalism, drawing its theoretical justification of the capitalist system from the concept of "justice in acquisition," which provides a defense of private property as opposed to other forms of ownership of productive resources.

Common Questions and Different Answers

This section examines how the alternative theories of distributive justice reviewed here attempt to answer some basic questions on inequality in order to provide a more integrative view of the subject.

Is Income and Wealth Inequality a Moral Problem?

A basic concern of political philosophy and ethics in the schools is the extent to which inequality of income and wealth is a moral (as well as an economic) problem.

Leaving aside the problem of absolute poverty and income deprivation, which all schools of thinking (including libertarianism) agree must be addressed through public policy, much less agreement exists regarding why (and, if so, how) income and wealth inequalities must be corrected.

It is fair to say that for liberals like Rawls and for socialists, inequality *is* a basic problem from a point of view of values. The social contract of Rawls, designed from a "veil of ignorance," say, from a situation in which the distribution of wealth is unknown, implicitly assumes that initial distributions of resources in society are not considered as necessarily fair and just.

Classical Marxist theory decidedly emphasizes the inequalities of capitalism stemming from an unequal distribution of wealth and property relations between a small group of wealth owners and a vast majority of people owning mainly their labor power. As mentioned earlier, Marxism is less prone to put the inequality issue in explicit ethical terms; it rather emphasizes its existence as a by-product of the capitalist system.

Utilitarianism and welfare economics are not explicit on the ethical implications of existing wealth ownership patterns and distributive outcomes in society. As welfare economics rests on the marginal productivity theory in competitive markets to determine the rewards of productive factors, there are no obvious injustices in observed factor remunerations. Moreover, if wealth patterns correspond to voluntary asset accumulation, hard work, and a sacrifice in consumption, then no ethical criticism would be justified according to neoclassic thinking.

For the libertarians à la Hayek, the resulting income and wealth distribution is not a problem to the extent that it reflects unintended outcomes of an extended market order.

In addition, any intervention in the market process—say, to correct income and wealth inequalities—is seen as highly detrimental to the functioning of the market mechanism and would negatively affect the incentives for wealth creation.

For Nozick, self-ownership and "justice in acquisition" are the key elements for judging inequality.

The Initial Position and the Origins of Inequality

An important issue in any theory of social justice is the origins of inequality. The concept of "original position" is intended to mean the influence of initial endowments of assets and talent on the future ability to generate income and satisfaction for individuals in life.

This is an area of disagreement between alternative theories. Utilitarians, neoclassical economists, and libertarians tend to assume that initial wealth reflects either family or parental preferences expressed in terms of bequests and inherited wealth. In general, there are no ethical objections by libertarians and neoclassical economists to the giver (and recipient) to the extent that savings, accumulations, and bequests are transferred in voluntary fashion; constitute the reward of effort, sacrifice, and risk taking; and are not the result of unlawful activities. Rawls's theory, in spite of being a theory based on rational choice, tends to attach great importance to "external" circumstances such as family, social background, inherited wealth, and talent in shaping the fortunes of individuals. According to Rawls, as the main determinants of individual welfare and distributive justice could be outside the individual's control and responsibility, they can be "arbitrary from a moral point of view," and inequality becomes an ethical issue. Then a concept of justice is needed in order to devise social institutions that assure fairness in the distribution of income and wealth in society.

Marxist theory also attributes to the initial distribution of property rights on productive wealth a central role in subsequent distributive results. The origin of private property rights can be due to different means (including arbitrary ones) and/or family inheritance often perpetuating preexisting inequalities in wealth and access to opportunities.

Concepts of Equality

An important task is to define the concept of equality. Ronald Dworkin (1982) made the important distinction between equality of welfare and equality of resources.

A central problem of equality of welfare is that its attainment depends on individual preferences. The problem arises when the formation of tastes may depend on resources. For example, what may be considered adequate well-being for the wealthy may be very different from that for the poor. Also, the adequate level of welfare for those with expensive tastes is different from that for those with "cheap" tastes. This renders the concept of equality of welfare a problematic criteria for distributive justice.

Another concept of equality is equality of resources. This approach states that what matters the most for personal success (or failure) and the attainment of individual well-being is access to and command of economic resources. Differences in outcomes, in turn, are largely related to personal responsibility, tastes, and ambition. The idea is certainly intuitive. A person born with inherited wealth (e.g., capital, land, or financial assets) is likely to have a higher stream of income and welfare than a person with less or no initial wealth. A crucial "policy issue" in the equalization of resources is how to compensate individuals for differences in initial endowments of wealth and talent.

Sen's "equalization of capabilities" (say, the capacities of people to achieve certain functions, achievements, or objectives that persons value)[16] and Rawls's difference principle can be viewed as variants of equality of resources, with Sen focusing on capabilities and Rawls on primary goods as inputs or resources required to achieve welfare or well-being.

An important distinction is between formal and effective equality of opportunity. Everybody may have legal (or formal) access to education and nondiscriminatory job opportunities; however, this may be just formal, but not effective, equality. The distinction between equality of opportunity and equality of outcome leads us to issues of freedom and individual responsibility. In this view, a person is *not* responsible for the opportunities he or she faces but *is* responsible for the transformation of those opportunities into actual outcomes.

Concluding Remarks: What Role for Social Reform?

What type of society do we want? The search for a "just" society is an ancient concern of political philosophers, (sometimes) economists, and social reformers.

The theme is extremely broad, and here only a few observations will be offered in light of our previous discussion.

A central question is how to make compatible a market economy or capitalism—a system that has an impressive ability to adapt and transform itself, something that the socialist system failed to do—with acceptable levels of equity in the distribution of income and wealth.

The utopia of utilitarianism and welfare economics is an undistorted pattern of resource allocation (and growth) resulting from competitive markets and corrected with lump-sum redistribution to correct distributive outcomes deemed to be socially undesirable.

Rawls adopts a different approach and focuses on the conditions for designing a just social contract, which may range from specific agreements on taxation and social policies that equalize access to private goods, income, and wealth to the type of constitutional charter and form of government that controls access to merit and public goods such as freedom, the rights of speech and the vote, the right to be elected to office, and the like.

Classical Marxism questioned the very right to exist of a capitalist system on the grounds that it is, in general, incompatible with an acceptable distribution of income to workers and other low-income groups in society.[17] The Marxist model (although not that explicit in Karl Marx) of the "good society" was a socialist system based on state ownership and planning. However, the ultimate collapse of classic socialism based on central planning and state ownership has led to a new search for a just and feasible economic system by neo-Marxists. What recent attempts in this direction share is the recognition that in modern and complex societies such an economic system has to encompass the market mechanism as an important coordination device of consumption, production, and investment decisions.

Libertarians, in contrast to liberals and socialists, vigorously reject the need for and convenience of implementing redistributive policies, though admitting the need for public policy to avoid absolute income deprivation and acute poverty.[18] The rejection of redistributive policies is based on two main reasons. First, policies of income redistribution would unavoidably lead to "inconvenient interference with the market-order" and therefore would discourage and hamper the process of wealth creation. In other words, libertarians believe in a sharp trade-off between economic growth and income distribution (for a thorough discussion of the relationship between economic growth and distribution, see chap. 4, this volume). The second objection to redistributive policies is of a more political nature. Redistributive policies increase the power of the state and empower it to expropriate the fruits of individual work and private wealth holdings, violating the basic natural rights of individuals. Moreover, these policies of state expansion can eventually lead to totalitarianism, which curtails personal freedom and leads to economic misery.[19]

Achieving a consensus on social reform across the different schools is very complex. An adequate balancing between equality of opportunity and resources, along with respect for individual responsibility and autonomy, is required to structure meaningful policies toward distributive justice. What forms of fiscal policy, property structures, governance mechanisms, and social institutions must complement (and correct) the market mechanism in order to ensure satisfactory levels of social equity is still an open question.

NOTES

Comments by Luis Ratinoff on a previous version of this chapter are acknowledged.

1. See Sen 1992; Roemer 1994a, 1994b, 1996; Rawls 1971; Nozick 1974; Dworkin 1981; Cohen 1995; and the many references cited therein.

2. Individualism and (neoclassical) rationality do not always come together. See Hayek 1948 on the distinction between utilitarian and nonutilitarian individualism.

3. The utilitarian notion that "society should seek to achieve the greatest good for the greatest number" (in Bentham's words) may amount to maximization of two objectives at once (see Roemer 1996, chap. 4).

4. See Sen 1970, 1979.

5. For utilitarianism, in a two-person situation, the utility pair (1,99) is indifferent to the pair (50,50), since they yield the same total sum of utility, although obviously the distributional outcome of the two pairs of utility configuration is very different (see Roemer 1996).

6. There is also a "post-Rawls" liberal literature, which will not be reviewed here (e.g., see Miller 1976); however, Rawls still represents the main exponent of nonutilitarian liberalism.

7. Quoting Rawls: "[T]he nature of the decision made by the ideal legislator is not, therefore, materially different . . . [from that] of a consumer deciding how to maximize his satisfaction by the purchase of this or that collection of goods. . . . This view of social cooperation is the consequence of extending to society the principle of choice of one man. . . . Utilitarianism does not take seriously the distinction between persons" (1971, 27).

8. Formal statements of the Marxist theory of exploitation can be found in Roemer 1988a, 1988b, 1994a; and Morishima 1973.

9. See particularly the work of Roemer (1994a, 1994b) in this context.

10. See Dworkin 1981.

11. For more on this, see Roemer 1994a (chap. 10).

12. An eloquent reference from Hayek is the following "This conception of 'social' justice is thus a direct consequence of that anthropomorphism or personification by which naive thinking tries to account for self-ordering processes. It is a sign of the immaturity of our minds that we have not yet outgrown these primitive concepts . . ." (1976, 62).

13. Hayek assumes that only in a centrally planned economy that correspondence (say, between "societal" actions and distributive outcomes) could be made. Interestingly, only in that system the concept of social justice makes sense. However, Hayek criticizes on moral grounds the validity of having a collectivist society in which a central authority replaces individual choice and freedom is lost.

14. This concept is weaker than John Locke's views on the morality of appropriation of external resources.

15. This, in turn, leads to the question of to what extent "common ownership" can be legitimately identified with ownership by the state, assuming that the state represents the interests of the people or the "common interests" of society.

16. See Sen 1992.

17. A permanent debate in left-wing politics is between "reformist" and "revolutionary" policies toward capitalism as the best way to achieve desired societal changes.

18. See Hayek 1976.

19. In the post–cold war era, and probably well before it, too, this contention seems obviously far-fetched. It is interesting to read again Hayek's *Road to Serfdom,* written in the early 1940s, to capture the mood and context prevailing at the time these arguments were first made.

REFERENCES

Cohen, G. A. 1995. *Self-Ownership, Freedom, and Equality.* Cambridge: Cambridge University Press.
Dworkin, R. 1981. "What Is Equality? Part 1: Equality of Welfare. Part 2: Equality of Resources." *Philosophy and Public Affairs* 10:185–246, 283–345.
Hayek, F. A. 1948. *Individualism and Economic Order.* Chicago: University of Chicago Press.
———. 1976. *Law, Legislation, and Liberty: The Mirage of Social Justice.* Vol. 2. Chicago: University of Chicago Press.
———. 1988. *The Fatal Conceit: The Errors of Socialism,* edited by W. W. Bartley. Chicago: University of Chicago Press.
Letwin, W. 1983. *Against Equality: Readings on Economic and Social Policy.* London: Macmillan.
Miller, D. 1976. *Social Justice.* Oxford: Clarendon.
Morishima, M. 1973. *Marx's Economics: A Dual Theory of Value and Growth.* Cambridge: Cambridge University Press.
Nozick, R. 1974. *Anarchy, State, and Utopia.* New York: Basic Books.
Rawls, J. 1971. *A Theory of Justice.* Cambridge: Harvard University Press.
———. 1993. *Political Liberalism.* New York: Columbia University Press.
Roemer, J. 1988a. *Analytical Foundations of Marxian Economic Theory.* Cambridge: Cambridge University Press.
———. 1988b. *Free to Lose: An Introduction to Marxist Economic Philosophy.* Cambridge: Harvard University Press.
———. 1994a. *Egalitarian Perspectives: Essays in Philosophical Economics.* Cambridge: Cambridge University Press.
———. 1994b. *The Future of Socialism.* Cambridge: Harvard University Press.
———. 1996. *Theories of Distributive Justice.* Cambridge: Harvard University Press.
Sen, A. 1970. "The Impossibility of the Paretian Liberal." *Journal of Political Economy* 78:152–57.
———. 1979. *Collective Choice and Social Welfare.* Amsterdam and New York: North-Holland.
———. 1992. *Inequality Reexamined.* New York: Russell Sage Foundation.

CHAPTER 3

How the Economy Is Constructed: On Scarcity and Desire

Stephen A. Marglin

By way of introduction I have two points to make. First, we economists are not neutral bystanders. I don't mean the practitioners among us. Everybody knows practitioners are not bystanders. I mean the academic wing of the profession, all of us who claim only to "tell it like it is," to describe the economy and evaluate alternative policies from a neutral vantage point. We, too, are more than bystanders. We participate in making society in the image of economics.

What economists take as human nature is largely contextual, largely constructed. Human beings are *not* the irreducible atoms of society; we do *not* naturally calculate and optimize at every turn; scarcity of means relative to unlimited ends is *not* the human condition. We are products of 400 years of a very particular historical experience, for which the economics profession has provided guidance and legitimacy, forming us into the kind of people who populate elementary economics texts.

John Stuart Mill warned us against this more than a century and a half ago. He begins by quoting Jeremy Bentham (Mill 1969, 14): "In every human breast . . . self-regarding interest is predominant over social interest; each person's own individual interest over the interests of all other persons taken together." According to Mill, believing is seeing:

> By the promulgation of such views of human nature, and by a general tone of thought and expression perfectly in harmony with them, I conceive Mr Bentham's writings to have done and to be doing very serious evil. It is by such things that the more enthusiastic and generous minds are prejudiced against all his other speculations, and against the very attempt to make ethics and politics a subject of precise and philosophical thinking. . . . The effect is still worse on the minds of those who are not shocked and repelled by this tone of thinking, for on them it must be perverting to their whole moral nature. It is difficult to form a conception of a tendency more inconsistent with all rational hope of good for the human species, than that

which must be impressed by such doctrines, upon any mind in which they find acceptance. . . .

[T]he power of any one to realize within himself the state of mind, without which his own enjoyment of life can be but poor and scanty, and on which all our hopes of happiness and moral perfection to the species must rest, depends entirely upon his having faith in the actual existence of such feelings and dispositions in others, and in their possibility for himself. It is for those in whom the feelings of virtue are weak, that ethical writing is chiefly needed, and its proper office is to strengthen those feelings. (15)[1]

My second point is this: as Mill hints, the society we are in the process of making, for all its material success, is a failure in human terms. We may or may not be destroying the resource base or polluting the environment beyond its capacity to absorb our wastes. We may or may not be. But we are surely making it more and more difficult to construct a society that provides even safety and security for its members, not to mention nurturance, or rhyme and reason, for our sojourn here on earth.

When I began this essay, I had thought to write about how an enlightened policy on income distribution might counter the destructive aspects of our society. But in the end I cannot make such an optimistic assessment. As Vito Tanzi and Ludger Schuknecht suggest (chap. 9, this volume), public policies to redistribute income reached a peak in the decades after World War II. There was a broad political consensus that the problems of market economies could be solved by selective government interventions, and the extraordinary performance of the leading market economies made it politically feasible to utilize some of the dividends of growth for redistributive purposes. The perception that these programs had failed to alleviate social problems, coupled with the slowdown in growth, created the backlash epitomized by Margaret Thatcher and Ronald Reagan, a reaction that, in the United States at least, has become quite mainstream. One does not have to share the cynicism that lies behind the Thatcher and Reagan revolutions to appreciate the illusory quality of any attempt to solve the problems created by the market without challenging fundamental assumptions of the market.

Our problems run deeper than *any* distributional policy can address. Concentration of income and wealth contribute to our obsession with growth, but concentration contributes as a secondary cause. The primary cause lies in the institutional structures we have built up over the last 400 years. In this essay, I invite you to look more closely at the basic assumptions of that system, a system for which not only our intellectual fathers (not many mothers in that lot) bear considerable responsibility, but which you and I further every time we teach a course in the principles of economics or publish a paper that takes these basic assumptions for granted.

In this essay, I explore one of these assumptions, the assumption that wants are unlimited, with its corollary that scarcity, or Scarcity (as I will term it), is therefore a pillar of the economy. But, before I address these issues analytically, I want to share with you two stories, the first intended to flesh out my assertions about the role of economics in constructing the economy, the second intended to give life to the discussion of scarcity and desire that follows.

Two Stories about Economics and the Economy

The Economist's Role in the Construction of Market Society

In 1993, a Finnish collaborator and I went to Moscow in an attempt to recruit Russians for an intellectual enterprise we were then putting together. In the end we got nowhere, but I learned a lot on the way. One afternoon we had a particularly lively discussion with a group that seemed somewhat sympathetic to our goals and methods, and there was a general interest in continuing into the evening. My collaborator and I suggested going to a restaurant, but the Russians reacted tepidly to this proposal. I had the impression that, as members of the salaried class, they were trapped by their new experience of poverty—uncomfortable with the idea of going to an "international" restaurant where a meal would cost more than a month's salary and most of the clients could hardly have come by the price honestly, but equally uncomfortable with the idea of going to a "national" restaurant, where mediocre food and service would be the best that one might reasonably expect.

The Russians' solution was to propose supper at the apartment of Sergei and Lena. Sergei was associated with the School of Cultural Politics where the afternoon meeting had taken place, but in fact we knew Lena much better. She had acted as our interpreter and translator and that morning had taken us to an exhibit of Soviet art of the 1920s and 1930s at the Tretyakov Gallery. Most striking was the grandiose canvas of Stalin and the military leadership of the mid-1930s; the pomp and splendor of the circle of generals, field marshals, and admirals grouped around Stalin reminded me at once of another group portrait I had seen many times in which rajas, maharajas, and assorted princes encircle the king-emperor (the occasion was a durbar held to celebrate the visit of Edward VII to India in 1910). Lena's comment was chilling: none of the high-ranking officers in the picture, she reminded us, survived Stalin's purge of the military in the late 1930s. These and other dark remarks made me believe that, despite a relatively spacious apartment and other indicators of present comfort, Lena's family had suffered under the Soviet regime.

Lena had already given us a warm welcome and an excellent dinner the evening before, so it took considerable reassurance from her to convince us that six or eight people descending upon her would not be a major inconvenience. Her only concession was to allow us to purchase some food and drink for the occasion. We went to a "gastronom," a grocery store, which, despite being a state enterprise, was reasonably well stocked. Because of both the long lines and the clumsy system (you get a ticket specifying your purchase, go to a cashier to pay, and then back to the salesperson for the goods), the process took a while, but for me the chance to see what more or less ordinary Muscovites could purchase in early 1993 outweighed any inconvenience. At last we were done—with a lot of smoked fish, some wine and vodka, and enough other things to make a reasonable supper.

As we emerged from the gastronom, Lena, quite out of the blue, said: "Terrible, terrible." Her observations at the Tretyakov had prepared me for some cryptic if not apocalyptic comment, but nothing seemed particularly terrible to my untrained eye. "What's terrible?" I asked.

"Milk."

"Milk?"

"Yes, milk. It's terrible. Here they sell milk for 54 rubles per liter [approximately nine cents at the then current rate of exchange], and at the kiosk in front of our apartment house it costs 92 rubles."

Jokingly, I responded: "That's not terrible; it's a great opportunity."

Now it was Lena's turn to be surprised: "Great opportunity? What do you mean?"

"Simple. You buy milk here for 54 rubles and sell it in front of your house for, say, 75. You make a lot of money and the folks in your apartment get their milk cheaper." Once an economist, always an economist.

Lena thought about this for a moment and then said "It won't work. You can't get the milk there. You can't buy gas."

"Listen," I said. "If you can make money from buying milk cheap, you can find gas."

Lena was silent for another moment and then shook her head, her exasperation with this uncomprehending foreigner showing: "No, it still won't work. Even if you could find gas, there is no transport."

Now I began to feel a challenge. Here was first-year economics. Here was the market to free Lena's apartment house from the bondage of 92-ruble milk and turn someone a tidy profit in the bargain. "Look, if there is enough money in it, all these obstacles can be overcome."

After some more back and forth, a light bulb went on just above my head: all this talk about "is" was really a cover for Lena's misgivings about "ought." The difficulties were not logistical but moral. As a matter of right, milk ought to sell for the same price in front of her apartment house as at the central gastronom. And it was immoral to bring this about through the mechanism of market and the incentive of profit.

Now the light got intense. I realized that what was second nature to me was totally alien to Lena. Doubtless the quickness and sureness of my responses owed not a little to my professional training, but my profession was only frosting on the cake of market culture. Most people reared in a market culture, economists or not, would have no trouble understanding the logic of arbitrage, even if they could not pronounce, much less define, this term.

I realized two other things. First, while it was certain that 70 years of communism were part of this story of cultural difference, Lena's resistance to market logic ran much deeper, the product more likely of centuries of wariness of the market than of decades of communist propaganda. Second, however ingrained market logic might be for the present generation of Americans, hardly a century ago Lena's suspicions of could have been found all over the United States. It oversimplifies to identify the populism that swept the prairies in the 1890s with wholesale condemnation of the logic of the market, but I do believe that many populists would have taken Lena's side of our exchange rather than mine.

But we don't have to go to Russia or back to nineteenth-century Kansas to see the process at work. Every year thousands of undergraduates all over the United States take courses in the principles of economics, partly, perhaps, because they are persuaded it is useful preparation for business or law school, but partly, I am sure, for enlightenment. Many ask (with Adam Smith) how morally to justify a world based on self-interest. Parents may have urged the importance of looking out for number one, but the idea that self-interest serves the general interest sounds too much like other forms of adult hypocrisy of which they become, as they grow up, increasingly aware. Imagine the relief, not to say exhilaration, at learning sophisticated arguments that demonstrate why looking out for number one is a social virtue. And if there remain any doubts students can always draw sustenance from remembering that the arguments come from neutral professors of economic *science,* who have no other ax to grind than that of Truth itself. (There remains an unconvinced minority. No matter how hard they try, they just don't get it. Needless to say, these students tend to limit their further exposure to economics.)

The light bulb burned brighter. I reflected on the change in American attitudes (and the lack of change in Russian attitudes). We economists have insisted on our scientific neutrality for a long time, claiming at least since the days of John Maynard Keynes's father (himself a noted economist who contributed a treatise on methodology to the corpus of nineteenth-century economics) that we do only two things: we describe how the economy actually works (so-called descriptive or positive economics) and we evaluate how well actual or hypothetical economic arrangements work (welfare or normative economics). We are neutral bystanders.

In reality, the spread of the market was hardly automatic. It needed reinforcement and legitimization. It needed the economics profession. We helped, and still help, to *construct* the market economy. Since long before Adam Smith, economists have been breaking down the resistance of the Lenas of the world to the logic of the market. Under the onslaught of the economics profession, either Lena is convinced or she is marginalized. The centuries it has taken to do so even in the most market-friendly society on earth is a measure of how deep the resistance to the logic of the market runs.

Envy

Long ago, in India, there was a Brahmin who was forced by poverty to leave his village in search of work. Before he left, he admonished his wife not, under any circumstances, to touch a particular lamp he had hidden away. She would get whatever she asked for if she rubbed the lamp, but something *else,* something very bad, would happen.

He was gone many months, and his wife, with no money and precious little grain left, grew more and more desperate. How would she feed her children? Finally, she disobeyed her husband and took down the lamp he had forbidden her to touch. No sooner had she rubbed the lamp than the proverbial genie appeared. "What is your command, my lady?" he asked. Afraid to compound her disobedience with greediness, the Brahmin's wife made a very modest plea: "Put enough grain in my storage bin to feed me and my children while my husband is away."

No sooner said than done. The Brahmin's wife and children never went hungry.

But a mysterious thing happened. The neighbors enjoyed a glorious windfall. Every one of the Brahmin's neighbors found not one but *two* storage bins filled to the brim.

After some time had passed and the Brahmin still had not returned, his wife decided to have another go with the lamp. She brought it out of its hiding place and rubbed it once again. This time she asked for a house, nothing too fancy, but something befitting the Brahmin's high ritual status. Before her very eyes, suddenly there appeared a beautiful if unpretentious bungalow. But once again something strange happened. Each of her neighbors suddenly found himself in a grand house, twice as large and twice as elegant as the Brahmin's.

One day, the Brahmin returned, clutching the few rupees he had managed to save during his sojourn away from the village. As he approached his own neighborhood, he noticed the new houses of his neighbors and at last saw his own bungalow, beyond his wildest dreams but modest in comparison with his neighbors' houses. It didn't take him long to figure out what had happened, and he returned home in a fury. "Didn't I tell you something awful would happen if you rubbed the lamp?" he berated his wife.

But anger only sharpened his wit. He seized the lamp and made a wish: "Let me be blind in one eye," he said to the genie. And for good measure he added: "Let there be an open well in front of my house."

The Brahmin would have had no trouble with a bumper sticker that made its appearance a few years ago. It read: "Whoever dies with the most toys wins."

Scarcity and Desire

As early as the seventeenth-century, economists developed the strategy of assimilating economic behavior to the mechanical models of the physical world developed by Galileo, Kepler, and Newton. If homo economicus flowed from human nature and operated according to the same kind of natural law that determined the orbit of Jupiter, then attempts to deflect economic man from his natural inclination would make as much sense as attempts to deflect Jupiter. One example will indicate the flavor of the argument. After explaining that the competition of buyers and sellers establishes the "Intrinsick value" of a commodity, the late-seventeenth-century pamphleteer, Charles Davenant, concluded that (quoted in Appleby 1977, 187):

> [in the] Naturall Course of Trade, Each Commodity will find its Price. . . .
> The supream power can do many things, but it cannot alter the Laws of Nature, of which the most originall is, That every man should preserve himself.

The emerging individualistic society was presented as freeing individuals from artificial shackles, the economist simply observing, describing, and analyzing the shackles and the positive effects that might be anticipated by letting nature run its course in the economic sphere.

In view of the success of Newton and his predecessors in cornering the market in physics, this strategy had obvious appeal. And the appeal has continued unabated—witness the rhetoric of the rational expectations folks and other new classical macroeconomists against the efficacy of government intervention. But all the rhetoric in the world does not hide the fact that market society is a social construction, one that would certainly have been more difficult and maybe even impossible without the active participation of economists. Economics is not only constructed in the image of market society; market society is society in the image of economics. Market society is society in which the economy, in the sense of the institutions that regulate human interaction in the processes of producing and distributing goods and services, merges with economy in the sense of individual calculation of economic advantage in a world ruled by Scarcity. In Karl Polanyi's terms (1957), the "substantive" economy of institutions merges with the "formal" economy of economizing behavior.

According to a standard definition, economics is the study of the allocation of limited means among unlimited ends. In this view, unlimited ends, like the maximizing individual, are universal, an attribute of the human condition. Thomas Hobbes, who (like Descartes) took Euclidean geometry as inspiration and model, made the inadequacy of means relative to ends the starting point of his politics. The rivalry, or "Competition" in Hobbes's terminology, that leads to the war of all against all begins with scarcity ([1651] 1968, 184).

> [I]f any two men desire the same thing, which neverthelesse they cannot both enjoy, they become enemies; and in the way to their End, (which is principally their owne conservation, and sometimes their delectation only,) endeavour to destroy or subdue one an other.

Evidently the argument is incomplete. Hobbes qualifies the simple relationship scarcity → competition in two ways. First is the assumption of equality. The paragraph from which the quotation is taken actually begins like this (184):

> From this equality of ability, ariseth equality of hope in the attaining of our Ends. And therefore if any two men desire the same thing . . .

Note the "therefore." For scarcity to beget competition, it is necessary that people be equal. Otherwise they will not look upon each other as rivals.

For Hobbes, equality is the relationship of men in the state of nature. Indeed, the chapter in which scarcity and rivalry are discussed is entitled "Of the Naturall Condition of Mankind, as concerning their Felicity, and Misery." It begins (Hobbes [1651] 1968, 183):

> Nature hath made men so equall, in the faculties of body, and mind; as that though there bee found one man sometimes manifestly stronger in body, or of quicker mind then [*then* in original] another; yet when all is reckoned together, the difference between man, and man, is not so considerable, as that one man can thereupon claim to himselfe any benefit, to which another may not pretend, as well as he.

There is a second qualification to the idea that scarcity leads to rivalry. The paragraph that begins with two men desiring the same thing develops into an argument for generalized rivalry, which in its own turn begets scarcity (Hobbes [1651] 1968, 184–85):

> And from hence it comes to passe, that where an Invader hath no more to feare, than an other mans single power; if one plant, sow, build or possesse a convenient Seat, others may probably be expected to come prepared with forces united, to dispossesse, and deprive him, not only of the fruit of his labour, but also of his life, or liberty. And the Invader again is in the like danger of another.

And from this diffidence of one another, there is no way for any man to secure himselfe, so reasonable, as anticipation; that is, by force, or wiles, to master the persons of all men he can, so long, till he see no other power great enough to endanger him . . .

In other words, diffidence (in its older sense of mistrust rather than its current sense of timidity) produces rivalry, which in turn leads to a strategy of deterrence. If you are the potential target, it makes sense to build up your defensive capability so that your potential opponent thinks better of attacking. Maybe it makes sense to think of a preemptive strike . . .

The logic is clear, for it is recognizable as the logic of the cold war of recent memory. What matters here is that there are no limits to acquisition in such situations, for the value of military means is determined by what the other side has. Deterrence requires us to have more, however much that might be. So it is rivalry that produces scarcity rather than the other way around.

Do not think that this counterlogic rivalry → scarcity is limited to military conflict. It is easy to find illustrations of the same logic closer, as it were, to home: it is generally recognized, for example, that cities have become increasingly unattractive and undesirable places for living, not to mention for raising a family. Whereas in the nineteenth, and perhaps even well into the twentieth, century the amenities of urban life improved markedly, in the latter part of this century cities have become increasingly dangerous, unhealthy, and dirty—and show no sign of getting better. The solution, for some at least, is escape—to the suburbs, increasingly to gated enclaves complete with private security guards, or at least to a vacation house in the country. Suburban homes and country retreats may involve a certain amount of conspicuous consumption, but they are much more: where people lack "voice" to take joint action to solve social problems, individual "exit" may be the only solution (Hirschman 1970). In individualistic societies, belief in the power of commodities need not be simply a form of fetishism nor a form of false consciousness, as Marxists often claim, but a realistic assessment of the available options. The mistaken belief is not that *being* is based on *having* but that this is the human condition rather than an artifact of the limited range of options available in individualistic societies.

The problem is that escape is not available to everybody. The cost of land suitable for a nice suburban home or a country retreat is determined precisely by the pressure of demand on the limited supply. As they say in the real estate trade, there are three factors that determine price: location, location, and location. In this case, it is the competition to escape urban blight that leads to the scarcity of suburban and vacation property.

There is yet another qualification to the logic scarcity → rivalry, or at least the seeds of one. According to Hobbes ([1651] 1968, 185), we are all after what he calls Glory:

[E]very man looketh that his companion should value him, at the same rate he sets upon himself . . .

It is a short step from here to Adam Smith's characterization of the spur to material acquisition. Smith begins with a question ([1759] 1976, 50):

[T]o what purpose is all the toil and bustle of this world? What is the end of avarice and ambition, of the pursuit of wealth, of power, and preheminence? . . . From whence, then, arises that emulation which runs through all the different ranks of men, and what are the advantages which we propose by that great purpose of human life which we call bettering our condition?

Here is his answer (50):

To be observed, to be attended to, to be taken notice of with sympathy, complacency, and approbation, are all the advantages which we can propose to derive from it. It is the vanity, not the ease, or the pleasure, which interests us.

We attract "sympathy . . . and approbation" by amassing wealth (50–51):

The rich man glories in his riches, because he feels that they naturally draw upon him the attention of the world, and that mankind are disposed to go along with him in all those agreeable emotions with which the advantages of his situation so readily inspire him.

Once again, the argument reverses causality. The point again becomes to have more than one's neighbors, no matter how much that might be. Rivalry causes scarcity.

The postulates that underlie the assumption of unlimited desires were drawn from the nascent market society of seventeenth-century Britain, but economists and political theorists, Hobbes and his successors, were not simply holding up a mirror to their society. They were helping to create it. Consider the postulate of equality, on which all Hobbes's arguments hinge. It is not that material equality had been achieved, and perhaps material equality had not even advanced in his day. But this doesn't matter, for it is a different kind of equality that is at issue. It is the equality of status, the absence of barriers to social mobility, and the equality of an individualistic society that actualize rivalry when two people want the same thing; it is equality of status that also leads to mistrust and the arms race. Finally, it is the erosion of status, the same individualistic equality, that encourages each man to believe that display of wealth will cause "his companion [to] value him, at the same rate he sets upon himselfe" ([1651] 1968, 185).

What made equality of status plausible as a characterization of people in Hobbes's day was the comparison with the status-oriented society that preceded market society. One example must suffice to illustrate the erosion of status. Earlier, dress and manners appropriate to one's social station had been regulated by custom, internalized norms supplemented by social sanctions for violators. The *bourgeois gentilhomme,* the townsman affecting the airs of a noble, was the object of ridicule. But with the growing anonymity of urban life it became more difficult to enforce social sanctions. In the early years of the seventeenth century, seven years before the birth of the author of *Le Bourgeois Gentilhomme,* Antoine de Montchretien could complain with reason of imposters who "dress like a gentleman . . . corrupting our ancient discipline" ([1615] 1889, 60; quoted in Lebergott 1993, 4).

The attempt to enforce dress codes by means of so-called sumptuary laws—the elaborate legal regulations to make dress accord with status that came into being at the end of the Middle Ages—was a total failure. Indeed, once sumptuary laws appeared on the scene, medieval society was clearly on its last legs. It is a sure sign of social breakdown when the internalized regulating mechanism has stopped working and social sanction no longer is effective. Indeed, once it no longer was unthinkable for a bourgeois to appear in public dressed like a noble, the game was clearly up. Sumptuary laws met the same fate as did the Volstead Act, which prohibited the consumption of alcoholic beverages in the United States early in this century.

It is far from my contention that scarcity exists only in conjunction with modernity. It is rather that scarcity takes on a specific form in the modern world. In the first place, scarcity emerges from the channeling of rivalry into the economic arena. I am prepared to concede, at least for the sake of argument, the universality of the two phenomena Hobbes elaborated, Competition and Diffidence, and the third, Glory, which Smith filled in for him. (The story about the Brahmin and his magic lamp has universal appeal because we all recognize the Brahmin's feelings toward his neighbors.) But the means by which we compete, the means by which we demonstrate our diffidence, the means by which we achieve glory—all these means vary from society to society. Rivalry may be expressed through oratory or song, mistrust may be expressed through spells and witchcraft, and admiration may be sought through display of physical courage. It is peculiarly modern to channel all this rivalry into the economy.

Second, scarcity becomes generalized. Instead of the isolated and incommensurable scarcities that have characterized human existence since time out of mind (remember Joseph, who made his name laying up grain against the famine foretold in Pharaoh's dream), in the modern world we have one big scarcity, Scarcity with a capital *S.* Scarcity structures our existence: since everything is interconnected, everything is scarce (Xenos 1989, 3).

How does this interconnection come about? Once Diffidence and Glory enter the picture, the specifics of goods become less important. If you are hungry, no amount of silk or jewelry will answer your need. But if the need is to command resources in general, as Diffidence requires, or if the need is for display to satisfy the urge for Glory, then goods are much more fungible. That is part of the story, the demand side so to speak. The other part of the story, the supply side, is the growth in commerce and monetization of the economy, which facilitates the substitution of goods and services for one another. King Midas might have thought he would never have a problem because he would always be able to exchange his gold for other commodities. He was, among other things, simply ahead of his time. In the modern world one can.

Finally, scarcity becomes Scarcity because the means become available to alleviate Scarcity. This sounds paradoxical, but Karl Marx and Sigmund Freud separately came up with the same explanation of the paradox, albeit at different levels. Marx ([1859] 1970, 21) said: "Mankind inevitably sets itself only such tasks as it is able to solve." Freud somewhere made a similar remark, I believe, about people in psychoanalysis. Not until the engine of production was sufficiently well developed could the genie of Scarcity be let out of the bottle. Not until the conditions were in place to satisfy desire could rivalry be safely channeled into the economy. Only in the seventeenth century did the European economy become sufficiently oriented toward expansion that demon Scarcity could be tamed by god Growth.

Hobbes's war of all against all was a struggle over the distribution of income. Economists of the seventeenth century finessed this struggle by proposing that the right policy would increase the economic pie overall, so that everybody could have a bigger piece. The economist's love affair with trickle down had begun in earnest, and Growth has been chasing Scarcity ever since. But, like the mechanical rabbit at the dog races, Scarcity has always managed to elude its pursuer.

We can learn something important about this race from a relatively little known work of Keynes, "Economic Possibilities for Our Grandchildren." This piece was published in the fall of 1930 in *The Nation and Athenaeum,* Keynes's vehicle for communicating views of generally Liberal (and liberal) persuasion—his own and others'. Keynes began by admitting to his readers that his purpose in writing the piece was to alleviate the doom and gloom that pervaded British society. The business slump through which the British had suffered during the 1920s was intensifying with the beginnings of the global depression that was to last until the outbreak of World War II.

Focus on the long-term possibilities of capitalism, not the short-run difficulties, Keynes suggested. He begins by introducing his readers into the mysteries of compound interest, tracing Britain's foreign capital of £4 billion to the original stake of £40,000 that Elizabeth I received as her share of the booty Sir Francis Drake stole from the Spanish (who in turn stole it from the Native

Americans—Keynes omits this last detail). This done, Keynes gets to his real point: "[T]he *economic problem* may be solved, or be at least within sight of solution, within a hundred years" (1931, 366 [italics in original]).

Keynes bases this startling prediction on the logic of compound interest. Surveying the economic performance of Europe and North America over recent decades, Keynes argues that it is reasonable to assume that per capita income can grow at the rate of 2 percent per year over the foreseeable future. Now, if income grows at the rate of 2 percent per year per person, we will see a doubling in approximately 35 years, in one generation more or less. Sustained over another generation, income will double again, and after a third generation, roughly 100 years, yet again. So after 100 years the average level of income will be eight times what it is at the start. For Keynes, and perhaps for most of us, an average level of income eight times what it presently is should provide enough for every citizen and then some.

The vista Keynes opens up is breathtaking. For the first time in human history, ordinary people will have time to be, and to become, what they will—for good or ill. On the one hand, the possibilities are endless. On the other, we are as a species totally unprepared to make constructive use of leisure. Keynes doubts whether the human race can adapt to the new freedom from economic scarcity that it will enjoy. "[W]e have been," he tells us (1931, 366),

> expressly evolved by nature—with all our impulses and deepest in-
> stincts—for the purpose of solving the economic problem. If the eco-
> nomic problem is solved mankind will be deprived of its traditional
> purpose.

Keynes fervently hopes that we will do better than what he refers to as the "advance guard," the wealthy classes of the present. But the ordinary folk are hardly more promising. Keynes quotes a traditional epitaph for a cleaning woman to show how limited is the working-class imagination with regard to leisure (1931, 367):

> Don't mourn for me friends, don't weep for me never,
> For I'm going to do nothing for ever and ever . . .
> With psalms and sweet music the heavens'll be ringing,
> But I shall have nothing to do with the singing.

Such passivity may be understandable for people whose lives have been spent in alienating work—the charwoman's ambition is not, after all, so different from that of the present-day couch potato whose work may be physically easier and financially more rewarding but in the end no more meaningful. "Yet," as Keynes says, "it will only be for those who have to do with the singing that life will be tolerable—and how few of us can sing" (1931, 367).

The most striking observation is that freedom from economic want will at last allow us to free ourselves from a system of ethics geared to solving the economic problem but opposed to goodness and decency, opposed to life.

We shall be able to rid ourselves of many of the pseudo-moral principles which have hag-ridden us for two hundred years, by which we have exalted some of the most distasteful of human qualities into the position of the highest virtues. We shall be able to afford to dare to assess the money-motive at its true value . . . a somewhat disgusting morbidity, one of those semi-criminal, semi-pathological propensities which one hands over with a shudder to the specialists in mental disease. All kinds of social customs and economic practices, affecting the distribution of wealth and of economic rewards, and penalties, which we now maintain at all costs, however distasteful and unjust they may be in themselves, because they are tremendously useful in promoting the accumulation of capital, we shall then be free, at last to discard. . . .

I see us free, therefore, to return to some of the most sure and certain principles of religion and traditional virtue—that avarice is a vice, that the exaction of usury is a misdemeanour, and the love of money is detestable, that those walk most truly in the paths of virtue and sane wisdom who take least thought for the morrow. We shall once more value ends above means and prefer the good to the useful. We shall honour those who can teach us how to pluck the hour and the day virtuously and well, the delightful people who are capable of taking direct enjoyment in things, the lilies of the field who toil not, neither do they spin. (Keynes 1931, 369–70, 371–72).

There is much here to chew on,[2] but for present purposes the most striking thing about this passage is its presupposition: the economy is socially constructed (albeit Keynes's social construction is a crude materialism on a par with Karl Marx's). For Keynes, social attitudes, "all kinds of social customs and social practices," not to mention ethics, reflect the needs and requirements of the economy. As long as the economy is geared toward the accumulation of capital, noneconomic institutions, structures of thought, and patterns of behavior must conform, and "we must pretend to ourselves and to every one that fair is foul and foul is fair; for foul is useful and fair is not" (Keynes 1931, 372). Only after sufficient capital has been accumulated can we drop the pretense.

In short, however much Keynes (and Marx as well) might reject the comparison, the Keynesian view differs little from the Marxist dynamic of the base driving the superstructure, with its implication that capitalism dictates the culture of market society—a culture must be tolerated until capitalism can lay the material foundations for a more decent society. As Keynes was writing these words, Josef Stalin was putting a more murderous version of the materialist vision into practice. Forced march, socialist accumulation also was to be temporary and temporarily to require us to "pretend to ourselves and to every one that fair is foul and foul is fair; for foul is useful and fair is not."

I do not wish to overstate the affinity between Keynes and Marx (and certainly not between either of them and Stalin). But their shared materialist conviction is no little thing. It is precisely his materialism that prompts Keynes to see the elimination of work as requiring us to learn to sing. A nonmaterialist view emphasizes that the problem is rather our inability to make our work sing.

But all this is preliminary to my real interest in Keynes's piece. We are now almost two-thirds of the way along the 100-year trek toward the solution of mankind's economic problem. So, how are we doing? *It may come as a surprise to find that we are right on track:* in 1990, the U.S. gross domestic product (GDP) per person had reached a level approximately 3.2 times its 1930 level (U.S. Bureau of the Census 1993, 445). From $6,079, GDP per capita had risen to $19,513, reckoned in terms of 1987 prices. This is almost exactly the increase that a 2 percent per capita growth trajectory would produce.

And yet. And yet, it hardly seems that we are solving our economic problem, even if we confine ourselves to the United States. We certainly do not see any of the signs that Keynes told us were posted on the way (1931, 372):

The course of affairs will simply be that there will be ever larger and larger classes and groups of people from whom problems of economic necessity have been practically removed.

What has gone wrong? I do not propose to examine all the possible answers to this question that challenge the meaningfulness of an aggregate like GDP (what is the appropriate price index; what about the changing role of the nonmonetized, or informal, economy; what about changes in income distribution; what about changes over time in the levels of negative externalities like pollution?). These are important issues, but my strong sense of the data is that when all is said and done we are not far from Keynes's 2 percent growth trajectory. So why is a solution to our economic problem so elusive?

Keynes himself recognized the problem but dodged it. Early on, he raises the issue of the boundlessness of desire: "Now it is true that the needs of human beings may seem to be insatiable" (1931, 365). But that is because we lump all needs together. In fact, needs

fall into two classes—those needs which are absolute in the sense that we feel them whatever the situation of our fellow human beings may be, and those which are relative in the sense that we feel them only if their satisfaction lifts us above, makes us feel superior to, our fellows. Needs of the second class, those which satisfy the desire for superiority, may indeed be insatiable; for the higher the general level, the higher still are they.

But this is not so true of the absolute needs—a point may soon be reached, much sooner perhaps than we are all of us aware of, when these needs are satisfied in the sense that we prefer to devote our further energies to non-economic purposes. (365)

But if to solve the economic problem is to solve a fraction of it, and that fraction the smaller one, then there is no reason to expect that multiplying output by a factor of eight will mean anything like the social upheaval that Keynes predicted. Indeed, no one might even notice that the economic problem was in the process of being solved—as we do not seem to notice today.

What Is to Be Done?

Recall that almost two centuries before Keynes, Adam Smith emphasized the relativity of wants. If the market is dedicated to fulfilling relative wants, and if these are insatiable, then far from being a solution to the problem of scarcity, growth may be its cause. The possibility of growth lets the genie of scarcity out of the bottle, but no amount of growth can ever give everybody more than his neighbor. The growth-driven society is the true zero-sum society.

Would greater equality in the distribution of wealth and income reduce the pressures for growth? My first instinct is to say yes because less concentration should mean less display and less cause for emulation. But this is at best only part of the story. For one thing, equality will presumably increase the demand for goods that satisfy absolute needs, at least for some time to come, and this may add more demand than the reduced role of relative needs takes away. Indeed, in the most prominent mainstream theories of demand, the life-cycle and permanent income hypotheses, redistribution does not affect aggregate demand at all since these theories make the propensity to save scale neutral. By contrast, one strand of theory inspired by Keynes's *General Theory* (1936) argues that the propensity to save is higher for higher income recipients, so that a more equal distribution of income would lead to higher aggregate demand.

But even if we could settle the effect of distribution on consumption demand, this would not settle the issue of the effect of distribution on growth. There remains the issue of the relationship of consumption demand to growth. My intuition that an increase in equality would reduce the demand for goods that satisfy relative needs, and thereby reduce aggregate demand, presupposes implicitly that investment demand responds positively to consumption demand. I am willing to defend this implicit assumption about investment demand even outside the short run to which contemporary mainstream economics has consigned Keynesian considerations of aggregate demand, but it should be recognized that this willingness runs counter to a savings-driven view of the world—be it of neoclassical or Marxist inspiration—in which what is not consumed is automatically invested in productive capital, so that consumption demand is rivalrous with investment demand rather than complementary. (My willingness is contextual: see Andrés Solimano, chap. 4, this volume; and Marglin and Bhaduri 1991.)

Of course, saving and investment do not have to be separated as they are in the Keynesian vision: particularly for the self-employed, saving and investment may be intimately linked, and Nancy Birdsall and her collaborators present a model of saving (chap. 5, this volume) according to which a redistribution of income toward the poor will increase not only saving but investment as well and therefore growth. Such redistribution allows the poor to overcome credit constraints that otherwise prevent them from investing in profitable opportunities.

Even in a savings-driven model, saving is not the only path through which distribution might affect growth. Solimano analyzes several channels, including a political channel through which voters pressure the government for more redistributively oriented policies, as against growth-promoting policies, the greater is the preexisting inequality (chap. 4, this volume).

If the theory is doubtful and contradictory, what about the empirical evidence? What do the data tell us about the relationship between distribution and growth? Unfortunately, they do not tell us much. There is support for the proposition that greater equality reduces measured saving and capital formation, but the evidence is hardly overwhelming (see Klaus Schmidt-Hebbel and Luis Servén, chap. 6, this volume).

A second counterargument to the proposition that greater income equality would reduce the pressure for growth has its roots in Hobbes and Tocqueville. Tocqueville in particular was very clear about the difference between an individualistic society like that of the United States and the old regimes of Europe: in the United States, everyone thought it within his power to improve his lot by competing with everyone else; in the old regimes, ordered by rank and privilege, hardly anyone thought it possible to improve his situation by striving against others. In this view, equality promotes competition and hence efficiency and growth. Indeed, it is the equality imminent in individualism that allows competition to become such a potent force in our society. Equality is the problem, not the solution.

But this line of reasoning reflects a confusion of categories. The equality immanent in individualism is *not* an equality of income or wealth but an equality of opportunity. It is an equality perfectly consistent with a lopsided inequality of outcomes, an inequality that nevertheless entices ever larger numbers of people to enter the Sisyphean quest for more, more, and still more.

However, we must keep distribution and redistribution in perspective. No practicable redistribution is going to eliminate, and maybe not even substantially reduce, the demand for goods that satisfy relative needs. Even with respect to absolute needs, it is by no means clear that we are closing in on the mechanical rabbit, so that later, if not sooner, we can expect to approach satiation, à la Keynes. Medical technology, the growth of which has contributed mightily to the enthusiasm for market rationing as a cure for the expansion of the elderly population, is likely to become even more complex and expensive. But medical care, in Keynesian terminology, is an absolute, not a relative, need. Triple bypasses have yet to become status symbols. As long as solipsistic individualism is the order of the day (see Marglin forthcoming), absolute as well as relative needs may be infinite.

It is only in a very different kind of society that we can even imagine limiting desire. It is the task of the economics of the next century to build such a society with the same care and devotion that we have applied to building the present one over the last four centuries.

But there is no reason to wait for the millennium. As John Kennedy reminded us, a journey of a thousand miles begins with a single step.

N O T E S

1. I am grateful to Professor Pratap Mehta of the Massachusetts Institute of Technology for this reference.

2. For one thing, it is extraordinary from the vantage point of the present how easily and unself-consciously Eurocentric Keynes was. When Keynes says "in the long run *mankind is solving its economic problem*" (1931, 364 [italics in original]), it may be anachronistic to accuse him of ignoring the 51 percent of the population that is female, but it is certainly the case that Africa, Asia, and Latin America are not part of "mankind." Second, one can hardly but be struck by the deliberate but casual anti-Semitism interspersed between the two long paragraphs just quoted, both of which emphasize Keynes's disgust at the love of money (371):

> Perhaps it is not an accident that the race which did most to bring the promise of immortality into the heart and essence of our religions has also done most for the principle of compound interest and particularly loves this most purposive of human institutions.

Even more striking is that such gratuitous calumny apparently offended neither editor (handpicked by Keynes) nor reader—not counting Jewish readers, perhaps.

R E F E R E N C E S

Appleby, Joyce. 1977. *Economic Thought and Ideology in Seventeenth-Century England.* Princeton: Princeton University Press.
de Montchretien, Antoine. [1615] 1889. *Traicte de l'Oeconomie Politique.* Paris: Plon, Nourrit.

Hirschman, Albert. 1970. *Exit, Voice, and Loyalty: Responses to Decline in Firms, Organizations, and States.* Cambridge: Harvard University Press.

Hobbes, Thomas [1651] 1968. *Leviathan.* Harmondsworth: Penguin.

Keynes, John Maynard. 1931. "Economic Possibilities for Our Grandchildren." In *Essays in Persuasion.* London: Macmillan.

―――. 1936. *The General Theory of Employment, Interest, and Money.* London: Macmillan.

Lebergott, Stanley. 1993. *Pursuing Happiness: American Consumers in the Twentieth Century.* Princeton: Princeton University Press.

Marglin, Stephen. Forthcoming. "Clarifying Individualism: A Step towards an Economics of Community." Manuscript.

―――, and Amit Bhaduri. 1991. "Profit Squeeze and Keynesian Theory." In *The Golden Age of Capitalism: Reinterpreting the Postwar Experience,* edited by S. Marglin and J. Schor. Oxford: Clarendon.

Marx, Karl. [1859] 1970. *A Contribution to the Critique of Political Economy.* Translated by S. Ryazanskaya, edited by M. Dobb. New York: International.

Mill, John Stuart. 1969. *Essays on Ethics, Religion, and Society,* edited by J. Robson. Toronto: University of Toronto Press.

Polanyi, Karl. 1957. "The Economy as Instituted Process." In *Trade and Market in the Early Empires: Economies in History and Theory,* edited by Karl Polanyi, Conrad Arensberg, and Harry Pearson. New York: Free Press.

Smith, Adam. [1759] 1976. *The Theory of Moral Sentiments.* Edited by D. Raphael and A. Macfie. Oxford: Clarendon.

Tocqueville, Alexis de [1835–40] 1969. *Democracy in America.* Translated by G. Lawrence, edited by J. Mayer. Garden City, NJ: Doubleday.

U.S. Bureau of the Census. 1993. *Statistical Abstract of the United States, 1993.* Washington, DC: Government Printing Office.

Xenos, Nicholas. 1989. *Scarcity and Modernity.* New York: Routledge.

PART II

Macroeconomic Growth and Developmental Dimensions

CHAPTER 4

The End of the Hard Choices? Revisiting the Relationship between Income Distribution and Growth

Andrés Solimano

1. Introduction

The 1990s are witnessing a renewed interest in issues of income distribution and growth. This contrasts with the relatively minor attention given to distributional matters in the 1980s, particularly in Latin America. Two main reasons stand as possible explanations for this feature. First, economic policies in the last 10 years or so were largely devoted to stabilization, adjustment, and market liberalization. The debt crisis of the 1980s and the ensuing macroeconomic crisis turned the attention of policymakers away from issues of social inequality. Second, the intellectual climate on economic policy since the mid-1970s and during the 1980s was shaped by the rise of free market economics initially associated with the advent of Thatcherism in the United Kingdom and Reaganomics in the United States, a trend that also permeated policy-making circles in Latin America and other areas of the developing world.

In contrast to Keynesianism and developmentalism, in the new paradigm distributive concerns are either largely absent or boil down to poverty issues, a less politically contentious area than is income and wealth distribution.

This situation is starting to evolve. At the mainstream academic level, the renewed interest in both endogenous growth theory and the endogenous theory of economic policy has encouraged new work on the interactions between income distribution and GDP growth. Moreover, this relationship is mediated through the political mechanism under the theory of the "median voter" in democracies. The main thrust of this approach is that inequality is harmful for economic growth.

The purpose of this chapter is to review the relationship among distribution, growth, and development across different theories and models. It examines how different models and theories address the following issues and questions.

49

1. Does economic growth bring greater income equality (or inequality)? Does greater equality hamper or foster economic growth? What do different theories say about the direction of causality and the sign of the relationship between income distribution and growth?
2. What are the main economic transmission mechanisms that mediate the relationship between income distribution and growth? What role do national savings, the rate of investment, productivity growth, education, and capital markets play in shaping that relationship?
3. What political mechanisms are specified (if any) by each theory that affect the relationship between distribution and growth? What role is played by voting mechanisms and social conflict?
4. What empirical evidence is available for both developing and advanced countries, say, regarding the relationship between income distribution and growth?
5. What policy implications can be drawn from alternative theories for fostering both economic growth and social equity?

The chapter is organized in five sections, including this introduction. Section 2 examines a wide range of macroeconomic theories, including classical, neoclassical (Solow), post-Keynesian (Kaldor), endogenous growth–endogenous policy, new structuralist views of wage- and profit-led growth regimes, and neo-Marxist.

The emphasis is on how the model closure adopted to obtain macroeconomic balance affects the sign of the relationship between income distribution and growth. The chapter highlights the main economic mechanisms (savings, profitability, and investment) and political mechanisms (voting and social conflict) at work. Empirical available evidence associated with these approaches, both cross section and time series, is assessed.

Section 3 turns to the analysis of the Kuznets curve, which shows increasing inequality at initial stages of development followed by a decline in inequality at later stages, as the levels of income per person rises above a certain threshold. Rationalizations of the Kuznets relation, as well as empirical evidence testing its shape and stability, are discussed.

Section 4 evaluates analytical and empirical features of the alternative theories reviewed in the chapter, and section 5 highlights policy implications for matching high growth with less social inequality.

2. Macroeconomic Approaches to Distribution and Growth

This section reviews macroeconomic theories of growth and distribution, highlighting transmission mechanisms at work and the sign of the relationship between the two variables.

The Classics

Classical economists such as Adam Smith, David Ricardo, Karl Marx, and others were, in general, skeptical on the possibility that capitalist growth could avoid income and wealth inequalities. Their implicit (and sometimes explicit) models supporting their views were savings-driven growth models in which the savings function provided the link between income distribution and growth. For the classics, the propensities to save were lower (or zero) for wage earners (workers) than for profit recipients (capitalists). In this setting, a more egalitarian income distribution would be associated with a lower (national) savings ratio, reduced capital formation, and sluggish output growth. Against the background of the eighteenth and nineteenth centuries, mainly in England, in which rapid growth and the Industrial Revolution coincided with increasing income and wealth concentration, this view did not seem at odds with reality.[1]

Growth and Distribution in the Neoclassical (Solow) and Post-Keynesian (Kaldor) Models

The neoclassical (Solow) and post-Keynesian (Kaldor) growth theories each have a specific theory of distribution related to the way macroequilibrium is achieved. As is well known, the main difference between the Solow and Kaldor theories is how they solve the Harrod-Domar problem of "knife-edge" instability of the growth process in an economy with fixed technical coefficients in production and a constant savings ratio. The solution proposed by Solow (1956) was to make the capital-labor ratio variable and dependent upon the wage-capital rental ratio. The assumptions of perfect competition and market clearing, constant returns to scale, and savings-driven growth (no independent investment function) give rise to a stable path of steady growth, with flexible factor prices guaranteeing full employment. In this model, growth is exogenous in a steady state and depends on the given rates of growth of the labor force and total factor productivity. In addition, factor prices are determined by the corresponding marginal productivities of capital and labor. In turn, factor shares (income distribution) are determined by capital output ratios and marginal productivities.

In the Solow model, saving is independent of the distribution of income with a constant economywide propensity to save equal for all agents. Under these conditions, income distribution does not directly affect economic growth.

In the model of Kaldor (1957), the Harrod-Domar instability problem is solved by changes in the income distribution between wages and profits as the central mechanism for the attainment of macroequilibrium. Kaldor makes the overall savings ratio the adjustment variable through a "forced savings" mechanism to meet an independent investment function at full employment.[2] Marginal productivity conditions are dropped out of the model, and changes in the profit rate or the wage share bring about the desired changes in savings. A central requirement for this adjustment pattern to occur is the adoption of a Cambridge savings function in which the propensity to save out of profits is greater than the propensity to save out of wages. The Kaldorian theory of distribution is macroeconomic rather than microeconomic in spirit, as in the neoclassical model in which real wages and rental rates on capital are given by marginal productivities and market-clearing conditions. Regarding causality, in the Kaldor model the causality goes from growth to income distribution and from investment to savings. In fact, in the Kaldorian golden age, the wage share and the capital output ratio depend on savings, investment, and technical progress.

Summarizing, in both the neoclassical and Kaldor models there is full employment.[3] Nevertheless, while in the Solow model growth is savings driven, in Kaldor growth is investment driven. Aggregate demand plays no role in the determination of output growth rates in Solow. Income distribution interacts with growth in Kaldor through a Cambridge savings function, a feature absent in the Solow model. A key implication of the growth model of Kaldor is the existence of an inverse relationship between income distribution to labor and growth, as a redistribution of income from high savers (profit recipients) to low savers (wage earners) depresses the national savings rate.

Endogenous Growth–Endogenous Policy Theories

The late 1980s and the first half of the 1990s witnessed a resurgence of academic work on income distribution and growth. These issues have been studied in a framework combining the endogenous growth theory with the theory of endogenous economic policy (see Alesina and Rodrik 1992, 1994; Persson and Tabellini 1992, 1994; Alesina and Perotti 1993; and Perotti 1992).

This new literature rests on three methodological assumptions. First, it reverses the direction of causality of the Solow model and the Kuznets curve. Now the causality runs from distribution to growth. Second, the new models are of investment-driven growth. Third, the new literature introduces a political mechanism along with an economic mechanism to map the effects of income inequality on growth.

The economic mechanism gives a prominent role to capital accumulation as the force that drives growth. Economic policies (the outcome of a political process) reflect citizens' preferences for redistributive vis-à-vis growth-oriented policies. Moreover, the channel through which policies affect growth is after-tax profitability of physical and/or human capital.

The political mechanism is a voting process in elections or referendums. Citizens' preferences for distribution and growth are a function of their endowments of capital, land, talents, skills, and raw labor. In this context, the asset distribution of capital vis-à-vis nonaccumulative assets (labor) will determine the outcome of the political process. The more concentrated is income distribution toward labor, the more biased policies might be toward redistribution as fewer people, relatively speaking, benefit directly from the rewards of capital accumulation and growth.[4] In turn, the more numerous and powerful is the capitalist class in society, the more likely it is that probusiness, progrowth policies will be adopted. The observed growth outcome, in turn, is the result of the political-economic equilibrium, often a reduced form of taxes, government expenditure, and technological parameters.[5]

The main thrust of this literature is that income inequality deters economic growth. In fact, societies with more unequal income distribution are expected to grow less than will economies that start from a more egalitarian distribution of income and wealth. Three reasons can be given to support the "inequality harms growth" view. First, the more unequal is income distributed in the society, the higher will be the level of taxation and other redistributive policies that discourage private accumulation of physical and human capital. A second reason is that a (highly) unequal distribution of income and wealth often generates social tensions, inducing a high level of political instability, which penalizes domestic investment and growth. A third reason is that wealth inequality leads to underinvestment in education by low-income groups that cannot finance it, therefore yielding a lower level of economic growth than otherwise.

Empirical Evidence

The empirics of this inequality-growth literature are largely dominated by cross-section or panel regression analysis.[6] In general, the empirical results reported in the works cited previously tend to support the hypothesis that inequality (an explanatory variable) has a negative, often statistically significant effect on the rate of output growth (the dependent variable in the regressions) after controlling for variables such as initial per capita income, levels of education, and political participation. This result seems to hold for separate samples of developed and less-developed economies (see Persson and Tabellini 1994) and is robust to alternative functional forms of the distribution-growth relationship and different measures of inequality (share of top quintile, Gini coefficient, or Theil coefficient; see Clarke 1992). On the influence of the political regime (democracies or nondemocracies) on the inequality and growth relationship, there seems to be less agreement. While Persson and Tabellini (1994) found that the negative relationship between inequality and growth holds only for democracies, Clarke (1992) and Alesina and Rodrik (1994) found no significant impact of the political regime on the sign and significance of the distribution parameter in the growth regressions. It is worth mentioning that all the models tested, including the economic and political mechanisms, are reduced forms. A structural test of the political mechanism (median voter) has not, to our knowledge, been performed.

A World Bank study by Deininger and Squire (1995a) shows that most of the recent tests of the negative relationship between initial inequality and subsequent economic growth are based on income distribution data of limited coverage and little cross-country and temporal comparability. Moreover, the results obtained in those studies have to be carefully interpreted, as they are estimates derived from reduced forms of a structural model in which other variables may determine the joint comovement of growth and income distribution observed in the data. Moreover, in a related study Liu, Squire, and Zou (1995), using recent and more consistent data on income distribution, show that income inequality is relatively stable within countries and over time, in stark contrast with the behavior of the rates of growth of GDP that do change rapidly and are characterized by very low persistence. These studies call into question the accuracy of the empirical tests of the new growth theory on income inequality.

Persistent Inequality and Growth: The Role of Capital Markets

A variant of the literature in the endogenous growth theory focuses on the existence of credit rationing and incomplete insurance markets for explaining the persistence of wealth and income inequalities (see Aghion and Bolton 1992; Galor and Zeira 1993; and De Gregorio and Kim 1994). The basic argument runs as follows: given an initial distribution of wealth, the future wealth and its distribution will be conditioned by access to financing for accumulation of physical and human capital. The wealthy have more access to credit than do the middle class and the poor since the affluent have assets that can be used as collateral for borrowing. Then, for a given set of accumulation opportunities potentially open to all individuals, only those who can finance projects (with their own wealth and/or through borrowing) can undertake them. As a consequence, the wealth of the rich and upper middle class will grow at a faster rate than will other people's wealth, generating persistent wealth inequality with no self-correcting mechanism at work.[7] The root of the problem is socially stratified access to capital markets, which generates underinvestment (from a social point of view) in physical and human capital and slower growth.

Wage-Led versus Profit-Led Growth Regimes Approaches: Keynesian-Structuralist Models

A different perspective on the relationship between (functional) income distribution and output growth is provided by authors in the structuralist and neo-Keynesian traditions (see Marglin and Bhaduri 1991 and Taylor 1991). These authors look at the relationship between distribution and growth through models in which aggregate demand plays a role in the determination of both short-term output and long-run growth. In their models, income distribution affects aggregate demand and the investment function.

The main policy question asked in this literature is whether income redistribution oriented toward workers is growth depressing (profit-led growth) or growth enhancing (wage-led growth).

The effect of income distribution on growth depends on the net effect of assuming that: (1) aggregate consumption is positively correlated with the wage share provided the marginal propensity to consume from wages is higher than from profits, (2) a higher wage share (lower profit share) can depress profitability and cut investment,[8] and (3) exports may decline with a higher wage share to the extent it reduces export competitiveness through an appreciation of the real exchange rate. To solve these indeterminancies a "wage-led growth regime" is distinguished from a "profit-led growth regime." The former is one in which an increase in the wage share increases output growth. For this effect to hold, the consumption effect, as well as the response of investment to increases in capacity utilization, must be strong.

In contrast, when investment profitability and export competitiveness effects dominate, an increase in the wage share cuts aggregate demand, capacity utilization, investment, and growth. In this case, we are in a "profit-led" growth regime in which progressive income redistribution reduces output growth.

Taylor (1991) introduces a full capacity constraint (and/or a foreign exchange constraint) into the model. These constraints set the limits to redistribution, showing how these policies can lead to inflationary pressures and/or balance of payments crises. This can help rationalize the Latin American experience, in which progressive redistribution often ended in macroeconomic crisis that reversed initial redistributive gains.[9]

Formal econometric testing of the wage- and profit-led hypothesis for industrialized economies shows a positive effect of real wages on aggregate demand in some Organization for Economic Cooperation and Development (OECD) countries. However, in other countries there is a negative correlation between real wages and aggregate demand (Bowles and Boyer 1995). Clearly, there is inconclusive econometric evidence for a "wage-led" macroregime in industrialized countries. In turn, interpreting the postwar experience in industrialized countries, Marglin and Bhaduri (1991) argue that in the United States the "golden age" period of 20 to 25 years of great prosperity after World War II could be characterized as a sort of wage-led growth regime in which higher wages led to high aggregate demand and higher profits. However, the demise of the golden age in the 1970s was associated with a "profit squeeze" according to Marglin and Bhaduri. In fact, the sustained wage expansion that took place in the 1950s and 1960s ultimately led to a cut in profit margins that hampered investment profitability and generated sluggish growth. In the new profit-led regime, the resumption of growth requires, according to the authors, the restoration of business profitability and wage moderation as well as institutional changes in the "rules of the game" that govern capital-labor relations.

TABLE 1. Summary of Distribution and Growth Theories

Models/Theories	Model Closure		Economic Mechanism		Sociopolitical Mechanism		Causality		Type of Relationship Inequality/Growth	
	Savings-driven Growth	Investment-driven Growth	Classic Saving Function	Profitability and Investment	Median Voter	Bargaining Power of Capitalists/Workers	Income Distribution to Growth	Growth to Income Distribution	Inverse	Direct
Classic	X		X				X			X
Solow	X							X		
Kaldor		X	X					X		X
New growth theory/ endogenous policy		X		X	X		X			
Wage-led and profit-led growth theories		X		X			X		X	
Neo-Marxist theories						X	X			
Long run	X		X			X	X			X
Profits squeeze/ social structures of accumulation		X		X		X	X			X

At the level of developing countries, the analysis of austerity and stabilization programs in the 1980s supported by the International Monetary Fund (IMF) and the World Bank, as reported in Taylor 1991, tends to show that the adoption of contractionary programs to reduce inflation and restore external balance often came with a worsening of income distribution, favoring a sort of wage-led regime hypothesis.

Neo-Marxist Approaches

The neo-Marxist view on the relationship between distribution and growth rests on several assumptions, some of them linked to the profit squeeze story just outlined. Three assumptions stand as important here. First, the profit rate and wages are determined by the relative bargaining power of capitalists versus workers. This bargaining process is influenced partly by economic considerations, such as the rate of unemployment in the labor market and the degree of slack or boom in the goods market, and partly by the bargaining power of capitalists vis-à-vis workers. In turn, class relations are mediated by social institutions both at the level of the firm (e.g., type of capital-labor industrial relations) and at the national level via the political system.

Second, profits are the main determinant of capital accumulation.

Third, capital accumulation and technological change are the main driving forces in the growth process.

At this point, it is useful to distinguish between three specifications sharing these assumptions. The first is provided by Marglin (1984, chap. 3), wherein the neo-Marxist model is cast in terms of steady state growth. The model drops the assumption of an independent investment function and assumes a classical savings function in which all profits are saved and all wages consumed. The resulting model is one of savings-driven growth with causality running from income distribution (exogenously given by social factors) to growth.

A second specification is the so-called high-employment profit squeeze, which focuses on the endogenous occurrence of economic crises after a long and protracted period of rapid growth, and high employment, which leads to the growing bargaining power of labor, higher real wages, and lower profit margins. The story is basically the one told by Marglin and Bhaduri (1991) in which a period of tight labor markets and high demand eventually conduces to a profit squeeze that leads to a decline in capital formation and a slowdown in output growth (see also Glyn, Hughes, Lipietz, and Singh 1991).

A third variant is the so-called social structures of accumulation view (see Weisskopf 1994; and Bowles, Gordon, and Weisskopf 1989). This approach retains the three assumptions just stated and emphasizes the institutional framework that mediates capital-labor conflict in order to support private investment and growth in a capitalist economy.

3. Inequality and Development: The Kuznets Curve

The relationship between the level of economic development and income distribution has been studied in the framework provided by the Kuznets curve, a sort of inverted U-shaped relationship between income per capita and income inequality (see fig. 1). The pattern, first found by Simon Kuznets, was one of rising income inequality at low to moderate levels of income per capita followed by a decline in inequality as the country began to reach higher levels of income and improve other indicators of overall economic development.

The Kuznets curve, however, is more an empirical regularity than a theory. In a way, it is like the Phillips curve in macroeconomics: an empirical finding (sometimes elusive) with an also elusive analytical grounding.

The rationalizations of the Kuznets curve focus on the transition, during the development process, from "traditional" agriculture (of low productivity) to "modern" sectors such as manufacturing (with higher productivity and more intensive requirements of skilled labor and new technologies). In the early stages of development, the existence of a labor surplus in the rural sector allows the transfer of workers from agriculture to industry to take place without any substantial increase in the real wage of unskilled labor. In contrast, the real earnings of skilled workers, in short supply, rise substantially during the agriculture-industry transition, generating a widening of the wage structure and a worsening of wage income distribution.[10]

A decline in inequality (the downward-sloping portion of the Kuznets curve) occurs when income per person rises, labor markets become tight (the "reserve army" of labor disappears), and, concomitantly, the premium on higher skills encourages an increase in the supply of qualified labor through education and training. As this process unfolds, the wage gap narrows and distribution improves.

Empirical Evidence

The Kuznets curve spurred a vast empirical effort devoted to testing its shape, determining its robustness to the selection of countries and time periods, and detecting turning points in which income distribution starts improving during the development process.

The empirical cross section work of Ahluwalia (1976), Lindert and Williamson (1985), Adelman and Robinson (1989), Bourguignon and Morrison (1990), and others tends to give (qualified) support to the existence of the Kuznets curve. In addition, for cross-country regressions, the inequality portion of the Kuznets curve tends to be more unstable than is the portion of declining inequality (see fig. 1a). Since the inequality part of the curve comprises countries in a range of lower to moderate income per capita levels, the relationship is more unstable for these countries.[11] In contrast, it seems a more

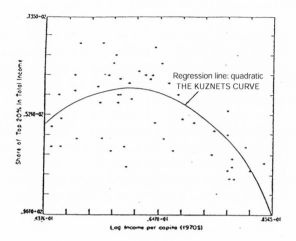

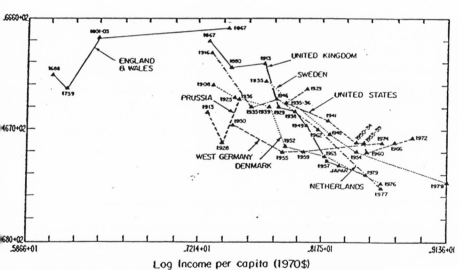

Log Income per capita (1970$)

Fig. 1. The Kuznets curve: (a) international 60-country cross-section from the 1960s and 1970s (from Ahluwalia 1976, table 8, pp. 340–41); (b) historical time series from five European countries and the United States (from Lindert and Williamson 1985). Reproduced from Lindert and Williamson 1985.

established fact that inequality tends to decline for countries at the intermediate and high levels of per capita income (see fig. 1b).[12]

However, studies for individual countries in Latin America (Colombia, Brazil, and Argentina) and for Asian countries are reported to conform to the Kuznets curve pattern (see Fields and Jakubson 1993) with a comparison of the impact of inequality on growth in Latin America and East Asia conducted in Birdsall and Sabot 1994.

Two World Bank studies (Deininger and Squire 1995a, 1995b) have produced an expanded data base on income distribution of improved coverage and consistency to reevaluate existing studies of the Kuznets curve. These World Bank studies, pooling cross-section with time-series data, show that the Kuznets curve holds only for only a very small set of countries (10 percent of the sample) and in general no statistically significant relationship between the level of income and inequality is found for over 75 percent of the sample. The "universal Kuznets curve" fails to be detected in the data. These studies thus cast doubt on the existence and robustness of the Kuznets curve.

4.   Integration and Evaluation

Economic Mechanisms

As the previous discussion suggests, the relationship between distribution and growth is largely shaped by the way macroeconomic equilibrium is attained. In fact, in full-employment, savings-driven growth models an inverse relationship between equality and growth is derived. Moreover, in these models the causality goes from growth to income distribution.

In investment-driven growth models, the causality is reversed and runs from distribution (often a predetermined variable) to subsequent growth. In political-economic growth models, income inequality deters economic growth by inviting, through the political process, the adoption of distortionary policies that depress the private incentives to accumulate physical and human capital. Moreover, large social inequalities can generate political instability and social conflict. As private investment is highly sensitive to uncertainty and political instability,[13] a more stable social environment certainly fosters growth.

In neo-Keynesian/structuralist models in which aggregate demand plays a role in determining long-run growth, inequality can be either growth depressing (a wage-led growth regime) or growth enhancing (a profit-led growth regime), depending upon the effects of income distribution on aggregate demand and private investment.

In neo-Marxist models of savings-driven growth, distribution and growth are inversely related, a result that also holds when the model is closed with investment-driven growth.[14] Clearly, distributional issues have to be discussed in *macroeconomic* terms when linked to growth, with savings and investment playing a central role both in the transmission process and in the sign of the relationship.

An important issue is how to reconcile the Kuznets curve with the macro-models of distribution and growth reviewed here.

The Kuznets curve shows that the relationship between both variables is contingent upon per capita income *levels.* At low levels of income per person, a certain degree of concentration in income distribution might be required to allow economic agents to finance a sufficient accumulation of human and physical capital for the growth process to take off. However, after the economy has reached a higher level of income, the same pattern of income distribution becomes dysfunctional and may hamper future economic expansion. Interestingly, this story emerges both from the endogenous growth–endogenous policy theories in which citizens who are dissatisfied with current distributive patterns vote for higher taxation on capital and from profit-squeeze theories predicting that after a long period of growth organized labor, pressing for higher wages and better working and social conditions, seeks a larger slice of the economic pie. The implication is clear: at certain development levels, and after a period of protracted growth with inequality, the system generates demands for some degree of redistribution as labor and other low-income groups seek a greater share of the benefits of development.

The Political Mechanism

The endogenous growth–endogenous policy theories reviewed here present a political mechanism that connects distribution with growth. That mechanism transmits the redistribution preferences of the citizens to the government, so that it can implement the corresponding policies. A central implication of this theory is that the initial asset distribution in society is an important force shaping the choice between pro-growth versus redistributive policies.

The voting mechanism for altering the distribution of income and wealth, and ultimately for changing the distribution of power in society, has several shortcomings worth mentioning. First, it seems a more relevant mechanism for inducing small to moderate changes in distributive patterns. The most radical changes in asset distribution—toward the state—in the twentieth century, the socialist revolutions of the Soviet bloc and other places, which expropriated the capitalists and eventually abolished most private property, were not the outcome of an exercise of public choice by informed citizens casting their votes in democratic elections.[15] On the contrary, they often followed a period of armed conflict and/or social uprisings.

Second, in general, in spite of voters' preferences to change the existing patterns of income distribution, actual redistributive policies can be blocked or resisted by those affected by higher taxes, increasing regulations, or downright expropriation. In this case, though the voting process can be reflected in the design of policies, this does not guarantee its implementation.

Third, the theory as stated is relevant for democracies, a feature that obviously reduces its degree of generality. In fact, even authoritarian governments need feedback mechanisms to detect citizens' preferences regarding the policy choices they make.

The political mechanism that maps distributive claims into actual policies embedded in the endogenous growth and policies theory is a direct extension of the "economic theory of democracy."[16] However, the strong links between citizens' preferences for redistribution (or growth) and government policies are weaker in other theories of the state. The "state autonomy" view takes a different perspective and argues that government policies are largely explained by preferences and values of state managers and the characteristics of state institutions. In this context, bureaucrats and politicians manage to become largely autonomous, even under democratic conditions, free to set and pursue their own policies with relatively weak links to citizens' preferences.

Another strand of theory, derived mainly from neo-Marxist political theory, posits that under capitalism the main role of the state is to respect and protect the claims of those who own the productive wealth of society (Przeworski 1990). Ultimately, citizens' preferences and state managers' goals are circumscribed by the public power of capital.

These other views of the state, thus, can provide additional perspectives that can help us to understand the U-turns or open failures of the redistributive policies of elected governments, as their implementation can undermine the prospects of government officials in power and/or affect created interests in society.

Empirical Issues

A central difficulty in testing reduced-form growth equations so as to discriminate between different theories of distribution and growth is that the empirical models are likely to be overidentified or observationally equivalent. Additional difficulties are associated with problems of reverse causality and omitted variables, and the quality, coverage and reliability of the data on income distribution is often weak (e.g., personal vs. household data, underreporting of non-wage incomes, and national vs. local coverage). For all these reasons, caution is required in drawing strong conclusions from the empirical work in this area. Moreover, it seems necessary to move from large, multicountry analyses to individual country studies of income distribution and growth patterns supplemented by more specific knowledge of historical and institutional characteristics.

5. Policy Concerns: Can We Have Social Equity and Sustained Growth?

A central policy question is whether public policies oriented toward improving income distribution can be compatible with high and sustained growth. The macrogrowth models reviewed here offer arguments to support both "conservative" views that redistribution deters growth and "progressive" views in which redistribution and growth are compatible, or even mutually reinforcing, goals. Analytically, the conservative view finds support in two models. In a full-capacity, growing economy, income distribution to relatively low savings groups can depress the aggregate savings ratio, therefore leading to a decline in growth. In investment-driven models, redistributive policies that entail higher taxation and/or regulation depress privately appropriated returns on human capital and physical investment and harm growth.

Are we thus condemned to accepting social inequality as the price for high growth policies? Is the "conservative equilibrium" inescapable? Not necessarily. Three arguments are in order here. First, the message of the Kuznets curve is that the growth process itself will be "equalizing" beyond a certain threshold of income per capita, making the fruits of progress and development available to a greater portion of the population. Second, beyond trickle down, policy intervention in assuring broad social access to education can have a big payoff. The market equilibrium can yield substantial underinvestment, particular in human capital, for those at the bottom of the income distribution scale, who cannot pay for education and face very limited access to capital markets. The rewards in terms of accelerated growth of education widening is bound to be sizable.

Third, a more equitable distribution of income and economic opportunities also contributes to social peace and political stability, key ingredients in a policy framework conducive to investment, innovation, and growth. Ultimately, social equity and economic growth can go hand by hand if properly articulated with respect to some key binding economic and political constraints in society.

NOTES

1. Lindert and Williams (1985) document peaks of (personal) income inequality around the 1860s in England and the second decade of the twentieth century in the United States, which declined thereafter in both countries (see fig. 1b).

2. Another strand of "Neo-keynesian" theory is given by Kaleckian models of growth and distribution. Those models differ from Kaldor (1957) in the sense of having an independent investment function determined by profitability and the rate of capacity utilization and assuming monopolistic competition. In the Kaleckian framework, aggregate demand and the distribution of income affect the determination of

output growth with causality running from distribution to growth (see Marglin 1984 and Lavoie 1992).

3. See Sen 1963.

4. The limits for the majority on the level of redistributive taxation they can vote for is given by the response of capital to taxation and other redistributive moves. The capitalist class and the business community are likely to withdraw their investment plans in the face of aggressive redistribution. This behavior was observed in Chile under the Allende government in the early 1970s, in Nicaragua under the Sandinistas in the 1980s, and in other places where radical redistribution has been tried.

5. The specifics of model formulation vary from author to author. Some work with personal income distribution and others with functional distribution. The asset to be privately accumulated can be physical or human capital (education). Policy interventions may be public investment, transfers, taxes on capital, capital controls, and regulation. However, the common result is that the higher the policy distortion the lower the investment rate and thus growth.

6. It is hard to find time-series, historically oriented studies of distribution and growth in this literature.

7. Bertola (1993) shows in a related case that initial class structures are perpetuated along a path of endogenous growth in a model of optimizing agents and an economywide Cambridge savings function.

8. The profit rate (profits over the value of capital stock) can be written as the profit share (profits over output) times the ratio of output over capital (or rate of capacity utilization). Then the effect of wage share on the profit rate depends on the net impact of a negative profit share effect and a potentially positive capacity utilization effect.

9. These were the cases of Chile under Allende in the early 1970s and Peru under Alan García in the mid to late 1980s among others (see Dornbusch and Edwards 1991).

10. Moreover, if profits rise in the process, the overall income distribution worsens.

11. A recent paper, Fields and Jakubson 1993, finds a reversal of the Kuznets curve using a "fixed effects" model that allows for different countries to lie on Kuznets curves with the same shape but different intercepts. However, in pooled models the standard Kuznets curve is maintained.

12. This does not rule out changes in the levels of inequality between periods as the result of changes in economic policies. This seems to have been the case in the United States under President Reagan and the United Kingdom under Prime Minister Thatcher, where inequality increased (see Krugman 1994).

13. See Pindyck and Solimano 1993 and Servén and Solimano 1993.

14. Neo-Marxist models are often supply-side models, with the investment function depending only on the profit rate. Keynesian models also introduce, as an argument of the investment function, the degree of capacity utilization. In this case, as already discussed, there is not necessarily an inverse relationship between distribution and growth.

15. An exception to this was, perhaps, the election in Chile in 1970 of the socialist candidate Salvador Allende, who promised a program of nationalization of large industrial firms and banks and radical agrarian reform. The Allende government, which actually implemented redistributive policies, lasted only three years (the constitutional

period was six years) and was ousted by a military coup in a context of acute economic and political crises (see Marcel and Solimano 1994). In some sense, the final outcome of the Allende experiment illustrates the limits of radical redistribution pursued through voting mechanisms.

16. See Przeworski 1990 for an excellent analysis of alternative theories of the state and the economy under capitalism.

REFERENCES

Adelman I., and S. Robinson. 1989. "Income Distribution in Development." In *Handbook of Development Economics,* edited by H. Chenery and T. N. Srinivasan. Vol. 2. Amsterdam and New York: North-Holland.

Aghion P., and P. Bolton. 1992. "Distribution and Growth in Models of Imperfect Capital Markets." *European Economic Review* 36:603–11.

Ahluwalia, M. 1976. "Inequality, Poverty, and Development." *Journal of Development Economics* 3:307–42.

Alesina, A., and R. Perotti. 1993. "The Political Economy of Growth: A Critical Survey of Recent Literature and Some Results." World Bank. Mimeo.

Alesina, A., and D. Rodrik. 1992. "Income Distribution and Economic Growth: A Simple Theory and Empirical Evidence." In *The Political Economy of Business Cycles and Growth,* edited by A. Cukierman, Z. Hercovitz, and L. Leiderman. Cambridge: MIT Press.

———. 1994. "Distributive Politics and Economic Growth." *Quarterly Journal of Economics* 109 (May): 456–90.

Bertola, G. 1993. "Factor Shares and Savings and Endogenous Growth." *American Economic Review* 83 (5): 1184–98.

Birdsall, N., and R. Sabot. 1994. "Inequality as a Constraint on Growth in Latin America." Inter-American Development Bank. Mimeo.

Bourguignon, F., and C. Morrison. 1990. "Income Distribution, Development, and Foreign Trade: A Cross Sectional Analysis." *European Economic Review* 34:1113–32.

Bowles, S., D. Gordon, and T. Weisskopf. 1989. "Business Ascendancy and Economic Impasse: A Structural Retrospective on Conservative Economics, 1979–1987." *Journal of Economic Perspectives* 3 (1): 107–34.

Bowles, S., and R. Boyer. 1995. "Wages, Aggregate Demand, and Employment in an Open Economy." In *Macroeconomic Policy after the Conservative Era,* edited by G. Epstein and H. Gintis. Cambridge: Cambridge University Press.

Clarke, G. 1992. "More Evidence on Income Distribution and Growth." Working Paper 1,064. World Bank.

De Gregorio, J., and S. Kim. 1994. "Credit Markets with Differences in Abilities: Education, Distribution, and Growth." Working Paper 94/97. International Monetary Fund.

Deininger, K., and L. Squire. 1995a. "Inequality and Growth: Results from a New Data-Base." World Bank. Mimeo.

———. 1995b. "Measuring Income Inequality: A New Data-Base." World Bank. Mimeo.

Dornbusch, R., and S. Edwards, editors. 1991. *The Macroeconomics of Populism in Latin America.* Chicago and London: University of Chicago Press.

Fields, G., and G. Jakubson. 1993. "New Evidence on the Kuznets Curve." Cornell University. Mimeo.

Galor, O., and J. Zeira. 1993. "Income Distribution and Macroeconomics." *Review of Economic Studies* 60:35–52.

Glyn, A., A. Hughes, A. Lipietz, and A. Singh. 1991. "The Rise and Fall of the Golden Age." In *The Golden Age of Capitalism,* edited by S. Marglin and J. Schor. Oxford: Clarendon and Oxford University Press.

Kaldor, N. 1957. "A Model of Economic Growth." *Economic Journal* 67:591–624.

Krugman, P. 1994. *Peddling Prosperity.* New York: Norton.

Larraín, F., and P. Meller. 1991. "The Socialist-Populist Chilean Experience, 1970–73." In *The Macroeconomics of Populism in Latin America,* edited by R. Dornbusch and S. Edwards. NBER Conference Report. Chicago: University of Chicago Press.

Lavoie, M. 1992. *Foundations of Post-Keynesian Analysis.* London: Edward Elgar.

Liu, H., L. Squire, and H. Zou. 1995. "Explaining International and Intertemporal Variations in Income Inequality." World Bank. Mimeo.

Lindert, P. H., and J. Williamson. 1985. "Growth, Equality, and History." *Explorations in Economic History* 22:341–77.

Marcel, M., and A. Solimano. 1994. "The Distribution of Income and Economic Adjustment." In *The Chilean Economy: Policy Lessons and Challenges,* edited by B. Bosworth, R. Dornbusch, and R. Laban. Washington, DC: Brookings Institution.

Marglin, S. A. 1984. *Growth, Distribution, and Prices.* Cambridge: Harvard University Press.

———, and A. Bhaduri. 1991. "Profit Squeeze and Keynesian Theory." In *The Golden Age of Capitalism: Reinterpreting the Postwar Experience,* edited by S. Marglin and J. Schor. Oxford: Clarendon and Oxford University Press.

Persson, T., and G. Tabellini. 1992. "Growth, Distribution, and Politics." *European Economic Review* 36:593–602.

———. 1994. "Is Inequality Harmful for Growth?" *American Economic Review* 84 (3):600–621.

Pindyck, R., and A. Solimano. 1993. "Economic Instability and Aggregate Investment." In *NBER Macroeconomic Annual,* edited by S. Fischer and O. Blanchard. Cambridge: MIT Press.

Przeworski, A. 1990. *The State and the Economy under Capitalism: Fundamentals of Pure and Applied Economics.* New York: Harwood Academic.

Sen, A. 1963. "Neo-classical and Neo Keynesian Theories of Distribution." *Economic Record* 39:53–64.

Servén, L., and A. Solimano. 1993. *Striving for Growth after Adjustment: The Role of Capital Formation.* World Bank.

Solimano, A. 1992. "Economic Growth and Income Distribution: Macro-Economic Trade-Offs Revisited." *Revista de Análisis Económico* (Santiago, Chile) 7 (Nov.): 43–68.

Solow, R. 1956. "A Contribution to the Theory of Growth." *Quarterly Journal of Economics* 70:65–94.

Taylor, L. 1991. *Income Distribution, Inflation, and Growth: Lectures on Structuralist Macroeconomic Theory.* Cambridge: MIT Press.

Weisskopf, T. 1994. "Alternative Social Structures of Accumulation Approaches to the Analysis of Capitalist Booms and Crises." In *Social Structures of Accumulation: The Political Economy of Growth and Crisis,* edited by D. Kotz, T. McDonough, and M. Reich. Cambridge: Cambridge University Press.

CHAPTER 5

Why Low Inequality Spurs Growth: Savings and Investment by the Poor

Nancy Birdsall, Thomas C. Pinckney, and Richard H. Sabot

1. Introduction

New empirical evidence on the relationship between inequality and growth contradicts an important dimension of the conventional wisdom regarding the nature of the process of transforming low-income into high-income economies. The conventional wisdom is that high rates of economic growth are likely to be associated with high levels of inequality in the distribution of income. This prediction, made decades ago, was largely based on economic theory. Kuznets (1955) saw rising inequality as the by-product of growth and structural change. As workers shift from a low- to a high-productivity sector there is a tendency for inequality to increase at first. Kaldor (1978) and—more specifically for developing countries—Galenson and Leibenstein (1955) saw the causality running the other way, from high inequality to rapid growth. If the rich have a higher marginal propensity to save than do the poor, greater concentration of income results in higher savings in the aggregate, hence in more rapid capital accumulation and growth.

There is evidence, however, that countries with relatively low levels of inequality in 1960 grew faster over the subsequent three decades than did countries in which the distribution of income was more skewed.[1] Rather than being associated with more rapid growth, high levels of inequality appear to be a constraint on growth. Thus, higher levels of inequality help to explain Latin America's slower growth relative to that of East Asia.

Figure 1 relates percentage growth in Gross Domestic Product (GDP) for the period 1965 to 1990 and income inequality, as measured by the ratio of the income share of the top and bottom quintiles. Latin American countries are concentrated in the southeast corner, indicating that they experienced slow growth and high inequality, while East Asian countries, having achieved both low inequality and rapid growth, stand alone in the northwest corner. Birdsall, Ross, and Sabot (1995) assess econometrically the relationship between inequality and growth, controlling for other determinants of growth. The addition

GDP growth per capita in percent

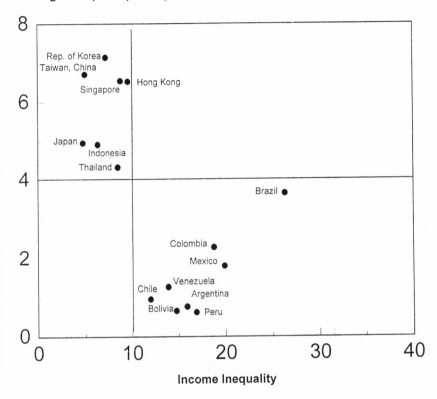

Income Inequality

Fig. 1.   Income inequality and growth of GDP, 1965–90. Income inequality is the average ratio of the income shares of the richest and poorest 20
percent of the population. (Data from World Bank 1993.)

of a measure of inequality, in 1970 or earlier, to the basic Barro function
explaining variations in growth rates among 74 countries over the period
1960–89 does not change the parameter estimates much. The results are presented in table 1. The education variables remain significantly positive. The
inequality variable is negative and significant (at the 10 percent level).

How important is high inequality as a constraint on growth? For this
sample of low- and middle-income countries in 1960, the average annual rate
of growth in per capita GDP between 1960 and 1985 was 1.8 percent. One
standard deviation increase in primary and secondary education raises growth

TABLE 1.   Per Capita Income of the Poor and Secondary Enrollment Rates

Country	Per Capita Income	Income Share, Bottom 20%	Per Capita Income, Bottom 20%	Secondary School Enrollment Rate
Indonesia, 1976	240	6.6	79	21
Kenya, 1976	240	2.6	31	17
Malaysia, 1987	1,810	4.6	416	59
Costa Rica, 1986	1,480	3.3	254	42
Brazil, 1983	1,880	2.4	226	35
Korea, 1976	670	5.7	191	88
Botswana, 1986	840	2.5	115	31
Indonesia, 1987	450	8.8	251	47
Philippines, 1985	580	5.5	160	68

Source: World Development Report, various years.

rates by 0.62 and 0.34 percentage points, respectively. One standard deviation decrease in the level of income inequality raises the predicted growth rate by 0.32 of a percentage point. Although the impact on growth of a change in inequality is smaller than similar changes in enrollment rates, the effect of reducing inequality is still substantial. Ceteris paribus, after 25 years, GDP per capita would be 8.2 percent higher in a country with low inequality than in a country with inequality one standard deviation higher.

Why are the predictions of the old theory contradicted by the new evidence? Some suggested explanations focus on the political implications of a highly skewed distribution of income. Higher inequality leads to the political alienation of the poor and hence to greater political and economic instability. Instability discourages investment, thereby lowering growth. Alternatively, in a democracy high inequality leads to popular demands for taxes on the capital of the rich, thereby discouraging investment and lowering growth.[2]

In this chapter, we suggest a different explanation for the negative relationship between inequality and growth, one that does not depend on the impact of inequality on the political process. Rather, we focus on the microeconomic behavior of poor households. We describe a set of circumstances that can trigger a savings and investment boom among the poor. The poor are credit constrained, implying that they cannot borrow to finance even those investments that yield extraordinary returns. And their poverty precludes much reduction of consumption as a means of financing investments. However, if the returns to labor are sufficiently high, the poor can intensify their work effort to generate additional income to finance high-return investments.[3] Under these circumstances, the marginal propensity to save from this additional income may be exceptionally high—100 percent or more.

An outward-looking, labor-demanding, growth strategy of the sort adopted by the rapidly developing countries of East Asia can generate the preconditions for a savings and investment boom by the poor. It can yield both high-return investment opportunities for the poor and high returns to labor. A boom in savings and investment among the poor can, in turn, simultaneously reduce poverty and income inequality and stimulate growth, thereby helping to explain the growth with equity achieved in East Asia. By contrast, an inward-looking, capital-intensive, growth strategy typical of Latin America may constrain the labor supply, savings, and investment of the poor, thereby contributing to both high inequality and low growth.

We develop these ideas in the rest of this chapter. The next section discusses in more detail our hypotheses regarding high-return investment and employment opportunities as determinants of savings by poor, credit-constrained households.[4] In section 3, we assess whether the assumptions of the model are realistic. Section 4 considers the implications of the model for the relationship between inequality and growth, with a focus on human capital investment in Brazil and Korea. Section 5 concludes.

2. Savings and Investment by the Poor

In high-income countries, economists normally distinguish between the determinants of savings and the determinants of investment. Because of financial intermediation, households can borrow to finance current investment that exceeds desired current saving and can accumulate financial assets in years that desired saving exceeds desired investment. Therefore, in permanent income and life-cycle models of savings behavior, while savings in any one year are influenced by current income—considered exogenous—over the long run households save in productive years to provide income for unproductive years in the future. A typical household first accumulates and then decumulates assets.

Savings behavior in high-income countries, however, does not typically follow the predictions made by life-cycle and permanent income models (Deaton 1992b; Carroll 1994). Precautionary motives and liquidity constraints are gaining more prominence as explanations. In low-income countries, where a high proportion of households are multigenerational (Deaton 1990), life-cycle and permanent income models are likely to be even less relevant. Adults expect their children to support them in their old age, as they themselves are supporting their parents. Thus, there may be little need for "hump" or retirement savings as a vehicle for transferring income between high- and low-productivity phases of the life cycle.

In such households, savings serve in part as a buffer against stochastic decreases in income. Deaton (1990, 61) asserts that "such households dissave as often as they save, do not accumulate assets over the long term, and have on average very small asset holdings." Deaton (1990, 1992a) develops a model of this precautionary savings behavior of low-income, multigenerational households.[5] His model assumes that households cannot borrow.[6]

Households may choose to hold precautionary savings in unproductive but liquid assets such as stocks of food, jewelry, and precious metals. When they choose to save in productive assets, however, the return to investment represents an incentive to save over and above the benefits in terms of risk reduction. In the absence of borrowing, household investment must be financed by—and thus can be no greater than—household savings. This implies that the expected returns to investment will be, in effect, the "interest rate" relevant for determining savings (as noted in McKinnon 1973). It also implies that an increase in the returns to investment will directly increase incentives for saving.[7] Schultz (1964) recognized this in his explanation of the correlation of low observed savings rates and the absence of profitable agricultural investment opportunities.

On the one hand, households can increase the share of present income allocated to savings only with substantial sacrifice. There are few luxuries to cut out of consumption bundles that are already scanty. And the poor are likely to have high rates of time preference given the pressing nature of many of their demands for cash. If the returns to investment are initially low, below the rate of time preference for the poor, then savings will result only from precautionary motives. In many environments, the incentives for the poor to invest are in fact low.

On the other hand, consider the impact of an increase in the returns to investment—such as might arise from the development of a new agricultural technology, more favorable agricultural price policies, the introduction of a new crop, an improvement in the quality of local schools, or a rise in the demand for educated labor—on income and savings of the poor. An increase in the returns to investment that raises the rate of return above the rate of time preference will, by definition, be attractive to the poor and will induce some poor households to search for ways of obtaining funds for investment.[8]

In the presence of credit constraints, the attractive new investment must be financed without borrowing. There are only two possibilities for a household in this situation: finance the investment by decreasing consumption or finance the investment by increasing work effort and thus income. This latter mechanism is vitally important. Past analyses of savings behavior by the poor, and the response of the poor to improvements in investment opportunities, have considered income to be exogenous. But a rational household faced with improved investment opportunities that will yield returns above the rate of time preference will respond by working harder to finance the investment as long as the marginal returns to additional labor are above zero (Birdsall, Pinckney, and Sabot 1995). Present income, then, is a function of the rate of return to investment.

In effect, the increase in the rate of return to investment increases the marginal utility of money in the initial period for a credit-constrained household. This induces the household to accept a lower level of leisure and a lower level of consumption initially, to allow the investment to take place.[9] The household is trading off a loss in utility in the initial period for a larger gain in utility in the future.

In this case, the marginal savings rate of a poor, credit-constrained household will be greater than one. When investment opportunities improve, all of the increase in income that results from increased labor supply is added to savings; in addition, savings increase by the amount that consumption decreases. This high marginal savings rate can lead to overall savings rates for the poor that are quite large, particularly when measured as a percentage of income prior to the increase in investment opportunities.

The dynamics of this response to improved returns to investment can lead to a virtuous circle as increases in investment and income reinforce each other. The rate of time preference of the poor is likely to decline as their income increases. Other investment opportunities then become attractive, and labor supply, savings, and investment will increase in order to match savings to desired investment.

The initial increments to savings and investment triggered by an increase in returns to investment will be positively related to the returns to labor. The marginal productivity of additional labor must be sufficiently large, and decline slowly enough, to allow for an increase in current income from decreased leisure.

Moreover, where returns to investment are already high, increases in the demand for labor, hence in returns to labor, can be another trigger for large increases in savings and investment. If at the margin returns to labor are low or decline rapidly, only slight increases in labor supply will occur. Therefore, nearly all of any increase in savings will result from decreases in current consumption. Given that small declines in consumption of the poor are likely to increase the marginal utility of consumption substantially, where the labor supply response is limited only small increases in savings are likely to result from improved investment opportunities. This implies that a boom in savings among the poor is unlikely to occur when there are conditions of surplus labor of the sort described by Lewis (1954).

In sum, there are two mechanisms that can lead to high marginal savings rates by poor, credit-constrained households: First, when the perceived rate of return to investment increases to the point where it is above the discount rate, poor households will have an incentive to invest and to decrease consumption and increase income to finance that investment. Second, if the return on investment is sufficiently high, an increase in returns to labor at the margin may lead to increases in labor supply, income, and savings. If both mechanisms are triggered, the total impact on savings is more than additive. A labor- and skill-demanding, agriculture-based, and export-oriented development strategy, such as those strategies adopted in East Asia, may raise returns on both investment and labor, thereby triggering both mechanisms (Birdsall, Ross, and Sabot 1995).

3. Assessing Key Assumptions

Without credit constraints there will be no boom in savings and investment. If households are able to borrow at an interest rate less than their discount rate, they will finance high-return investments by borrowing rather than decreasing either consumption or leisure. A household that can borrow will respond to an increase in the rate of return to investment, hence in permanent income, by borrowing more. The household will also consume more and work less in the first period.[10] So our story requires that credit constraints be binding.

Poor households do borrow: Deaton (1992a) reports that 25 to 40 percent of rural households surveyed in the Cote d'Ivoire and Ghana had outstanding loans. In Nigeria, Pakistan, Kenya, and Tanzania, surveys indicate that 65 to 90 percent of households borrowed at some point during a twelve-month period (Udry 1993; Alderman and Garcia 1993; Kimuyu 1994). However, nearly all of these loans are for short terms, one cropping season or less. The present year's crop is often used as collateral. In East Africa, less than 1 percent of surveyed households had loans that extended beyond the next harvest (Kimuyu 1994).[11] It appears as though borrowing to finance multiyear investments, such as the planting of tree crops or augmenting human capital, is simply not feasible for poor households without collateral.[12]

In our story, households can only produce income via self-employment or by investing. If anything, taking account of a market in which labor can be purchased or sold strengthens our results. Household labor supply would still depend on the marginal utility of leisure as well as on the returns to investment, the discount rate, and the marginal product of labor. Allowing households to sell labor in a perfect market, with the possibility of negative "sales" if the demand for leisure is high enough, would lead to one important change: the output of the own-produced good would no longer increase in the first period in response to an increase in the returns to investment. However, the basic thrust of our story—that households increase work effort, and hence income and savings, in response to an improvement in investment opportunities—still holds. Consumption would still decrease in the first period, but rather than increasing labor in self-employment households would raise income by increasing labor market activity. At the margin, as investment opportunities improve, households will either decrease the amount of labor hired or increase the amount of labor sold so as to obtain the income necessary to finance investments. If the labor market is large, then marginal returns to labor are constant, *increasing* the impact on savings of improved investment opportunities.

4. An Application

We have suggested that a boom in savings and investment—for example, in agriculture and in human capital—by the poor may help explain the association of rapid growth and low inequality in East Asia. Data on savings and investment disaggregated by income are not readily available. However, aggregate data on agricultural growth and productivity, and on educational change, comparing East Asia and Latin America, are consistent with our story. It appears that in East Asia the poor participated through their own investments in the agricultural growth and educational change that fueled East Asia's economic success—but they did not participate in Latin America.

It is commonplace that the agricultural sector included a large portion of poor households in developing countries, especially in the early postwar decades. Thus, policies that penalized agriculture almost certainly penalized the poor. Schiff and Valdés (1992) report that countries in East Asia, such as Korea and Malaysia, taxed agriculture (directly and through exchange rate and other policies) much less than did countries in Latin America. It is also the case that agricultural production and income grew much more rapidly in East Asia, at more than three times the rate of growth of the agricultural labor force, compared with only 50 percent greater in Latin America (Turnham 1993). Obviously, measured increases in total factor productivity in agriculture in East Asia were substantial—an annual rate of 2.2 percent from 1965 to 1988. These measured increases may in fact reflect in part increased but unmeasured investments in agriculture by poor smallholder households (Timmer 1995) and unmeasured increases in labor hours and work effort by households that saw returns to their investments rising as urban workers' consumption demands increased (Fei, Kuo, and Ranis 1981 documents this process for Taiwan).

In short, in East Asia, unlike in Latin America, the poor in the agricultural sector had increasing opportunities for high-return investments. These opportunities occurred in a context of rapidly growing labor demand as wages and the labor force in the manufacturing sector expanded rapidly (manufacturing sector employment in Korea increased by 58 percent from 1975 to 1985). Their savings and investment have not been systematically measured but surely contributed to the rapid growth of agricultural production.

A similar story can be told about high rates of investment in education, including by the poor, in East Asia. Birdsall, Ross, and Sabot (1995) provide evidence of rates of enrollment in education in East Asia above those predicted for countries at their level of income; high enrollments represented investments by families in the human capital of their children. They also provide evidence that rapid accumulation of human capital both stimulated growth and reduced inequality. In the remainder of this section, we show how marked differences between Korea and Brazil in investment in human capital contributed to differences between the countries in growth rates and levels of inequality, and we suggest that policies conducive to a boom in savings and investment among the poor contributed to Korea's superior growth rate and its success in reducing inequality.

Regressing secondary school enrollment rates on per capita national income for more than 90 developing countries for the years 1965 and 1987 indicates that Korea was well above the regression line—secondary enrollment rates were higher than predicted for countries at its level of income—while Brazil was well below the line.[13] Where enrollment rates are low, children of the poor are the least likely to be enrolled. A corollary of the difference in enrollment rates between Brazil and Korea is a higher rate of investment in human capital by the poor in Korea.

The cross-country growth regression estimated by Birdsall, Ross, and Sabot (1995) can be used to estimate the impact of this difference in enrollment rates on growth. If Korea had had Brazil's 1960 enrollment rates, its growth rate would have been 5.6 rather than 6.1 percent, resulting in 1985 per capita GDP 11.1 percent less than Korea actually attained. This estimate only establishes a lower bound for the costs to Brazil of low investment in human capital; for one thing, it assumes that quality of schooling did not decline, with concomitant declines in the economic returns to schooling, which it almost certainly did.[14]

Low investment in schooling, especially for the poor, also appears to have prevented any improvement in the highly unequal distribution of income in Brazil. In Korea, with rapid educational expansion in the 1960s and 1970s, the relative abundance of educated workers increased and the scarcity rents that the educated earn were eroded, leading to reductions in the inequality of pay in the 1970s and 1980s. By contrast, in Brazil the absolute increment to the labor force of relatively well educated workers was so small in the 1970s that it did not take much of an increase in the demand for educated workers to offset any wage compression effect of the increase in supply. The educational structure of wages barely changed. The net effect of educational expansion in Brazil over the decade was to increase the log variance of wages by roughly 4 percent, in marked contrast to the 22 percent decline that resulted from educational expansion in Korea.[15]

Marked differences in educational performance help explain why Korea has had both faster growth and lower inequality than Brazil. But why have enrollment rates, particularly among the poor, been so high (and dropout and repetition rates so low) in Korea? Why have enrollment rates, particularly among the poor, been so low (and dropout and repetition rates so high) in Brazil? The story we have told suggests some hypotheses.

Growth in Korea from 1970 to 1990 was export oriented and labor demanding. Over two decades, wage increases in the manufacturing sector were an estimated 8.7 percent, while annual increases in wage employment were an extraordinary 18.7 percent.[16]

This employment and wage growth dramatically raised the returns at the margin for the labor of the poor, making it attractive to increase time allocated to work in order to finance high-return investments, including investments in the education of children. The labor-demanding growth path became increasingly skill intensive over time, contributing to high expected rates of return to schooling, hence to strong household demand for education. Public policy also ensured high-quality schooling even in poor districts, thereby contributing to the high rates of return to investment in schooling. In sum, in Korea there were strong incentives for the poor to invest in their children and to work more to finance that investment. It is our supposition that marginal savings rates among the poor were exceptionally high, as households saved in the form of investing in their children's education. This new savings among relatively poor households, as primary and secondary enrollments rose dramatically over two decades, helped ensure education's contribution to aggregate growth set out earlier.

By contrast, in Brazil the inward-looking growth strategy was not labor demanding, and so for the poor the returns to additional labor time allocated to work were quite low. Lack of dynamism in the demand for labor and skill held down expected returns to investment in schooling. In addition, school quality for the poor tended to be abysmal. Because of the limited supply of educated workers, average returns to investment in schooling were high, but for the poor returns to investment in schooling were low (Birdsall and Sabot 1996). In sum, in Brazil public policy created incentives for high levels of leisure and low levels of savings among the poor.

More generally, our story predicts higher investment in schooling in countries with lower inequality. Where inequality is low, the poor are likely to benefit from high returns to labor and investment in human capital, and thus they are likely to save and invest more, including in education. Table 1 presents data from four sets of countries. Within each set per capita incomes are roughly the same. However, the share of GDP going to the poorest quintile, hence the mean absolute income of the poorest quintile, varies considerably. In all but one case, the country with lower inequality has higher secondary enrollment.

5. Conclusions

We have told a story about savings for households that cannot borrow, in which an increase in returns to investment can raise savings, income, and the labor supply. We have suggested that improvements in investment opportunities and returns to labor—features of a labor-demanding growth strategy—can lead to exceptionally high marginal savings rates by the poor. Reductions in poverty and income inequality may result. Low inequality and its corollaries— higher absolute incomes of the poor and higher returns to the poor's labor and investment—can also result in higher aggregate savings and investment rates. The implications of our story are therefore potentially far reaching: ensuring that the poor face incentives to invest and work more can result not only in higher incomes for the poor but in faster growth and lower overall levels of inequality. Our story suggests a microeconomic explanation for the cross-country relationship between low inequality and rapid growth that does not rely on the political benefits of low inequality.

Our analysis is of particular relevance to Latin America. The distribution of income is more unequal in Latin America than in other developing regions, in part because policies have been more biased against the poor. Low inequality combined with high growth in East Asia over three decades suggests that sustained growth requires that the poor contribute to as well as benefit from the development process. Ensuring that the poor have opportunities to contribute to growth in Latin America is thus not a matter of altruism but of enlightened self-interest. The challenge in Latin America is to find ways to reduce inequality and make growth more inclusive, not by imposing growth-inhibiting transfers and regulations but by improving investment opportunities for the poor and shifting to a more labor-demanding growth path.

It is important that the poor be beneficiaries of the growth process. Our analysis of savings and investment suggests they can be an engine of growth as well.

NOTES

Special thanks to Jere Behrman, Roger Bolton, John Knight, Michael Lipton, David Ross, Joseph Stiglitz, Peter Timmer, and participants in seminars at Williams College, Harvard University, Oxford University, the Inter-American Development Bank, and in an International Monetary Fund and World Bank sponsored conference in Escorial, Spain, for helpful comments on a related essay. The usual disclaimer applies.

1. For estimates of growth rate functions in which the impact of initial inequality is econometrically assessed for a large number of developing countries while controlling for other determinants of growth, see Birdsall, Ross, and Sabot 1995 and Clarke 1995.

2. See, for example, Alesina and Perotti 1994; Alesina and Rodrik 1994; and Persson and Tabellini 1994.

3. Unlike the labor surplus models that follow Lewis 1954, we assume that marginal returns to labor are greater than zero.

4. The analysis in this section summarizes the implications of a formal model developed in Birdsall, Pinckney, and Sabot 1995.

5. Much recent research has investigated the saving and dissaving response of rural households to income shocks. See, for example, Townsend 1995 and Paxson 1992.

6. ". . . [A]t least for some households, borrowing restrictions are real and necessary to explain what we observe" (Deaton 1990, 67).

7. Where there is financial intermediation, the improvement in incentives to save when expected returns to investment improve is indirect, through increased demand for loanable funds and consequent increases in interest rates.

8. Bruton (1985) argues that search behavior plays a key role in development. He contends that the impact of a policy change that increases returns to investment by the poor could be greater than the change in marginal conditions suggests, by inducing search for yet more profitable investments.

9. There is no "income effect" of the increase in investment returns on consumption in the first period; with a binding credit constraint, the positive impact on consumption of that increase in returns is realized only in the second period. In each period, the marginal utility of leisure must equal the marginal utility of consumption times the marginal productivity of labor. An increase in the returns to investment induces more work and *reduced* consumption in period 1 to finance the investment; labor supply increases and consumption decreases in such a way as to maintain the equality.

10. See Shibli 1991 for a discussion of households' borrowing response to improved investment opportunities.

11. See Behrman, Foster, and Rosenzweig 1995 for convincing evidence that the poor in rural Pakistan are credit constrained even in the short period between planting and harvesting. See also Bhalla 1978, Jacoby 1994, and Rosenzweig and Wolpin 1993 for indirect evidence of the importance of borrowing constraints in developing countries. On the macrolevel, liquidity constraints are being used increasingly to explain savings behavior even in rich countries (Deaton 1992a).

12. Income and credit constrain investment in human capital only when expected returns to schooling are high. If these returns are low, an increase in the income of the poor may have little or no impact on investment in schooling. Thus, empirically estimated income elasticities of demand for schooling, as conventionally measured, are of little relevance for assessing the model's assumptions. To test our model, the demand equations need to include controls for expected returns to investment.

13. While inequality of access by socioeconomic background is higher, inequality of access by gender is nearly as low in Latin America as in East Asia.

14. Public expenditures per eligible school-age child rose more than 350 percent in Korea between 1970 and 1989, while they rose just 191 percent in Brazil. The increase in Brazil, combined with declines in administrative efficiency, was insufficient to ensure maintenance of quality, as the rapid enrollment increases brought a much poorer pool of students into the system. Completion rates, an indicator of quality, fell in Brazil; in the same period, they rose in Korea (Birdsall and Sabot 1996).

15. Birdsall and Sabot 1996; Knight and Sabot 1990.

16. Banerji, Campos, and Sabot 1994, citing World Bank 1993, and the *ILO Yearbook of Labor Statistics* (various issues).

REFERENCES

Alderman, Harold, and Marito Garcia. 1993. *Poverty, Household Food Security, and Nutrition in Rural Pakistan.* Research Report 96. Washington, DC: International Food Policy Research Institute.

Alesina, Alberto, and Roberto Perotti. 1994. "The Political Economy of Growth: A Critical Survey of the Recent Literature." *World Bank Economic Review* 8 (3): 351–71.

Alesina, Alberto, and Dani Rodrik. 1994. "Distributive Politics and Economic Growth." *Quarterly Journal of Economics* 109 (May): 465–90.

Banerji, A., E. Campos, and R. Sabot. 1994. "The Political Economy of Pay and Employment in Developing Countries." World Bank. Washington, D.C. Mimeo.

Behrman, Jere R., Andrew Foster, and Mark R. Rosenzweig. 1995. "Dynamic Savings Decisions in Agricultural Environments with Incomplete Markets." Philadelphia: University of Pennsylvania. Mimeo.

Bhalla, Surjit S. 1978. "The Role of Sources of Income and Investment Opportunities in Rural Savings." *Journal of Development Economics* 5:259–81.

Birdsall, Nancy, Thomas C. Pinckney, and Richard H. Sabot. 1995. "Inequality, Savings, and Growth." Memorandum 148. Williams College Center for Development Economics Research. Mimeo.

Birdsall, Nancy, David Ross, and Richard Sabot. 1995. "Inequality and Growth Reconsidered: Lessons from East Asia." *World Bank Economic Review* 9 (3): 477–508.

Birdsall, Nancy, and Richard H. Sabot. 1996. *Opportunities Foregone: Education in Brazil.* Washington, DC: Inter-American Development Bank.

Bruton, Henry J. 1985. "The Search for a Development Economics." *World Development* 13:1099–1124.

Carroll, Christopher D. 1994. "How Does Future Income Affect Current Consumption?" *Quarterly Journal of Economics* 109 (Feb.): 111–47.

Clarke, George. 1995. "More Evidence on Income Distribution and Growth." *Journal of Development Economics* 47 (2): 403–27.

Deaton, Angus. 1990. "Savings in Developing Countries: Theory and Review." In *Proceedings of the World Bank Annual Conference on Development Economics, 1989. World Bank Economic Review, special issue:* 61–96.

———. 1992a. "Household Saving in LDCs: Credit Markets, Insurance, and Welfare." *Scandinavian Journal of Economics* 94 (2): 253–73.

———. 1992b. *Understanding Consumption.* Oxford: Clarendon.

Fei, John, Shirley W. Y. Kuo, and Gustav Ranis. 1981. *The Taiwan Success Story: Rapid Growth with Improved Distribution in the Republic of China: 1952–1979.* Boulder: Westview.

Galenson, Walter, and Harvey Leibenstein. 1955. "Investment Criteria, Productivity, and Economic Development." *Quarterly Journal of Economics* 80 (Aug.): 342–70.

International Labor Organization (ILO). Various years. *Yearbook of Labor Statistics.* Geneva: International Labor Organization.

Jacoby, Hanan G. 1994. "Borrowing Constraints and Progress through School: Evidence from Peru." *Review of Economics and Statistics* 76 (Feb.): 151–60.

Kaldor, Nicholas. 1978. "Capital Accumulation and Economic Growth." In *Further Essays on Economic Theory,* edited by Nicholas Kaldor. New York: Holmes & Meier.

Kimuyu, Peter K. 1994. "Credit and Financial Markets." In *Policy and Rural Develop-*

ment: Two Communities in East Africa, edited by Thomas C. Pinckney. Williamstown, MA: Williams College Center for Development Economics.

Knight, John, and Richard Sabot. 1990. *Education, Productivity, and Inequality.* New York: Oxford University Press.

Kuznets, Simon. 1955. "Economic Growth and Income Inequality." *American Economic Review* 45 (1): 1–28.

Lewis, W. Arthur. 1954. "Economic Development with Unlimited Supplies of Labour." *The Manchester School* 22 (May): 139–91.

McKinnon, Ronald L. 1973. *Money and Capital in Economic Development.* Washington, DC: Brookings Institution.

Park, Young-Bum, David Ross, and Richard Sabot. 1992. "Educational Expansion and the Inequality of Pay in Brazil and Korea." Washington, DC: World Bank. Mimeo.

Paxson, Christina H. 1992. "Using Weather Variability to Estimate the Response of Savings to Transitory Income in Thailand." *American Economic Review* 82:15–33.

Persson, Torsten, and Guido Tabellini. 1994. "Is Inequality Harmful for Growth?" *American Economic Review* 84 (3): 600–621.

Rosenzweig, Mark R., and Kenneth I. Wolpin. 1993. "Credit Market Constraints, Consumption Smoothing, and the Accumulation of Durable Production Assets in Low-Income Countries: Investment in Bullocks in India." *Journal of Political Economy* 101 (2): 223–44.

Schiff, Maurice, and Alberto Valdés. 1992. *The Political Economy of Agricultural Pricing Policy.* Vol. 4: *A Synthesis of the Economics in Developing Countries.* Baltimore and London: Johns Hopkins University Press.

Schultz, T. W. 1964. *Transforming Traditional Agriculture.* New Haven and London: Yale University Press.

Shibli, M. Abdullah. 1991. *Investment Opportunities, Household Savings, and the Rates of Return on Investment: A Case Study of the Green Revolution in Bangladesh.* Lanham, MD: University Press of America.

Timmer, C. Peter. 1995. "Getting Agriculture Moving: Do Markets Provide the Right Signals?" *Food Policy* 20 (5): 466–68.

Townsend, Robert M. 1995. "Consumption Insurance: An Evaluation of Risk-Bearing Systems in Low-Income Economies." *Journal of Economic Perspectives* 9:83–102.

Turnham, David. 1993. *Employment and Development in New Review of Evidence.* Paris: Development Centre, Organization for Economic Cooperation and Development.

Udry, Christopher. 1993. "Credit Markets in Northern Nigeria: Credit as Insurance in a Rural Economy." In *The Economics of Rural Organization: Theory, Practice, and Policy,* edited by Karla Hoff, Avishay Braverman, and Joseph E. Stiglitz. Oxford: Oxford University Press.

World Bank. 1993. *The East Asian Miracle.* New York: Oxford University Press.

World Bank. Various years. *World Development Report.* New York: Oxford University Press.

CHAPTER 6

Income Inequality and Aggregate Saving: The Cross-Country Evidence

Klaus Schmidt-Hebbel and Luis Servén

1. Introduction

For the most part, the empirical literature based on cross-section microdata suggests a positive relation between personal income inequality and overall personal saving. However, the evidence from aggregate (typically cross-country) data is more mixed. Some studies also find positive effects of personal income inequality on *aggregate* saving, but others do not. Reconciling these conflicting results is difficult because empirical studies based on macrodata use widely different samples and specifications, different measures of saving and inequality and, in most cases, income distribution information of questionable quality.

This chapter reexamines the empirical evidence from macrodata on the links between the distribution of personal income and aggregate saving, controlling for relevant saving determinants. The focus on aggregate (national) saving and the use of macroeconomic data is justified on two grounds. First, our objective is to test for the overall impact of income distribution on *total* saving, encompassing both direct and indirect mechanisms affecting personal, firm, and public saving. Second, we want to look at the *long-run* relations in a cross-country perspective including a large sample of both industrial countries (those that belong to the Organization for Economic Cooperation and Development [OECD]) and developing countries—something that would not be possible with household data.

The main conclusion of the chapter—supported by empirical evidence based on new income distribution data constructed by Deininger and Squire (1996)—is that cross-country data do not reveal a strong association between income distribution and aggregate saving. More precisely, after controlling for other saving determinants, aggregate saving ratios do not appear to be significantly related to standard income distribution indicators. This conclusion holds for our full cross-country sample, as well as for its industrial and developing-country subsamples, and is robust to alternative saving measures, income distribution indicators, and functional forms.

The chapter is organized as follows. Section 2 presents the stylized facts on saving, income, growth, and distribution, using data for a large number of industrial and developing countries, and relates the empirical regularities present in our sample to those reported in the literature. Section 3 provides a brief survey of alternative views of saving determination, with emphasis on the saving consequences of different income distribution profiles. Section 4 reviews previous empirical studies of the impact of income distribution on saving, and section 5 presents new cross-country econometric evidence using our data set. Section 6 concludes.

2. Saving and Distribution: The Stylized Facts

We begin by reviewing the empirical regularities on saving, income, and distribution. To do this, we use annual macroeconomic data on 52 industrial and developing countries from the World Bank data bases and income distribution data from a new data base recently constructed by Deininger and Squire (1996). In principle, the data cover the years 1965 to 1994—although for some countries some of the variables of interest (notably income distribution data) are not available every year within this time span. The ensuing discussion focuses on the cross-country dimension of the data, making use of the averages of the relevant variables over the three-decade period.[1] Unless otherwise noted, here and in the rest of the chapter we use the term *saving* (*saving ratio*) to refer to gross national saving (GNS)—respectively, its ratio to gross national product (GNP). We choose national saving and national product data as the relevant variables because they are closer to the relevant units (households or individuals) for which income distribution data are available than are the domestic saving and domestic product measures. In this respect, we differ from most previous empirical studies, which are based on the less adequate domestic measures.

A preliminary issue that merits comment is that of measurement error. As is well known, this is a central problem in empirical studies of saving, due not only to the inadequacy of the very saving concept used by the national accounts (which, e.g., exclude capital gains from the definition of income and treat human capital expenditures as consumption) but also to the unreliability of measured saving, which stems largely from the fact that saving is often computed as the residual from another residual (consumption). The upshot is that saving measures may contain large errors, particularly in poorer countries (see Schmidt-Hebbel, Servén, and Solimano 1996 for further discussion). Measurement error is an even more serious problem in the case of income distribution statistics. The latter are primarily derived from household survey data, which typically understate the income of the richer households. As a result, income inequality is likely to be underestimated. Although no firm evidence is avail-

TABLE 1.   Income Distribution Indicators: Descriptive Statistics

	Number of Observations	Gini Coefficient		Income Share Ratio of Top 20% to Bottom 40%		Income Share of Middle 60%	
		Mean	Std. dev.	Mean	Std. dev.	Mean	Std. dev.
World	52	39.62	2.70	2.72	0.04	0.48	0.02
OECD countries	20	33.34	1.92	2.08	0.04	0.54	0.01
Developing countries	32	43.68	3.17	3.65	0.03	0.45	0.05
Take-off countries	10	40.31	2.87	2.63	0.04	0.47	0.02
Other developing countries	22	45.21	3.31	4.00	0.05	0.43	0.03

able, most observers would probably agree that such underestimation again is probably more severe in poorer countries because the statistical apparatus involved in the collection of household data is likely to be weaker.

Keeping in mind these limitations of the available data, we turn to the review of the stylized facts. Since our income distribution information is new, we first provide some summary statistics (a detailed description is given in Deininger and Squire 1996). Table 1 presents means and standard deviations of three conventional indicators of inequality: the Gini coefficient, the ratio between the income shares of the richest 20 percent and poorest 40 percent of the population, and the income share of the "middle class," defined as the middle 60 percent of the population (which is often used as an indicator of equality). The statistics are computed for three country groups: industrial countries, developing countries, and, as a subset of the latter, the so-called "take-off" countries. The latter group is defined as consisting of those developing countries that during the sample period successfully shifted from a low to a high saving and growth path.[2]

As table 1 shows, developing countries are more unequal than industrial countries by any of the three indicators presented. Take-off countries, however, possess on average an income distribution more equitable than that of other developing countries, also by all three indicators considered.

The Stylized Facts

The first stylized fact concerns the relationship between saving ratios and level of development—as measured by real per capita GNP. Figure 1 presents the scatter plot of the 1965–94 averages of these two variables for the sample countries; using per capita income at the initial year of the sample instead of its average value yields a very similar picture. In the figure, countries appear clustered in rough correspondence to their development level. On average, saving rates are lower for developing countries (denoted as LDC in the figure)

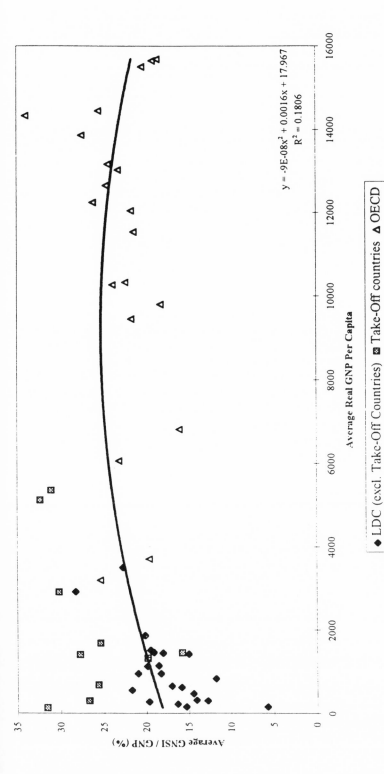

Fig. 1. Long-term world saving and income. Gross national saving rate, including net current transfers and real GNP per capita, 1965–94 averages, by country.

$$y = -9E\text{-}08x^2 + 0.0016x + 17.967$$
$$R^2 = 0.1806$$

Average Real GNP Per Capita

Average GNSI / GNP (%)

• LDC (excl. Take-Off Countries) ⊠ Take-Off countries △ OECD

TABLE 2. Correlation Matrix of Basic Regressors

	GNS/GNP	Per Capita GNP	Growth Rate of Per Capita GNP	Gini Coefficient	Income Share of Top 20% to Bottom 40%	Income Share of Middle 60%	Old-Age Dependency Ratio
GNS/GNP							
Per capita GNP	0.311						
Growth rate of per capita GNP	0.632	-0.001					
Gini coefficient	-0.278	-0.551	-0.238				
Income share of top 20% to bottom 40%	-0.277	-0.469	-0.233	0.951			
Income share of middle 60%	0.335	0.652	0.204	-0.957	-0.919		
Old-age dependency ratio	0.177	0.860	-0.012	-0.627	-0.536	0.705	
Young-age dependency ratio	-0.394	-0.872	-0.211	0.683	0.603	-0.763	-0.933

than for industrial countries. The exceptions are the take-off economies in our sample, whose saving ratios exceed even the industrial country average.

The figure shows that saving rates tend to rise with per capita income: the correlation coefficient between the two variables is .31, significantly different from zero at the 5 percent level, and it is even higher (.60) among developing countries (see the matrix of correlations between the saving rate and related variables in table 2). A similar association has been found in a number of empirical studies of saving (e.g., Collins 1991; Schmidt-Hebbel, Webb, and Corsetti 1992; Carroll and Weil 1994; Masson, Bayoumi, and Samiel 1995; and Edwards 1995).

The figure also suggests that at high levels of per capita income saving ratios appear to level off—for example, the relationship is not linear and possibly not even monotonic. As a more formal check on this, the solid line in figure 1 plots the fitted values from regressing the saving rate on a quadratic polynomial in per capita income; the estimated coefficients are significant at conventional levels. The fitted curve shows that the positive association between saving and development appears, indeed, to be confined to the early stages of development, ceases to hold at about US $8,000 per capita GNP (in 1987 dollars), and turns into a negative association at higher income levels.

A second stylized fact is the strong positive association between saving ratios and real per capita growth, which has been amply documented in cross-country empirical studies.[3] However, its structural interpretation remains controversial, as it has been viewed both as proof that growth drives saving (e.g., Modigliani 1970 among many other studies) and that saving drives growth through the saving-investment link (e.g., Levine and Renelt 1992; Mankiw, Romer, and Weil 1992).[4]

As figure 2 shows, our data conform to these findings. Aggregate saving ratios and real per capita GNP growth are positively associated, and their correlation coefficient equals .63, significantly different from zero at the 5 percent level. However, the figure also suggests that this relationship might be driven by the fast-growing, high-saving, take-off economies, most of which are clustered at the upper right corner of the graph. In fact, if these countries are removed from the sample the correlation drops to .40 but still remains significant.

Is the association between saving and income distribution as clear-cut as that between saving and income (or its growth rate)? Figure 3, which plots saving ratios against Gini coefficients of income distribution, shows a less clear-cut pattern than is found in the preceding two figures. Nevertheless, the full sample correlation between both variables is − .28, just statistically significant at the 5 percent level. The correlation pattern is, however, rather different in the industrial (.10) and developing country (− .26) subsamples; in neither is it significantly different from zero. Interestingly, the figure also reveals a sharp distinction between both sets of countries from the point of view of inequality:

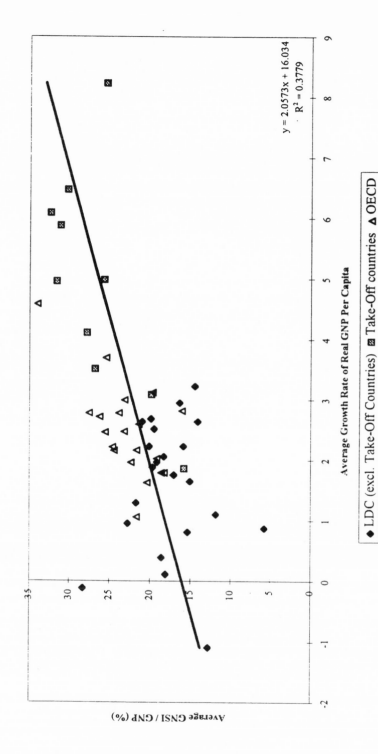

$y = 2.0573x + 16.034$

$R^2 = 0.3779$

Average Growth Rate of Real GNP Per Capita

Average GNSI / GNP (%)

● LDC (excl. Take-Off Countries) ▨ Take-Off countries ▲ OECD

Fig. 2. Long-term world saving and growth. Gross national saving rate, including net current transfers and growth rate of real GNP per capita, 1965–94 averages, by country.

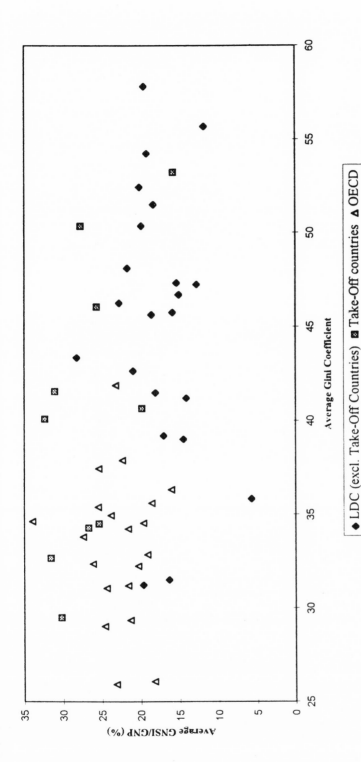

Fig. 3. Long-term world saving and income distribution. Gross national saving rate, including net current transfers and Gini coefficient, 1965–94 averages, by country.

virtually all non-take-off developing countries possess a more unequal income distribution (as measured by the Gini coefficient) than that of the most unequal OECD country.

These facts lead to the much discussed relationship between income inequality and level of development—with the latter measured, as before, by real per capita GNP. According to the well-known finding by Kuznets (1955), the relationship between these variables follows an inverted U-shape: inequality rises in the early stages of development and then decreases as per capita income continues to rise. This stylized fact has been replicated to varying extents in a number of cross-country studies (for recent examples, see Bourguignon and Morrison 1990 and Clarke 1992), but its interpretation is far from clear (see Adelman and Robinson 1989 for a discussion).[5]

Figure 4 shows that our sample fits the Kuznets curve. Keeping with convention, the figure plots Gini coefficients against the log of per capita income (with both variables measured by their 1965–94 averages). The curved line in the graph depicts the fitted values from regressing the Gini coefficient on the log of per capita income and its square; the estimated coefficients are highly significant. As can be seen from the figure, developing countries account for the upward-sloping portion of the empirical curve, and industrial countries cluster along the declining portion.

One methodological issue that arises is whether these findings are sensitive to our choice of the Gini coefficient as the relevant statistic. A number of alternative indicators are found in the literature—for example, Theil's index, the coefficient of variation of income across households, the income share of the poorest 20 or 40 percent of the population, the ratio of the latter to the income share of the richest 20 percent, or the income share of the middle class.[6] Among all them, the Gini coefficient, Theil's index, and the coefficient of variation are generally preferable because they use more information than do the commonly encountered quintile-based indicators. At the same time, the Gini coefficient has the well-known drawback that it is not uniquely related to the shape of the underlying distribution, so that very different redistribution schemes can be reflected in the same change in the Gini coefficient. Finally, income shares (in levels) and Gini coefficients may pose cross-country comparability problems more severe than those derived from the use of share ratios (Deininger and Squire 1996).

In practice, however, the informational content of all these indicators is usually very similar, as is shown by the fact that they typically are very highly correlated—even though they may yield different orderings for a few sample observations (see, e.g., Clarke 1992). This applies also in our case. By way of example, figure 5 plots the Gini coefficient against the ratio of the income share of the richest 20 percent of the population to that of the poorest 40 percent for those countries in our sample for which both kinds of data are available. The plot reveals a strong positive association between both distribution mea-

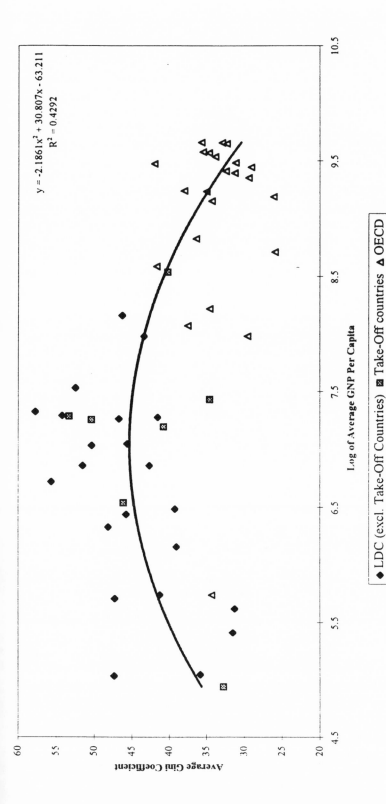

Fig. 4. Long-term world income distribution and development. Gini coefficient and log of average GNP per capita, 1965–94 averages, by country.

The chart axes and legend read:

- Y-axis: Average Gini Coefficient (20 to 60)
- X-axis: Log of Average GNP Per Capita (4.5 to 10.5)
- Equation: $y = -2.1861x^2 + 30.807x - 63.211$
- $R^2 = 0.4292$

Legend: ◆ LDC (excl. Take-Off Countries) ▨ Take-Off countries △ OECD

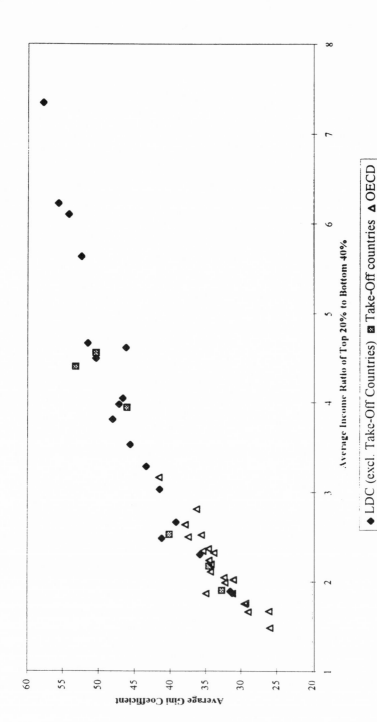

Fig. 5. Long-term world income distribution measures. Gini coefficient and ratio of income of top 20 percent to bottom 40 percent of population, 1965–94 averages, by country.

sures; indeed, their correlation coefficient equals .95, so they are virtually indistinguishable.

To summarize this section, our data conform to three stylized facts found in cross-country studies. First, saving rates appear to rise with development (as measured by per capita GNP)—at least at its early stages. Second, saving and growth rates are positively correlated across countries. Third, income inequality seems to rise at early stages of development and decline beyond certain levels of per capita income, as is predicted by the "Kuznets curve."

For the overall sample, we also find a negative association between aggregate saving rates and standard measures of income inequality, although the relationship is not robust across subsamples. More importantly, this refers only to the simple correlation between saving and income distribution. The more substantive question is whether the association between both variables continues to hold once other standard saving determinants are taken into consideration. To answer this question, we need to examine the theoretical underpinnings of the saving-inequality link and place the latter in a broader framework, encompassing other relevant determinants of saving. This task is undertaken in the next section.

3. Saving and Income Distribution: A Brief Survey

Aggregate saving is the outcome of individual saving efforts by heterogeneous members of different classes of savers. Heterogeneity among savers is a key feature that helps us to understand how aggregate saving is affected by changes in saving determinants, including policies. Heterogeneity may be related to the fact that different types of individuals determine their consumption/saving plans according to different objectives (i.e., their preferences are not identical). Alternatively, even if all individuals possess identical preferences, their behavior may differ because they face different institutional constraints (e.g., in their access to borrowing) or behavior may vary, depending on the values of exogenous variables relevant for their consumption/saving decisions (e.g., no saving can be made below a certain threshold of income needed for subsistence).

Heterogeneity is important, of course, because when agents are dissimilar the aggregate levels of those variables relevant for *individual* saving decisions are not sufficient to determine *aggregate* saving—the latter also depends on the distribution of such variables across individual savers. Even if all agents have identical preferences and face the same constraints, distribution still matters as long as their (common) decision rule for saving is not linear in the relevant variables. In such a case, a given change in the aggregate value of a saving determinant (such as disposable income or wealth) can have very different consequences for aggregate saving, depending on how it impacts different types of savers. Likewise, purely redistributive policies can have an impact on aggregate saving—for example, public transfers to the poor financed by taxes on the rich may reduce total saving if the former have a higher propensity to spend than do the latter.

In section 3.1, we review briefly the literature on consumption and saving determination, with a focus on income (or wealth) distribution in particular. We adopt an aggregate perspective, although some reference is made to the distinction between private and public saving, or firm and household saving, where relevant. Our approach is selective rather than exhaustive. We first examine the relationship between saving and three basic determinants: income, the rate of return, and uncertainty.[7] Then we highlight different channels through which distribution affects the relationship between these basic variables and aggregate saving.

3.1. Basic Saving Determinants

Income.   Income or wealth is the main driving force behind consumption (and hence saving), and therefore it has attracted the most attention among all potential saving determinants. But beyond this very general statement there is very little in common among different saving theories. The differences start with the appropriate measure of income: current income (in the conventional Keynesian hypothesis, henceforth KH), permanent income net of taxes over the life cycle (the life-cycle hypothesis, LCH), permanent income net of taxes over an infinite horizon (the permanent income hypothesis, PIH), or, as a variant of the latter, permanent income net of government spending over an infinite horizon (REH, the Ricardian equivalence hypothesis).

As a benchmark, consider either the PIH or its REH variant for a representative consumer.[8] A rise in net permanent income leads to a proportional increase in consumption levels without any effect on saving. Temporary income changes are smoothed out through appropriate levels of saving. If both current and permanent income rise by the same amount, consumption and saving ratios to current income remain unaltered; in turn, purely temporary income changes result in movements of the saving (consumption) ratio in the same (opposite) direction.

According to the PIH, income growth—for example, the increase of future income relative to current income levels—must reduce saving rates, as consumers raise current consumption in anticipation of higher future income. This, however, is at odds with the positive saving-growth correlation observed in the data and reviewed in the previous section, and it has prompted several lines of research attempting to explain why rational consumers may fail to adjust their consumption levels in the face of rising income.[9] The explanations are mostly based on nonstandard preferences incorporating consumption habits (which prevent rapid changes in consumption levels), subsistence consumption levels (below which no saving takes place, so that the saving propensity is effectively zero), or wealth as an argument of the utility function (the classical "capitalist spirit" model). Under each of these formulations, higher income can generate increases in saving, at least transitorily. On the other hand, as we shall see, once the representative-agent framework is abandoned, some of these preference specifications provide possible channels through which income distribution could affect overall saving.

At the other end of the theoretical spectrum is the LCH of Modigliani and Brumberg (1954, 1979)—the main competitor of the PIH-REH theories. As opposed to the representative-agent framework of the latter, agent heterogeneity is the cornerstone of the LCH. Aggregate saving results from the addition of saving by different age-specific cohorts. Each cohort smooths consumption over a finite horizon, given lifetime resources that—in the simple LCH hypothesis—are not transferred across generations. Over the life cycle, saving and consumption follow hump-shaped patterns, with dissaving at young age, the peak of saving at working age, and dissaving during retirement as households run down their accumulated assets. Hence, saving propensities depend on age and differ systematically across cohorts.

The impact of growth on saving in the LCH framework is ambiguous. On the one hand, the earnings and saving of the working-age population will rise relative to retirees' dissaving, thus pushing up aggregate saving. On the other hand, however, workers will anticipate higher earnings during their working age, and this will depress their saving just like in the PIH framework. The overall effect is therefore indeterminate.

As mentioned, there is, of course, an alternative interpretation of why standard models of saving have such a hard time generating a positive growth-saving association. Rather than saving behavior, the latter could just reflect the combination of two well-established empirical facts: the positive association between investment and growth (Levine and Renelt 1992) and the equally positive saving-investment correlation (Feldstein and Horioka 1980; Feldstein and Bachetta 1990), often interpreted as evidence of international capital immobility (see Schmidt-Hebbel, Servén, and Solimano 1996).

The Rate of Return.   The second key factor governing the intertemporal allocation of consumption, and hence saving, is the rate of return. However, its impact on saving in the representative-agent framework of the PIH is ambiguous because changes in the rate of return have both income and substitution effects, which run in opposite directions (except in particular cases, as when the consumer is a net debtor). The situation is similarly ambiguous in the LCH framework. Here changes in interest rates entail transfers among cohorts, and the net impact on aggregate consumption and saving depends on the different cohorts' saving propensities as well as on their relative size (see Deaton 1992).

In practice, empirical studies support these theoretical ambiguities and typically fail to find significant effects of interest rate changes on saving.

Recent work by Ogaki, Ostry, and Reinhart (1994) adds a new dimension to the effect of the rate of return on saving. They present a model in which the elasticity of intertemporal substitution (and hence the interest rate sensitivity of saving) rises with the level of income. Empirical estimation of the model on a cross-country data set provides some support for this view.

Uncertainty. Recent work on saving has moved away from the simple versions of the PIH and LCH models toward broader frameworks incorporating uncertainty about future income, the rate of return to savings, the length of life, and so on. One line of work has relaxed the certainty-equivalent utility function of Hall's (1978) PIH, allowing the marginal utility of consumption to be nonlinear, typically convex. This convexity creates precautionary motives for saving whenever uncertainty about future consumption is introduced: it is prudent for individuals to limit borrowing and not consume too much until they know more about their future—an effect that is stronger the greater is the uncertainty about lifetime income.[10]

The existence of the precautionary motive for saving is less in doubt than is its actual magnitude. While empirical testing has been limited, it is likely that precautionary saving may represent well the short-term consumption-smoothing behavior of the average consumer but not explain the bulk of saving, which in most societies appears to be carried out by a relatively small number of wealthier households (see Carroll and Summers 1991 and Deaton 1995).

3.2. Income Distribution and Saving

Let us now focus in more detail on the impact of changes in the distribution of income (or wealth) on aggregate saving. We examine four topics: (1) links between saving and the *functional* distribution of income; (2) links between saving and the *personal* distribution of income; (3) borrowing constraints, distribution, and saving; and (4) indirect effects of distribution on saving.

Functional Distribution and Saving. The link between the functional distribution of income and saving (and growth) is at the heart of the neoclassical growth model (Solow 1956) as well as the neo-Keynesian growth models of Lewis (1954), Kaldor (1957), and Pasinetti (1962). These models are general equilibrium in nature, with both saving and income distribution as endogenous variables.

Unlike the neo-Keynesian models, in the neoclassical framework workers and capitalists do not necessarily differ in their saving patterns. Aggregate saving behavior in conjunction with production characteristics determines income distribution. The reason is that saving influences investment and thus the capital stock. An increase in the propensity to save will increase the long-run capital-labor ratio, and capital's income share will rise or fall depending on whether the elasticity of factor substitution is greater or smaller than one, respectively.

By contrast, the neo-Keynesian growth models of Lewis and Kaldor assume from the outset that workers and capitalists have different saving behavior.[11] Lewis (1954) argues that most saving comes from the profits of the entrepreneurs in the modern industrial sector of the economy, who save a high fraction of their incomes, while other groups in the economy save less. The more fervent the activities of the capitalists, the faster does the distribution of income tilt toward profits, increasing the aggregate saving ratio. Income redistribution from the low-saving group to the entrepreneurs raises aggregate saving.

Likewise, in the simplest form of Kaldor's (1957) model, workers spend what they earn (their propensity to save is zero) and the share of profits in national income depends positively on the investment-output ratio and inversely on the propensity to save of the capitalists. Thus, as in Lewis's model, an increase in investment raises the income share of profits at the expense of the wage share, and the more the capitalists spend the more they earn—the "widow's cruse" is never empty.

Pasinetti (1962) assumes that saving propensities differ among classes of individuals rather than classes of income. Workers' saving is not zero; indeed, they are assumed to own shares of the capital stock and receive part of the profits. Nevertheless, the implications for the share of profits in income are the same as those obtained by Kaldor. The fact that workers save does influence the distribution of income between capitalists and workers, but it does not influence the distribution of income between profits and wages.

While these neo-Keynesian models establish a clear relation between the functional distribution of income and saving, it is worth noting that their implications in terms of the inequality-saving link are less automatic. The reason is that in many societies wage earners do not necessarily represent the poorer segments of the population, which are likely to include instead small rural landowners and self-employed individuals in the informal sector. As a result, the association between the functional and personal distributions of income is empirically rather weak (Atkinson 1994).

Personal Distribution and Saving. With consumer heterogeneity, standard consumption theories also generate links between personal income distribution and aggregate saving that, unlike the classical theories just referred to, do not depend on the exogenous distinction of two groups of savers and nonsavers. These links result from a nonlinear relationship between individual saving and income, which can have different sources but in most cases—although not invariably—leads to a positive relationship between inequality and aggregate saving.

A starting point is again the LCH, amended to include bequests. The latter were absent from the early formulations of the LCH because they were thought to be insignificant. Only 20 percent of total U.S. wealth was believed to come from bequests, with the remaining 80 percent due to the saving of living individuals. More recent studies have virtually reversed this 20–80 rule to 80–20 (Kotlikoff and Summers 1981, 1988). This is an important finding from the theoretical viewpoint because, with a fully developed intergenerational bequest motive, the distinction between the LCH and the PIH virtually vanishes, as different age cohorts become mutually linked.

The view that bequests as a saving motive are more important than life-cycle considerations, and that the elasticity of bequests with respect to lifetime resources exceeds unity, helps explain a number of empirical puzzles on the LCH model (see Deaton 1992, 1995, for further discussion and references). First, there is little evidence that the old dissave, as implied by the simple LCH; on the contrary, their saving rates appear to be as high or even higher than those of young households. Second, if bequests are a luxury (at least over a relevant wealth range), saving rates should be higher among wealthier consumers and richer countries than in the rest, which empirically seems to be the case. Third, the fact that saving appears to be concentrated among relatively few richer households, which may be accumulating mostly for dynastic motives, is also in agreement with a central role of bequests in driving saving.

If bequests by the wealthy are a chief force behind saving, as this literature suggests, the situation is close to that described by the "capitalist spirit" model, mentioned earlier, in which wealth is accumulated for its own sake (see, e.g., Zou 1994), and higher wealth prompts further accumulation—because consumption and wealth are gross substitutes in the agent's utility function. More generally, the apparent concentration of saving in a small group of richer individuals suggests that a better understanding of their saving behavior is essential to understanding aggregate saving patterns.

The key issue is that, if the elasticity of bequests with respect to lifetime resources is greater than unity (so that bequests are a luxury good), income redistribution from rich to poor will unambiguously reduce aggregate saving (Blinder 1975). As we shall see, this view has received some empirical support.

An alternative route through which income distribution may matter for aggregate saving was suggested by Becker (1975). If there are decreasing returns to human capital, the poor will invest relatively more in human capital than will the rich. Since human capital expenditures are considered to be consumption in standard national accounting, the measured saving rates of the poor will appear lower than those of the rich, even if their "overall" saving rates (including human capital accumulation) are identical.

In turn, precautionary saving also implies a link between distribution and saving. Consumers with low assets tend to compress consumption to avoid running down their precautionary balances, so that their marginal propensity to consume out of income is higher than that of those consumers holding large asset stocks—they would devote most of any extra income to consumption. Thus, redistribution from the wealthy to the poor would depress overall saving. The opposite could happen, however, if the poor face greater uncertainty, are more risk averse, or have more limited access to risk diversification than the rich; under such circumstances, a transfer from the latter to the former would lead to higher aggregate saving. A related view, advanced by Friedman (1957), holds that, if the cross-sectional distribution of income reflects future income uncertainty, then greater income inequality should raise precautionary saving.

Consumption habits, the theoretical interest of which lies mainly in their ability to generate positive saving-growth correlations through the slow adjustment of consumption,[12] also have implications for the saving-distribution link. This can be most clearly seen in an LCH framework. Consumption is costlier for young households—because the habit it induces has to be fed for the rest of one's life—and cheaper for old consumers. Thus, the young will tend to save more than the old, and income redistribution from the latter to the former will raise overall saving. Redistribution from rich to poor can also raise saving under the (not too implausible) assumption that habits make it more difficult to adjust future consumption down than up. In such case, richer consumers would reduce their consumption level by the full amount of the transfer, while poorer consumers would be reluctant to raise their consumption by the same amount.

Borrowing Constraints, Saving, and Distribution. The inability of some consumers to borrow forges a powerful link between income distribution and saving. Consumption models with borrowing constraints divide consumers into savers and nonsavers. Unlike in the classical models of functional income distribution, however, this does not arise from the exogenous distinction of two classes of people or preferences but from the distribution of preferences among the population, interest rates, the variability of earnings, and their rate of growth.

Borrowing constraints act in a way similar in many respects to the precautionary saving motive. Given the inability to borrow, consumers use assets to buffer consumption, accumulating when times are good and running them down to protect consumption when earnings are low. In the theoretical models, borrowing constraints mostly affect impatient consumers who face high earnings growth (Deaton 1991).

The empirical relevance of borrowing constraints is well established. However, they help explain mostly short-term saving for consumption buffering, not long-term saving for old age or bequests. For example, Hayashi (1985) finds that for a significant fraction of the Japanese population the behavior of consumption over time is consistent with the existence of credit rationing and differential borrowing and lending rates. Borrowing constraints appear particularly important with regard to saving for housing purchases. Jappelli and Pagano (1994) show that credit constraints reflected in housing mortgage regulations are an important explanatory factor behind cross-country differences in saving.

In practice, borrowing constraints affect mostly poorer households and not the rich who hold large asset stocks. Thus, like the precautionary saving motive, borrowing constraints likely are a chief force behind the saving behavior of lower- and middle-income groups but not richer households. Income redistribution away from the latter makes the borrowing constraints less likely to bind and reduces the importance of buffer-stock saving, thus lowering aggregate saving rates.

Indirect Links.   Other recent literature brings out some indirect links between distribution and saving operating through third variables that affect saving. One particularly active line of research is the "political economy" literature, which has underscored the positive association between income equality and economic growth in a framework of endogenous growth and endogenous economic policy.[13] In this approach, causality runs from distribution to growth via investment. In addition, these models include a political mechanism that provides a link between income inequality and economic policy.

The main line of argument is that a highly unequal distribution of income and wealth causes social tension and political instability (violent protests, coups, etc.); the result is a discouragement of investment through increased uncertainty along with adverse consequences for productivity and thus growth (Persson and Tabellini 1994; Alesina and Rodrik 1994; Perotti 1995; Alesina and Perotti 1996). In addition, income distribution may affect growth through taxation and government expenditure: in a more unequal society, there is greater demand for redistribution and therefore higher taxation, lower returns to investments in physical and human capital, and less investment and growth.

These arguments have received some empirical support. From the point of view of saving, the implication is that if saving is positively dependent on growth then higher inequality will, through the channels just described, depress aggregate saving—in contrast to the positive impact of inequality on saving implied by most of the theories examined so far. Additionally, distributive inequality may also tend to lower *public* saving, as governments engage more actively in redistributive expenditures, as in the populist experiences examined by Dornbusch and Edwards (1991); in the absence of strict Ricardian equivalence, this would in turn reduce aggregate saving.

It is important to note that the existence of an inverse relationship between inequality and investment, as suggested by the literature, could also imply a negative association between inequality and saving through firms' earnings retention. The latter is typically the primary source of financing for private investment, so that if higher inequality lowers investment it should also reduce firm saving. What happens with *aggregate* saving, however, depends on whether firm owners (i.e., households) can pierce the "corporate veil" that separates household and firm decisions. Unless this is the case, a fall in firm saving will be less than fully offset by a rise in household saving, thus lowering aggregate saving.

Summing Up. What can be concluded from this brief review of the links between income concentration and saving? On the one hand, income concentration affects household (and hence aggregate) saving directly through several channels, positively in most (but not all) cases. On the other hand, however, there are indirect, negative effects of income concentration on aggregate saving operating through lower corporate and public saving. In view of the opposing signs of the different mechanisms at work, we conclude that the overall impact of changes in income distribution on aggregate saving is ambiguous on theoretical grounds and can be established only empirically.

4. Empirical Studies

Empirical tests of the impact of income distribution on saving are rather scarce. Some early studies followed the Kaldor-Lewis approach and focused on the functional distribution of income. Along these lines, Houthakker (1961), Williamson (1968), Kelley and Williamson (1968), and Gupta (1970) found some evidence that the propensity to save from nonlabor income exceeds that from labor income.

More recent empirical studies focus on the effect of personal income inequality on saving. Blinder (1975) uses U.S. time-series data for 1949–70 to estimate an equation for aggregate consumption, including income distribution indicators. He finds that higher inequality appears to raise aggregate consumption (and thus lower saving), although the estimated effect is in general statistically insignificant. He attributes this result to the lack of correspondence between his analytical framework—which predicts the opposite result—and his empirical model and proposes as a preferable empirical test the estimation of separate consumption equations by income class. This suggestion is taken up by Menchik and David (1983), who use disaggregated U.S. data to test directly whether the elasticity of bequests to lifetime resources is larger or smaller for the rich than for other income groups. They find that the marginal propensity to bequeath is unambiguously higher for the wealthy, so that higher inequality leads to higher lifetime aggregate saving.

A related approach is that of Bunting (1991), who uses consumer expenditure survey data for the United States to estimate consumption as a function of income level and distribution by income quintile. He finds strong evidence that household spending depends on both the level and distribution of income: the estimated marginal propensities to consume uniformly decline (and propensities to save therefore rise) as the quintile share of income rises. The coefficients are highly significant, and the model explains over half of the variation in household consumption in the sample.

Two early studies by Della Valle and Oguchi (1976) and Musgrove (1980) use cross-country data on both industrial and developing countries to investigate the relationship between saving and income distribution. In both cases, the results show no statistically significant effect of income distribution on saving. The exception is the OECD countries included in the study by Della Valle and Oguchi, for which they find some evidence that increased inequality may increase saving; Gersovitz (1988) suggests that their failure to obtain a similar result for the developing countries may be due to poor quality of the corresponding income distribution data. In turn, Lim (1980) finds that inequality tends to raise aggregate saving rates in a cross-section sample of developing countries, but his coefficient estimates are significant at conventional levels only in some subsamples.

Venieris and Gupta (1986) examine the pattern of average saving propensities across income groups in a cross-section sample of 49 countries, using an econometric specification that includes also political instability as a saving determinant. Their results show that poorer households have the lowest saving propensities, but somewhat surprisingly they also find that the highest average saving propensity corresponds to the middle-income group, so that redistribution that does not favor the rich may raise or lower the aggregate saving ratio depending on whether the favored group is the middle class or the poor, respectively. However, the interpretation of their results is somewhat unclear due to their use of constant-price saving as the dependent variable, which has no clear analytical justification.

Sahota (1993) tests a reduced-form relationship between saving and income distribution, controlling for the effects of per capita income on saving. Using data on 65 industrial and developing countries for the year 1975, he regresses the saving/GDP ratio on the Gini coefficient and a quadratic polynomial in per capita income (he includes also regional dummy variables to remove cultural and habit effects). The parameter estimate on the Gini coefficient is found to be positive, implying a positive impact of inequality on aggregate saving, but the estimate is somewhat imprecise and significantly different from zero only at the 10 percent level.

More recently, Cook (1995) presented estimates of the impact of inequality on aggregate saving ratios in LDCs from a conventional saving equation, including also the level and growth rate of real income, dependency ratios, and a measure of capital inflows. A dummy for Latin American countries is also added to the regressions, although its justification is unclear since no other regional dummies are included. Using decade averages for the 1970s for 49 developing countries, he finds a positive and significant effect of inequality on saving, which appears robust to some changes in specification and to the choice of alternative indicators of income inequality.

Finally, Hong (1995) reports econometric results on the effect of income inequality on gross domestic saving ratios in cross-country samples of 56 to 64 developing and industrial countries, using 1960–85 averages for each country. He finds that the income share of the top 20 percent of the population has a positive effect on saving rates, controlling for old-age dependency, income (and/or education) level, and income growth.

Last, Edwards (1995) estimates private saving equations using panel data for developing and OECD countries for the years 1970–92. While the main focus of the study is not on the relation between income distribution and saving, he reports two regressions for mostly OECD countries that control for income inequality, finding that the latter has a significant positive effect on private saving if combined with one set of regressors but negative and insignificant when combined with a different set.

In summary, most empirical studies based on microhousehold data show evidence of a positive effect of income concentration on household saving. Regarding the studies based on cross-country aggregate data, the results are more mixed, although some do find a positive impact of income inequality on total saving. Independently of their results, however, most of the cross-country studies utilize inadequate saving measures and use income distribution data of highly heterogeneous quality, mixing both income- and expenditure-based measures. Their robustness to alternative specifications and data samples is also unclear. These drawbacks justify a more systematic empirical search for the effect of income inequality on aggregate saving across different specifications, saving and income distribution measures, and data samples.

5. Econometric Results

In this section, we present new empirical results on the cross-country relationship between saving and income distribution. Our objective is to assess the impact on national saving of alternative income distribution indicators after controlling for income and demographic variables. Our basic sample includes 52 countries (see data appendix). The focus on aggregate (national saving) data and the use of macroeconomic data is justified on two grounds. First, we want to test the overall impact of income distribution on saving, encompassing both direct and indirect mechanisms at work. Second, we want to look at the long-run relationships, in a cross-country framework that includes a large sample of OECD and developing countries, and microhousehold data are not available for such a sample.

We limit our model search to variants of simple specifications found in comparable cross-country studies of saving (see e.g., Edwards 1995 and Masson, Bayoumi, and Samiel 1995). The basic equation to be estimated is the following.

$$\text{GNS/GNP} = \alpha_0 + \alpha_1 \text{ gnp} + \alpha_2 \text{ (gnp)}^2 + \alpha_3 \text{ growth} + \alpha_4 \text{ old} \\ + \alpha_5 \text{ young} + \alpha_6 \text{ distrib,}$$ (1)

where GNS/GNP is the ratio of current-price gross national saving to current-price gross domestic product, gnp is real per capita gross national product, growth is the (geometric) average annual rate of growth of real per capita gross national product, old is the old-age dependency ratio (ratio of population age 65 and above to total population), young is the young-age dependency ratio (ratio of population ages 0 to 15 to total population), and distrib is an income distribution variable.

The basic specification in equation 1 embeds both a linear and a quadratic term in real per capita income to encompass the nonlinear relation between the saving rate and income described in section 2; accordingly, we should expect $\alpha_1 > 0$, $\alpha_2 < 0$. All other variables enter linearly in our basic equation.[14] The majority of empirical studies suggest that the coefficient on growth should be positive, while those on the dependency ratios should be negative according to standard life-cycle arguments.[15]

As the income distribution indicator, we use the Gini coefficient, although we present also some regressions using instead the ratio of the income share of the poorest 40 percent of households to that of the richest 20 percent and the income share of the middle 60 percent of the population. The latter variables, however, are available only for a smaller sample.

The correlation matrix of our basic set of regressors in table 2 shows three striking features. First, as mentioned, all three income distribution indicators are very highly correlated with each other, with correlation coefficients in all cases exceeding .90 in absolute value. Second, the (negative) correlation between young-age and old-age dependency ratios is also very large ($-.93$). Third, both dependency ratios are closely correlated with real per capita income (the corresponding correlation coefficients exceed .88). It will be useful to keep in mind these features of the data for the subsequent discussion of the empirical results.

Table 3 shows estimation results using the basic equation for a variety of samples. As a benchmark, the first column reports parameter estimates using a specification excluding income distribution indicators. As expected, the second and third rows show that saving ratios rise with income levels (a result also found by Carroll and Weil [1994] and Edwards [1995]) but taper off at high income, as indicated by the negative coefficient on squared GNP per capita. Specifically, the estimates in column 1 imply that, if the other variables are set at their sample means, the saving rate peaks (at a level around 22 percent) when per capita income reaches $9,000 (in 1987 dollars).

TABLE 3. Cross-Section Estimates of Saving Equations—Dependent Variable: GNS/GNP (t-statistics in parentheses)

Sample	Equation								
	1	2	3	4	5	6	7	8	9
	Full	Full	OECD	LDC	Full	OECD	LDC	Full without take-off countries	LDC without take-off countries
Constant	36.506	36.055	28.209	39.844	37.632	30.999	41.447	32.57	52.299
	(2.762)	(2.666)	(1.261)	(2.149)	(2.708)	(1.348)	(2.144)	(2.155)	(2.616)
Real GNP per capita (1987 constant dollars)	0.001	0.001	0.002	0.004	0.001	0.001	0.004	0.002	0.011
	(1.736)	(1.667)	(1.906)	(1.151)	(1.375)	(1.196)	(1.054)	(2.165)	(2.070)
Real GNP per capita squared	$-5.67E-08$	$-5.5E-08$	$-7.22E-08$	$-3.26E-07$	$-4.20E-08$	$-4.61E-08$	$-4.13E-07$	$-7.96E-08$	$-1.84E-06$
	(-1.429)	(-1.376)	(-1.603)	(-0.727)	(-0.979)	(-0.823)	(-0.730)	(-1.903)	(-1.475)
Real GNP growth rate	1.479	1.495	3.265	1.074	1.502	3.202	1.107	0.923	0.341
	(3.055)	(3.042)	(2.757)	(1.779)	(2.843)	(2.687)	(1.738)	(1.308)	(0.729)
Old-age dependency ratio	-1.258	-1.253	-0.927	-1.36	-1.271	-0.878	-1.671	-1.188	-2.742
	(-2.643)	(-2.618)	(-1.490)	(-1.061)	(-2.522)	(-1.452)	(-1.106)	(-2.055)	(-1.819)
Young-age dependency ratio	-0.413	-0.439	-0.647	-0.402	-0.425	-0.593	-0.455	-0.426	-0.518
	(-1.620)	(1.672)	(-1.218)	(-1.143)	(-1.521)	(-1.219)	(-1.202)	(-1.503)	(-1.631)
Gini coefficient		0.035	0.105	-0.095				0.094	-0.238
		(0.381)	(0.982)	(-0.734)				(1.054)	(-1.613)
Income share ratio of top 20% to bottom 40%					-0.019	0.222	-0.649		
					(-0.033)	(0.165)	(-0.921)		
Adjusted R^2	0.528	0.520	0.539	0.511	0.506	0.525	0.497	0.455	0.413
Standard error	3.875	3.912	2.691	4.446	4.092	2.817	4.742	3.681	3.458
Number of observations	52	52	20	32	45	18	27	42	22

Note: The *t*-statistics were computed using heteroskedasticity-corrected standard errors.

In turn, the fourth row in the table indicates that saving ratios are positively associated across countries with per capita GNP growth rates. A 1 percent increase in real growth raises the national saving ratio by about 1.5 percentage points. Finally, it can be seen from the fifth and sixth rows in column 1 that both young and old-age dependency ratios have the expected negative effect on national saving rates.

The simple specification in column 1 accounts for nearly 60 percent of the observed cross-country variation in national saving rates. However, the estimated coefficients on per capita income and its square, as well as on the young-age dependency ratio, have rather large standard errors. The obvious reason for this lack of precision is the strong cross-correlation between age dependency ratios and real income described in table 2.[16] Indeed, a joint F-test of the null hypothesis that young-age dependency, real income, and real income squared have no impact on saving yields a test statistic of 5.49, which overwhelmingly rejects the null at the 1 percent level.

Columns 2 through 4 in table 3 augment the specification in the first column using the Gini coefficient as the income distribution indicator in different country samples. The sign pattern of the parameter estimates in the first six rows remains unchanged, and the full sample estimates in column 2 are virtually identical to those in column 1. However, the saving-growth relationship does not appear robust across country groups: it is much stronger among industrial countries (col. 3) than among developing countries (col. 4)—the same cross-country pattern found by Carroll and Weil (1994). Controlling for other factors, a 1 percent increase in the growth rate raises national saving ratios by 3.3 percentage points among OECD countries and by only 1.1 percentage point among LDCs.

The seventh row reports the parameter estimates for the Gini coefficient. They are positive for the full sample and the OECD subsample and negative for LDCs. In all three cases, however, they are insignificantly different from zero. As before, real income, its square, and the dependency ratios are not individually significant, but F-tests cannot reject their joint significance even at the 1 percent level.

Columns 5 through 7 use as the income distribution indicator the ratio of the income shares of the top 20 and bottom 40 percent of the population. This results in a loss of seven observations (two industrial and five developing countries) due to unavailability of the share data. Apart from a general loss of precision, the estimation results are otherwise very similar to those obtained using the Gini coefficient, as should be expected in view of the very high correlation reported above between the two income distribution indicators.

Columns 8 and 9 show the results of excluding from the sample the group of take-off developing countries, which some might argue are "exceptional" from the viewpoint of saving (and also growth). For both the full and the LDC samples in columns 8 and 9, the main consequence is that the estimated coefficient on growth loses all significance, a finding similar to that reported by Carroll and Weil (1994) when excluding from their sample the East-Asian "tigers." In addition, in the LDC sample (col. 9) the estimated coefficient on the income distribution indicator becomes larger in absolute value and closer to statistical significance, suggesting a *negative* effect of inequality on saving. The interpretation of this result, however, is a bit unclear. By dropping the take-off countries, we are eliminating eight of the 10 highest-saving countries (see fig. 1), so that in effect we are truncating the sample from above. It is well known that under such circumstances OLS estimates are biased, although the direction of the bias is not known in general (e.g., Maddala 1983).

Next we check the robustness of our main result—that income inequality does *not* affect aggregate saving—by estimating alternative specifications that have been used in previous studies. Table 4 presents the results using the full sample. The first two columns explore possible nonlinear effects of income distribution, interacting the Gini coefficient with real per capita income and adding a quadratic term, respectively. Neither specification proved successful. Column 3 adds income variability to the basic set of regressors, with variability measured by the standard deviation of real per capita GNP around a trend relative to the average GNP level; according to the precautionary saving motive, it should have a positive impact on saving ratios. In fact, the estimated coefficient is negative but insignificant. The likely reason is that aggregate income variability is very different from—actually much lower than—individual income variability, as was shown by Pischke (1995). Column 4 introduces regional dummies, as was done, for example, by Sahota (1993), with industrial countries as the omitted category. However, the dummies are not significant, either individually or jointly (a joint F-test yields $F[3, 42] = 0.681$, far below conventional significance levels). The last two columns in table 4 investigate alternative inequality indicators: column 5 uses the income share of the middle class, and column 6 adds to this the ratio of income shares of the top 20 and bottom 40 percent of the population. In neither case do we find any significant effects on saving.

As a final check on our results, and also to facilitate comparability with other empirical studies, table 5 presents estimation results using gross domestic saving and real per capita GDP as the relevant measures of saving and income, respectively. The first two columns estimate our basic specification on the full and LDC sample, respectively. As can be seen, the main difference with the estimation results in table 3 is the loss of significance of income growth as a saving determinant. For the full sample, the parameter estimate on the Gini coefficient is very similar to that reported by Sahota (1993) but falls far short of statistical significance. For the LDC sample, the estimate turns positive (recall that it was negative when using the national saving ratio as the dependent variable), but its precision is extremely poor.

The remaining columns in table 5 report alternative specifications adding

TABLE 4. Cross-Section Estimates of Saving Equations—Dependent Variable: GNS/GNP (t-statistics in parentheses)

	Equation					
	1	2	3	4	5	6
Sample	Full	Full	Full	Full	Full	Full
Constant	38.740	23.249	41.816	33.354	35.140	27.395
	(2.654)	(1.480)	(2.709)	(2.425)	(2.061)	(1.170)
Real GNP per capita (1987 constant dollars)	0.001	0.001	0.001	0.002	0.001	0.001
	(0.517)	(1.614)	(1.211)	(2.032)	(1.402)	(1.251)
Real GNP per capita squared	−5.33E-08	−5.63E-08	−3.76E-08	−6.99E-08	−4.22E-08	−3.84E-08
	(−1.334)	(−1.377)	(−0.933)	(−1.734)	(−0.995)	(1.251)
Real GNP growth rate	1.420	1.453	1.291	1.234	1.497	1.504
	(2.710)	(2.912)	(2.429)	(2.065)	(2.817)	(2.765)
Old-age dependency ratio	−1.241	−1.256	−1.349	−0.997	−1.273	−1.287
	(−2.556)	(−2.591)	(−2.638)	(−2.002)	(−2.498)	(−2.471)
Young-age dependency ratio	−0.444	−0.484	−0.455	−0.485	−0.407	−0.411
	(−1.656)	(−1.794)	(−1.655)	(−1.736)	(−1.445)	(−1.439)
Gini coefficient	−0.024	0.763	−0.032	0.022		
	(−0.180)	(1.541)	(−0.347)	(0.191)		
Income share ratio of top 20% to bottom 40%					0.548	0.548
					(0.526)	(0.526)

	(1)	(2)	(3)	(4)	(5)	(6)
Income share of middle 60%					0.038 (0.218)	0.173 (0.526)
GNP variability			−16.185 (−1.317)			
Multiplication of GNP and Gini coefficient	2.15E-05 (1.099)					
Gini coefficient squared		−0.009 (−1.410)				
Latin America regional dummy				4.413 (1.129)		
Africa regional dummy				3.975 (1.001)		
Asia regional dummy				5.164 (1.403)		
Adjusted R^2	0.516	0.520	0.535	0.508	0.507	0.496
Standard error	3.925	3.911	3.848	3.960	4.089	4.134
Number of observations	52	52	52	52	45	45

Note: The t-statistics were computed using heteroskedasticity-corrected standard errors.

TABLE 5. Cross-Section Estimates of Saving Equations—Dependent Variable: GDS/GDP (t-statistics in parentheses)

				Equation		
Sample	1	2	3	4	5	6
	Full	LDC	Full	Full	Full	Full
Constant	39.011	51.769	28.699	40.523	34.594	41.524
	(2.444)	(2.158)	(1.857)	(2.305)	(2.116)	(2.558)
Real GDP per capita (1987 constant dollars)	0.002	0.005	0.002	0.002	0.003	0.002
	(2.260)	(1.615)	(2.792)	(1.199)	(2.897)	(1.965)
Real GDP per capita squared	−7.94E-08	−5.58E-07	−8.44E-08	−7.81E-08	−1.03E-07	−6.49E-08
	(−1.822)	(−1.198)	(−2.008)	(−1.777)	(−2.304)	(−1.353)
Real GDP growth rate	0.430	−0.213	0.582	0.385	0.130	0.447
	(0.664)	(−0.251)	(1.003)	(0.558)	(0.163)	(0.688)
Old-age dependency ratio	−1.695	−1.791	−1.574	−1.688	−1.196	−1.695
	(−3.256)	(−1.121)	(−3.121)	(−3.219)	(−2.144)	(−3.026)
Young-age dependency ratio	−0.548	−0.716	−0.359	−0.552	−0.644	−0.480
	(−1.812)	(−1.589)	(−1.210)	(−1.780)	(−2.000)	(−1.443)

	(1)	(2)	(3)	(4)	(5)	(6)
Gini coefficient	0.149 (1.368)	0.012 (0.087)	0.134 (1.219)	0.117 (0.7340)	0.097 (0.673)	
Income share ratio of top 20% to bottom 40%						0.546 (0.726)
GDP variability			14.945 (1.760)			
Multiplication of GDP and Gini coefficient				1.16E-05 (0.483)		
Latin America regional dummy					9.324 (2.337)	
Africa regional dummy					8.848 (1.952)	
Asia regional dummy					9.176 (2.540)	
Adjusted R^2	0.355	0.323	0.385	0.342	0.373	0.290
Standard error	4.770	5.447	4.656	4.816	4.704	5.013
Number of observations	52	32	52	52	52	45

Note: The *t*-statistics were computed using heteroskedasticity-corrected standard errors.

income variability (computed now on the basis of real GDP) and regional dummies and using the ratio of income shares as the indictor of distribution. The main novelties are that the estimated coefficient on income variability has the correct (positive) sign and the regional dummies are individually significant. In every specification, however, we fail to find any significant effects of income distribution on saving.[17]

While our findings are in accordance with the theoretical ambiguity surrounding the impact of income inequality on aggregate saving, they stand in contrast with some of the empirical literature reviewed earlier (Sahota 1993; Cook 1995; Hong 1995), which finds a positive effect of income concentration on saving. In view of our extensive empirical experiments, the likely conclusion is that the results reported by this literature are not robust to changes in sample coverage, saving measure employed, empirical specification, and— perhaps most important—to the use of the new and improved cross-country data set on income distribution constructed by Deininger and Squire (1996).

6. Conclusions

Both the historical literature on distribution and aggregate saving based on functional income distribution and neoclassical consumption theory based on the personal distribution of income bring out a number of channels through which inequality affects personal saving. Most of these mechanisms (but not all) suggest positive direct effects of income inequality on overall personal saving. However, recent political-economy research brings out negative indirect links from inequality (through investment, growth, and public saving) to aggregate saving. Taken together, these two strands of the literature imply that the overall impact of inequality on aggregate saving is ambiguous and can only be assessed empirically.

The empirical literature on the links between personal income distribution and personal saving based on household data typically finds a positive relation between personal income inequality and overall personal saving. In turn, some empirical studies based on macro (national accounts) saving data, typically conducted on cross-country samples, also report positive effects of personal income inequality on *aggregate* saving. Other studies, however, find the opposite result or no effect whatsoever. Reconciling these conflicting results is difficult because macro-based empirical studies use widely different samples and specifications, different measures of saving and inequality, and, in most cases, income distribution information of questionable quality.

This chapter has presented new econometric evidence on the saving-inequality link. Using a new data set on income distribution for a large cross-country sample, on the whole we do not find evidence of any significant association between standard inequality indicators and saving ratios, once other key saving determinants are taken into consideration. This conclusion holds for a variety of samples, income distribution indicators, and empirical specifications, and is consistent with the theoretical ambiguity summarized earlier.

There are, however, some caveats that make our empirical results tentative. First, because of the unavailability for most countries of long time series on income distribution, only the cross-country dimension of the data has been exploited here. While this entails some loss of information, it is well known that income distribution indicators generally display little variation over time relative to that across countries, and thus on the whole we do not think that omission of the time dimension has any major consequences for our results. Second, our empirical estimates—like those reported in the vast majority of the literature on saving—are based on the implicit assumption that causality runs from income, growth, and distribution to saving. While we are aware of the potential simultaneity between these variables, we also believe that the search for valid instruments is not a trivial task, and we leave it for future work. Third, related to this, our empirical estimates focus only on the *direct* effects of inequality on saving ratios, ignoring possible indirect effects operating through other saving determinants—for example, the negative impact of inequality on growth that the recent political-economy literature suggests. To explore the *total* effect of inequality on saving in a satisfactory manner one would need an analytical and empirical framework encompassing these indirect channels.

Ideally, the starting point for addressing the latter two caveats would be to specify a complete theoretical model describing, as a minimum, the determination not only of saving but also of the distribution of income and its growth rate. This, however, is likely to be a formidable task, well beyond the scope of this chapter.

DATA APPENDIX

The variables introduced in sections 2 and 5 and their definitions and sources are the following.

Variable Name	Definition and Source
Gross domestic saving ratio	Gross domestic saving relative to gross domestic product in current prices, average over 1960–94; World Bank
Gross national saving ratio	Gross national saving, including net current transfers relative to gross national product in current prices, average over 1965–94; World Bank
Real GDP per capita	In constant 1987 U.S. dollars, average over 1960–94; World Bank

Real GNP per capita	In constant 1987 U.S. dollars, average over 1965–94; World Bank
Real GDP per capita growth rate	Average over 1960–94
Real GNP per capita growth rate	Average over 1965–94
Gini coefficient and income share of top 20 percent / bottom 40 percent of population	Average over 1965–94; Deininger and Squire data set
Income share of middle 60 percent of population	Average over 1965–94; Deininger and Squire data set
Old-age dependency ratio	Population aged 65 and over relative to total population, average over 1965–94; World Bank
Young-age dependency ratio	Population aged 14 and below relative to total population, average over 1965–94; World Bank
GDP variability	Ratio of standard deviation of residuals of regression of real GDP per capita on time trend to real GDP; authors' calculation
GNP variability	Ratio of standard deviation of residuals of regression of real GNP per capita on time trend to real GNP; authors' calculation

The number of countries in the full sample is 52. The country classification is the following. *OECD countries:* Australia, Austria, Belgium, Canada, Denmark, Finland, France, Germany, Greece, Ireland, Italy, Japan, Netherlands, New Zealand, Norway, Portugal, Spain, Sweden, United Kingdom, and United States. *Take-off countries:* Chile, China, Hong Kong, Indonesia, Korea (Rep.), Malaysia, Mauritius, Singapore, Taiwan (China), and Thailand. *Other developing countries:* Bangladesh, Brazil, Colombia, Costa Rica, Dominican Republic, Egypt, Guatemala, India, Jamaica, Mexico, Morocco, Pakistan, Panama, Peru, Philippines, Sri Lanka, Tanzania, Trinidad and Tobago, Tunisia, Turkey, Venezuela, and Zambia.

Not all countries have Gini and income distribution measures available for each year. Countries are included in the sample only if they have at least one observation in each of two different decades. The distribution of countries according to the number of annual observations is the following: 38 (31) countries with less than 10 Gini (income distribution) observations, 11 (11) countries with 10 to 20 Gini (income distribution) observations, and 3 (3) countries with more than 20 Gini (income distribution) observations.

NOTES

We are grateful to Klaus Deininger and Lyn Squire for kindly making available to us their data base on income distribution. We thank Steve Marglin, Branko Milanovic, Vito

Tanzi, and an anonymous reviewer for useful comments and suggestions on an earlier draft. Excellent research assistance by Wanhong Hu is gratefully acknowledged.

1. The sample countries were selected on the basis of availability of income distribution data (kindly made available to us by Klaus Deininger and Lyn Squire). The 1965–94 average for each country is computed over those years for which the information is available. To ensure the long-term nature of the averages, the sample includes only those countries with at least one income distribution observation in each of two of the three decades that span the 1965–94 period. This leaves us with 20 industrial and 32 developing countries out of the 20 industrial and 66 nontransition developing countries in the data base of Deininger and Squire. More details are given in the data appendix.

2. The group includes China, seven market-economy East-Asian countries (Hong Kong, Indonesia, Korea, Malaysia, Singapore, Thailand, and Taiwan [China]), Chile, and Mauritius.

3. See, for example, Modigliani 1970, Maddison 1992, Bosworth 1993, and Carroll and Weil 1994.

4. On saving-growth causality, see the recent overviews by Carroll and Weil (1994), Deaton (1995), and Schmidt-Hebbel, Serven, and Solimano (1996).

5. As is well known, Kuznets's explanation of his empirical finding was based on the shift of population from traditional to modern activities. See Anand and Kanbur 1993 for an analytical reassessment of this view.

6. For a discussion of the properties of these indices, see, for example, Cowell 1977.

7. Uncertainty refers basically to the variability of income and the rate of return, and therefore it is really not a separate variable. However, because the literature emphasizes the distinction between the effects on saving of income (or rate of return) variability and those of their respective levels, we treat them separately.

8. See Friedman 1957, Hall 1978, and Flavin 1981.

9. See Carroll and Weil 1994 and Deaton 1995.

10. Unlike in the simple PIH, in this framework intertemporal transfers of resources that leave the present value of lifetime income unaffected can still affect saving behavior. Higher present taxes with lower future taxes leads to a decline in consumption if individuals have to rebuild their precautionary balances (and cannot borrow against the future tax break).

11. See Marglin 1984 for in-depth analyses of the classical, neoclassical, neo-Marxian, and neo-Keynesian approaches.

12. See Carroll and Weil 1994 and Carroll, Overland, and Weil 1994.

13. For a general overview of the different strands of the literature on income distribution and growth, see Solimano 1998.

14. All variables (except the variability of income, defined later) are measured by their means over 1965–94 (or the available sample, if shorter).

15. See Leff 1969 and Modigliani 1970. The dependency ratio is often defined to include also the population under 15. See Gersovitz 1988 for an analytical discussion of the effects of these and other demographic variables on saving.

16. The correlation between real per capita GNP and its square, not presented in table 2, equals .98.

17. The same result was obtained in other regressions (not reported) using alternatively the income shares of the top 20, middle 60, and bottom 40 percent of the population as inequality indicators.

REFERENCES

Adelman, I., and S. Robinson. 1989. "Income Distribution and Development." In *Handbook of Development Economics,* edited by H. Chenery and T. N. Srinivasan. New York: North-Holland.

Alesina, A., and R. Perotti. 1996. "Income Distribution, Political Instability, and Investment." *European Economic Review* 40:1203–28.

Alesina, A., and D. Rodrik. 1994. "Distributive Politics and Economic Growth." *Quarterly Journal of Economics* 109:465–90.

Anand, S., and S. Kanbur. 1993. "The Kuznets Process and the Inequality-Development Relationship." *Journal of Development Economics* 40:25–52.

Atkinson, A. 1994. "Seeking to Explain the Distribution of Income." WSP Discussion Paper 106. London School of Economics. Mimeo.

Becker, G. 1975. *Human Capital.* Cambridge: National Bureau of Economic Research.

Blinder, A. 1975. "Distribution Effects and the Aggregate Consumption Function." *Journal of Political Economy* 87:608–26.

Bosworth, B. P. 1993. *Saving and Investment in a Global Economy.* Washington, DC: Brookings Institution.

Bourguignon, F., and C. Morrison. 1990. "Income Distribution, Development, and Foreign Trade: A Cross Sectional Analysis." *European Economic Review* 34: 1113–32.

Bunting, D. 1991. "Savings and the Distribution of Income." *Journal of Post Keynesian Economics* 14:3–22.

Carroll, C., J. Overland, and D. Weil. 1994. "Saving and Growth with Habit Formation." Manuscript.

Carroll, C., and L. Summers. 1991. "Consumption Growth Parallels Income Growth: Some New Evidence." In *National Saving and Economic Performance,* edited by B. D. Bernheim and J. B. Shoven. Chicago: University of Chicago Press.

Carroll, C., and D. Weil. 1994. "Saving and Growth: A Reinterpretation." *Carnegie-Rochester Conference Series on Public Policy* 40:133–92.

Clarke, G. 1992. "More Evidence on Income Distribution and Growth." World Bank Policy Research Working Paper 1,064. Mimeo.

Collins, S. 1991. "Saving Behavior in Ten Developing Countries." In *National Saving and Economic Performance,* edited by B. D. Bernheim and J. B. Shoven. Chicago: University of Chicago Press.

Cook, C. 1995. "Savings Rates and Income Distribution: Further Evidence from LDCs." *Applied Economics* 27:71–82.

Cowell, F. 1977. *Measuring Inequality: Techniques for the Social Sciences.* New York: Wiley.

Deaton, A. 1991. "Saving and Liquidity Constraints." *Econometrica* 59:1121–42.

———. 1992. *Understanding Consumption.* Oxford: Clarendon.

———. 1995. "Growth and Saving: What Do We Know, What Do We Need to Know, and What Might We Learn?" Princeton University, Research Program in Development Studies. Manuscript.

Deininger, K., and L. Squire. 1996. "A New Data Set Measuring Income Inequality." *World Bank Economic Review* 10:565–92.

Della Valle, P., and N. Oguchi. 1976. "Distribution, the Aggregate Consumption Function, and the Level of Economic Development: Some Cross-Country Results." *Journal of Political Economy* 84:1325–34.

Dornbusch, R., and S. Edwards. 1991. "The Macroeconomics of Populism." In *The Macroeconomics of Populism in Latin America,* edited by R. Dornbusch and S. Edwards. Chicago: University of Chicago Press.

Edwards, S. 1995. "Why Are Saving Rates So Different across Countries? An International Comparative Analysis." NBER Working Paper 5,097. Mimeo.

Feldstein, M., and C. Horioka. 1980. "Domestic Saving and International Capital Flows." *Economic Journal* 90:314–29.

Feldstein, M., and P. Bachetta. 1991. "National Saving and International Investment." In *National Saving and Economic Performance,* edited by B. D. Bernheim and J. Shoven. Chicago: University of Chicago Press.

Flavin, M. 1981. "The Adjustment of Consumption to Changing Expectations about Future Income." *Journal of Political Economy* 89:974–1009.

Friedman, M. 1957. *A Theory of the Consumption Function.* Princeton: Princeton University Press.

Galor, O., and J. Zeira. 1993. "Income Distribution and Macroeconomics." *Review of Economic Studies* 60:35–52.

Gersovitz, M. 1988. "Saving and Development." In *Handbook of Development Economics,* edited by H. Chenery and T. N. Srinivasan. Amsterdam: North-Holland.

Gupta, K. 1970. "Personal Saving in Developing Nations: Further Evidence." *Economic Record* 46:243–49.

Hall, R. 1978. "Stochastic Implications of the Life-Cycle Permanent Income Hypothesis: Theory and Evidence." *Journal of Political Economy* 86:75–96.

Hayashi, F. 1985. "Tests for Liquidity Constraints: A Critical Survey." NBER Working Paper 1,720. Mimeo.

Hong, K. 1995. "Income Distribution and Aggregate Saving." Harvard University. Manuscript.

Houthakker, H. 1961. "An International Comparison of Personal Saving." *Bulletin of the International Statistical Institute* 38:55–69.

Jappelli, T., and M. Pagano. 1994. "Saving, Growth, and Liquidity Constraints." *Quarterly Journal of Economics* 109:83–109.

Kaldor, N. 1957. "A Model of Economic Growth." *Economic Journal* 67:591–624.

Kelley, A. C., and J. G. Williamson. 1968. "Household Savings Behavior in Developing Countries: The Indonesian Case." *Economic Development and Cultural Change* 16 (3): 385–403.

Kirman, A. 1992. "Whom or What Does the Representative Individual Represent?" *Journal of Economic Perspectives* 2:117–36.

Kotlikoff, L., and L. Summers. 1981. "The Role of Intergenerational Transfers in Aggregate Capital Accumulation." *Journal of Political Economy* 90:706–32.

———. 1988. "The Contribution of Intergenerational Transfers to Total Wealth: A Reply." In *Modelling the Accumulation and Distribution of Wealth,* edited by D. Kessler and A. Masson. Oxford: Clarendon.

Kuznets, S. 1955. "Economic Growth and Income Inequality." *American Economic Review* 89:1–28.

Leff, N. H. 1969. "Dependency Rates and Savings Rates." *American Economic Review* 59:886–96.

Levine, R., and D. Renelt. 1992. "A Sensitivity Analysis of Cross-Country Growth Regressions." *American Economic Review* 82:942–63.

Lewis, W. A. 1954. "Economic Development with Unlimited Supplies of Labor." *The Manchester School* 22:139–91.

Lim, D. 1980. "Income Distribution, Export Instability, and Savings Behavior." *Economic Development and Cultural Change* 26:359–64.

Maddala, G. 1983. *Limited-Dependent and Qualitative Variables in Econometrics.* Cambridge: Cambridge University Press.

Maddison, A. 1992. "A Long-Run Perspective on Saving." *Scandinavian Journal of Economics* 94:181–96.

Mankiw, N., D. Romer, and D. Weil. 1992. "A Contribution to the Empirics of Economic Growth." *Quarterly Journal of Economics* 107:407–38.

Marglin, S. 1984. *Growth, Distribution, and Prices.* Cambridge: Harvard University Press.

Masson, P., T. Bayoumi, and H. Samiel. 1995. "Saving Behavior in Industrial and Developing Countries." International Monetary Fund. Manuscript.

Menchik, P., and M. David. 1983. "Income Distribution, Lifetime Savings, and Bequests." *American Economic Review* 73:672–90.

Modigliani, F. 1970. "The Life Cycle Hypothesis of Savings and Intercountry Differences in the Savings Ratio." In *Induction, Growth, and Trade,* edited by W. A. Eltis, M. F. G. Scott, and J. N. Wolfe. Oxford: Oxford University Press.

———, and R. Brumberg. 1954. "Utility Analysis and the Consumption Function: An Interpretation of Cross-Section Data." In *Post-Keynesian Economics,* edited by K. K. Kurihara. New Brunswick, NJ: Rutgers University Press.

———. 1979. "Utility Analysis and the Consumption Function: An Attempt at Integration." In *The Collected Papers of Franco Modigliani,* edited by A. Abel. Vol. 2. Cambridge: MIT Press.

Musgrove, P. 1980. "Income Distribution and the Aggregate Consumption Function." *Journal of Political Economy* 88:504–25.

Ogaki, M., J. Ostry, and C. M. Reinhart. 1994. "Saving Behavior in Low- and Middle-Income Developing Countries: A Comparison." International Monetary Fund. Manuscript.

Pasinetti, L. 1962. "Rate of Profit and Income Distribution in Relation to the Rate of Economic Growth." *Review of Economic Studies* 29:267–79.

Perotti, R. 1995. "Growth, Income Distribution, and Democracy: What the Data Say." Columbia University. Manuscript.

Persson, T., and G. Tabellini. 1994. "Is Inequality Harmful for Growth? Theory and Evidence." *American Economic Review* 84:600–621.

Pischke, J-S. 1995. "Individual Income, Incomplete Information, and Aggregate Consumption." *Econometrica* 63 (4): 805–40.

Sahota, G. 1993. "Saving and Distribution." In *The Economics of Saving,* edited by J. H. Gapinski. Boston: Kluwer.

Schmidt-Hebbel, K., L. Servén, and A. Solimano. 1996. "Saving, Investment, and Growth in Developing Countries: An Overview." In *Road Maps to Prosperity:*

Essays on Growth and Development, edited by A. Solimano. Ann Arbor: University of Michigan Press.

Schmidt-Hebbel, K., S. Webb, and G. Corsetti. 1992. "Household Saving in Developing Countries: First Cross-Country Evidence." *World Bank Economic Review* 6:529–47.

Solimano, A. 1998. "The End of the Hard Choices? Revisiting the Relationship between Income Distribution and Growth." Chap. 4, this volume.

Solow, R. 1956. "A Contribution to the Theory of Economic Growth." *Quarterly Journal of Economics* 70:65–94.

Venieris, Y., and D. Gupta. 1986. "Income Distribution and Sociopolitical Instability as Determinants of Savings: A Cross-Sectional Model." *Journal of Political Economy* 94:873–83.

Williamson, J. 1968. "Personal Saving in Developing Nations: An Intertemporal Cross-Section from Asia." *Economic Record* 44:194–202.

Zou, Heng-Fu. 1994. "The Spirit of Capitalism and Long-Run Growth." *European Journal of Political Economy* 10:279–93.

CHAPTER 7

Income Distribution, Investment, and Growth

Felipe Larraín B. and Rodrigo Vergara M.

1. Introduction

This chapter carries out an empirical investigation on the determinants of economic growth in a comprehensive group of countries within the context provided by the new growth theory. The main working hypothesis is that economic growth is affected by a structural factor of the country: the distribution of income. Our presumption is that a greater inequality in income distribution retards the growth process of countries because the higher the inequality the greater the possibility of social conflict. The mere perception of higher instability has a depressing effect on investment and thus on economic growth.

A quick look at the international evidence provides preliminary support for this argument. Figure 1 shows the relation between an index of income distribution inequality[1] and the average annual per capita economic growth for a large group of countries during the period 1965–85. The correlation between both variables is clearly negative. Countries with more egalitarian distribution tend to show a higher rate of per capita growth and vice versa. Figure 2 shows the relation between income distribution and private investment. Once again, the correlation is clearly negative: the greater income inequality is the lower private investment tends to be. Of course, the figures only show a simple correlation between the variables in question and do not control for the influence of other variables that can affect this relationship. We address this issue later in the chapter when we study the empirical evidence with an econometric model.

The chapter is organized as follows. Section 2 contains a brief review of the literature on income distribution and growth. The next section compares the actual experience of Latin America and East Asia in this matter. Section 4 contains a formal empirical analysis of the central hypothesis of this chapter, and section 5 offers some conclusions.

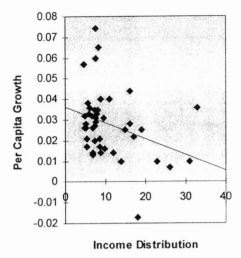

Fig. 1. Per capita growth and income distribution

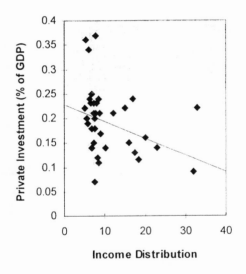

Fig. 2. Private investment and income distribution

2. Income Distribution and Growth: A Brief Review of the Literature

The existence of a relationship between income distribution and growth is not a new idea. One of its first expressions is the famous inverted-U curve of Simon

Kuznets (1966). According to him, income distribution is more egalitarian in extreme stages of development, while it is more unequal at the intermediate level of development. The causality of the Kuznets relation, however, goes from the level of economic development to income distribution. For many years, this was the way in which the relationship that concerns us here was studied. Our interest is precisely in the inverse relation because we believe that income distribution is an important determinant of economic growth. This idea is considerably newer and more unexplored, and it only began to appear in a formal way toward the end of the last decade.[2]

Berg and Sachs (1988) studied the structural characteristics that influenced some countries to restructure their external debt, on finding themselves incapable of servicing it, while other highly indebted countries did not. From our perspective, the most interesting result of their essay is that the more unequal the distribution of income the greater the probability that a country would be forced to restructure its debt. The authors attribute this to the difficulties of political management derived from social conflict in economies having large distributive inequalities.

Galor and Zeira (1993) focus their analysis on access to credit. The authors argue that credit is restricted to the poor, who consequently face great difficulties in investing in human capital. The more unequal the distribution of income, the smaller is the number of people who have access to education, and as a result there is lower growth. In Greenwood and Jovanovich 1990, income distribution and growth correlate through time as the financial system develops.

The empirical evidence presented by Larraín and Vergara (1993) indicates that one of the most significant factors explaining the differential of private investment rates between Latin American and East Asian countries is that the latter present much greater macroeconomic stability. As a measure of stability, they use the coefficient of variation of different macroeconomic variables. These authors suggest that the greater instability in Latin America may be associated with the fact that these countries present much more unequal income distributions than do the East Asian countries. Thus, Latin American nations are much more susceptible to populist pressures, changes in economic policies, expropriations, violent changes of authorities, and so on, a fact that harms credibility, produces indefinition of property rights, and has adverse effects on investment.

Persson and Tabellini (1994) develop a model in which growth is determined, to a great extent, by the accumulation of knowledge employed in the production of goods and services. In a society in which the distribution of income is more unequal, it is more likely that tax and regulatory measures will be adopted, which can hinder the private appropriation of the fruits of this knowledge. This damages growth. The empirical analysis they perform confirms a negative relation between inequality in income distribution and growth.

Alesina and Rodrik (1994) use an endogenous growth model with

distributive conflicts. In this framework, they show that, in a democratic society where the median-voter theorem is applied, the more unequal the income
distribution the lower the growth will be. In their reasoning, this is due to the
fact that the average voter has a low stock of wealth, and thus he favors higher
capital levies, which retard growth. These authors also present empirical evidence supporting their hypothesis.

Both Persson and Tabellini (1994) and Alesina and Rodrik (1994) study
the relation between distributive inequality and growth in democracies since it
is the result of a political process. In our chapter, the type of political regime is
not of great significance since unequal income distribution produces instability
regardless of the political regime. In democracies, it is possible that the reasoning of these authors may apply—in other words, that a large majority of the
population supports the application of higher levies on capital, which have a
negative effect on growth. However, this is only one of the many channels
through which distributive inequality can affect growth.

In other types of political regimes (and also in a democracy), an inequitable distribution can provoke unexpected variations in the rules of the game,
expropriations, abrupt changes of orientation in economic policy, and other
effects that can cause instability and indefinition of property rights. These, in
turn, have a negative effect on investment and growth.

On the other hand, one of the explicit mechanisms whereby growth is
affected in our analysis is through private investment. And, although in some
previous studies one could infer that the theoretical transmission channel is
investment, this is never explicitly put forward. Furthermore, no empirical
evidence is presented in this respect. As analyzed in section 4, our results
support the conceptual reasoning that a greater inequality in income distribution exerts a negative influence on economic growth.

3. East Asia and Latin America: Two Regions in Contrast

As a motivation for the hypothesis advanced in this chapter, perhaps the most
illustrative comparison is that of Latin America and East Asia. One of the most
profound structural characteristics of Latin America is the great inequality it
has permanently exhibited in income distribution, at least ever since reliable
measurements have been available. This region has also been characterized by
unstable democracies (frequently interrupted by authoritarian regimes), great
instability in the rules of the game, and poor economic performance. Precisely
the opposite can be said of the East Asian countries, with the obvious exception
of the reference to the authoritarian type of political regime, which has also
been present there.

Table 1 shows the income distribution and the rate of growth of per capita

TABLE 1. Income Distribution and Growth in Latin America and Asia

Country	Percentage of National Income			Per Capita GDP (rate of growth) (3)
	Poorest 20% (1)	Richest 20% (2)	Quotient (2/1)	
Asia				
Korea	5.7	45.3	7.9	6.0
Hong Kong	5.4	47.0	8.7	6.6
Indonesia	6.6	49.4	7.4	3.7
Malaysia	3.5	56.1	16.0	4.5
Singapore	6.5	49.2	7.6	7.4
Thailand	5.6	49.8	8.9	4.1
Taiwan	8.8	37.2	4.2	5.7
Average	6.0	47.7	8.0	5.4
Latin America				
Argentina	4.4	50.3	11.4	0.5
Brazil	2.0	66.6	33.3	3.5
Chile	4.2	60.4	12.2	0.7
Mexico	2.9	57.7	19.9	2.5
Peru	1.9	61.0	32.1	0.8
Venezuela	3.0	54.0	18.0	−1.6
Average	3.1	58.3	18.8	1.1

Source: Income distribution: World Bank 1989, 1990, and specific country sources; Chile: Instituto Nacional de Estadísticas, September 1989; per capita income growth: Summers and Heston 1988.

income in the two regions. The tremendous difference between both groups of countries is self-evident. Income distribution is much more egalitarian in East Asia, where the richest 20 percent of the population has, on the average, about eight times more income than the poorest 20 percent. This coefficient ranges from 4.2 in Taiwan (the most equitable of them all) to 16 in Malaysia. On the other hand, the average per capita growth between 1960 and 1985 was 5.4 percent. The average inequality coefficient (DISTY) for Latin America, however, is 18.8, more than double the Asian average. The most dramatic case of inequality is that of Brazil, where the richest 20 percent has 33 times more income than the poorest 20 percent. And the average per capita growth for Latin America was 1.1 percent over the same period, remarkably lower than that of East Asia.

Recent studies have conjectured that this distributive problem is behind the great instability of macroeconomic policies in Latin America. Sachs (1990) and Dornbusch and Edwards (1991) have analyzed economic populism in the region. Their hypothesis starts from a marked inequality in income distribution, which generates social pressures to reduce it. On several occasions, Latin American countries have yielded to the temptation of applying populist policies in order to diminish social problems. The general pattern is strong fiscal and monetary expansion that generates an economic boom and a false sensation of well-being for one or two years (at the most). After this period, inflation takes off, real wages fall, unemployment increases, and output declines. At the end of the populist cycle, the country is worse off than it was initially and requires a drastic adjustment. This cycle has been absent in Asia, largely because income distribution is much more equitable.

Thus, distributive inequalities give rise to social pressures, and these, in turn, generate great instability in economic policies. It is not surprising, then, that key macroeconomic variables, such as inflation, output growth and the real exchange rate, present much greater volatility in Latin America. Larraín and Vergara (1993) have calculated that, on average, the instability of the real exchange rate in Latin America is more than double that in East Asia. The situation is even more extreme regarding the rate of output growth, the volatility of which in Latin America is 10 times higher than that recorded in Asia.[3] It is clear that more unstable macroeconomic environments discourage investment and impair growth.

4. Empirical Evidence

This section presents empirical evidence that supports the relation between income distribution and growth set forth in the preceding sections. In performing this analysis, 45 countries were considered, including developed as well as developing ones. We run Barro (1991) types of regressions when we additionally include income distribution variables.

Most of the data are obtained from Barro and Wolf (1989). However, the income distribution series—a key variable in our study—comes from World Bank information. Unfortunately, this information is available for a considerably lower number of countries (45) than is contained in the Barro and Wolf data base (1989). This is why the maximum number of countries included in our regressions with income distribution is 45.

Two types of regressions were carried out. In some, per capita growth was taken as the dependent variable. In others, the variable to be explained was private investment as a percentage of GDP. Thus, the regressions to be estimated are:

$$\text{GRTH6085} = B0 + B1*\text{GDP60} + B2*\text{PRIM60} + B3*\text{GOVCONS} \\ + B4*\text{REVCOUP} + B5*\text{DISTORT} + B6*\text{DISTY} + \text{error}$$

and

$$\text{PRINV} = D0 + D1*\text{GDP60} + D2*\text{PRIM60} + D3*\text{GOVCONS} \\ + D4*\text{REVCOUP} + D5*\text{DISTORT} + D6*\text{DISTY} + \text{error.}$$

4.1. The Variables

The dependent variable (GRTH6085) represents the mean rate of growth of per capita GDP for the 1960–85 period. The original source of this information is Summers and Heston (1988), who, to make the GDPs of the different countries comparable, adjust them according to purchasing power parity.

GDP60 represents the per capita GDP at the beginning of the estimation period (1960). A negative coefficient is expected for this variable, which would support the convergence theory, for example, that countries with higher initial per capita GDP (in 1960) have grown less than those with lower per capita GDP in that year. The original source of this series is Summers and Heston 1988.

The variable PRIM60 represents the percentage of pupils of primary school age who were actually attending primary school in 1960. This variable represents a proxy for human capital, which is presumed to be positively correlated with growth. The series was obtained from Barro and Wolf (1989), where United Nations Education, Scientific and Cultural Organization (UNESCO) and the International Labour Office (ILO) are cited as original sources.

GOVCONS represents government consumption net of spending on education and defense (which in many cases pertains more to investment than to consumption) as a percentage of GDP. With greater government consumption, it is probable that more taxes and distortions will exist in the economy. Therefore, this variable is expected to be negatively correlated with growth. Once again, the series is obtained from Barro and Wolf (1989), wherein Summers and Heston 1988, government finance statistics (IMF), and the UNESCO data are cited as original sources.

REVCOUP is the number of revolutions and coups d'état per year during the 1960–85 period. This variable is included to capture in a direct manner the climate of political instability that would be negatively correlated with growth. The source is Barro and Wolf (1989), who cite Banks (1979) as the original source.

DISTORT is a proxy variable for the distortions present in the economy. More specifically, it measures the deviation of the price of capital goods with respect to the mean of the sample. In this sense, a positive or negative deviation would indicate a move away from their market price. This variable comes from Barro and Wolf 1989, who cite Summers and Heston 1988.

The PRINV variable measures private investment in capital assets (in real terms) as a percentage of GDP. The figures are obtained from Barro and Wolf 1989, where Summers and Heston 1988 is cited as the original source.

Last, DISTY is the variable used as an income distribution proxy. This is the ratio between the total income received by the richest 20 percent of the population and the income that goes to the 20 percent with the lowest income. Thus, a higher value of this ratio indicates a more unequal income distribution.

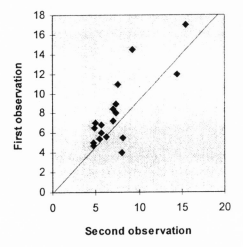

Fig. 3.   Income distribution at two points in time

According to the hypothesis set forth here, this variable should be negatively correlated with growth as well as with private investment. The source of these figures is World Bank 1989 and Larraín and Vergara 1993 (for a number of countries not included in that report). Table 2 shows the information on income distribution and per capita growth for the 45 countries of our sample.

The income distribution figures, although taken from a recent work, generally pertain to information from the 1970s, and the more recent ones (a few) are from the early 1980s. Ideally, it would have been desirable to have the income distribution at the beginning of the estimation period (as close as possible to 1960) such that the causality between income distribution and growth is adequately reflected. The absence of a reliable series of this nature for a significant number of countries left us with no option but to use figures such as those already described. In any event, the use of these figures can be defended with three arguments. In the first place, the income distribution figures are very stable over time. In countries where figures are available for 1960 and 1985, it can be seen that the figures show very little variation (see fig. 3). Second, the figures generally pertain to an intermediate point in the sample period and not to the end of that period. And, third, we estimated the regressions with instrumental variables, using as instruments only variables of the year 1960.

Another variable—the GINI coefficient for the different countries—was also used to measure income distribution. The sample in this case drops to 41 observations, which correspond to the number of countries where this coefficient was available.[4] Table 3 shows the main information concerning the DISTY and GINI variables.

TABLE 2. Income Distribution and Growth Data

Country	DISTY	GINI	Percentage of Average Growth (1960–85)
Egypt	8.3	0.38	3.5
Ivory Coast	25.6	0.52	0.9
Kenya	23.2	0.51	1.0
Mauritius	15.1	n.d.	2.5
Bangladesh	6.9	0.36	1.5
Hong Kong	8.7	0.38	6.6
India	7.1	0.38	1.4
Israel	6.7	0.32	3.2
Japan	4.3	0.27	5.8
South Korea	7.9	0.36	6.0
Malaysia	16	0.47	4.5
Philippines	10.1	0.42	1.8
Singapore	7.6	n.d.	7.4
Sri Lanka	8.6	0.39	1.8
Taiwan	4.2	n.d.	5.7
Thailand	8.9	0.4	4.1
Belgium	4.6	0.27	3.2
Denmark	7.1	0.32	2.7
Finland	6	0.3	3.3
France	7.7	0.34	3.2
Germany	5	0.3	2.9
Ireland	5.1	0.3	2.9
Italy	7.1	0.35	3.3
Netherlands	4.4	0.26	2.6
Norway	6.4	0.3	3.7
Portugal	9.4	0.4	3.8
Spain	5.8	0.31	3.9
Sweden	5.6	0.31	2.6
Switzerland	5.8	0.29	1.8
Turkey	16.1	0.47	2.8
United Kingdom	5.7	0.31	2.2
Canada	7.5	0.33	2.8
Costa Rica	16.6	0.46	1.9
El Salvador	8.6	0.38	0.5
Mexico	19.9	0.49	2.5
Trinidad and Tobago	11.9	0.42	1.4
United States	7.5	0.33	2.1
Argentina	11.4	0.41	0.5
Brazil	33.3	0.56	3.5
Chile	14.4	n.d.	0.7
Peru	32.1	0.54	0.8
Venezuela	18	0.47	− 1.6
Australia	8.7	0.38	2.1
New Zealand	8.8	0.37	1.4
Indonesia	7.5	0.41	3.7

Source: Income distribution: World Bank, 1989, 1990, and specific country sources; Chile: Instituto Nacional de Estadisticas, September 1989; per capita income growth: Summers and Heston 1988.

Note: n.d. = no data available.

TABLE 3. Income Distribution Variables

	DISTY	GINI
Mean	10.6	0.38
Highest value	33.3	0.56
Lowest value	4.2	0.26
Standard deviation	7.0	0.08
Number of observations	45	41

Source: See table 2.

4.2. Empirical Results

Table 4 presents the results of the regressions with per capita growth as the dependent variable. Given that in cross-sectional studies it is usual to encounter heteroskedasticity problems, the standard errors have been obtained in accordance with White's variance-covariance matrix in all the regressions.

Per capita income as the dependent variable. All the coefficients in regression 1 have the expected signs and are significant. In particular, the coefficient that most interests us in this work, the one associated with inequality in income distribution, is negative and significant. Its value (-0.0009) indicates that for every 10 points of increment in the inequality coefficient the long-term average annual per capita growth rate diminishes by 0.9 percent. Certainly, this is not an insignificant result, since it indicates that the difference in average per capita growth between the most egalitarian country of our sample (Taiwan) and the least egalitarian one (Brazil), attributable to their different inequality indexes (controlling for all the other variables), would be around 2.5 percentage points per year.

Figure 4 shows the partial correlation between per capita growth and the DISTY variable. That is to say, from the GRTH6085 variable is subtracted the predicted value for all the other variables, with the exception of DISTY. On doing this, it can be seen that the correlation between both variables is negative and significant.

Regression 2 uses the GINI variable (instead of DISTY) as an inequality proxy, and the results are practically the same. This confirms our presumption that inequality in income distribution has a negative effect on growth, a result that is robust to different ways of measuring that inequality. The coefficient (-0.0825) indicates that for each 0.1 increase in the GINI, per capita growth drops an average of 0.8 percent. The highest GINI coefficient of our sample is that of Brazil (0.56) and the lowest is that of the Netherlands (0.26),[5] so the difference between the two, all else remaining constant, would explain 2.5 percentage points of annual difference in rates of growth. Thus, these results are perfectly consistent with those of the first regression. Furthermore, the quantitative effects are exceedingly similar.

TABLE 4. Per Capita Growth (dependent variable: per capita growth)

Variables	1	2	3	4	5
Constant	0.0525	0.071	0.0544	0.0709	0.0273
	(0.0101)	(0.016)	(0.0103)	(0.0166)	(0.0073)
GDP60	−0.0068	−0.0067	−0.007	−0.0068	−0.0053
	(0.0011)	(0.0012)	(0.0011)	(0.0013)	(0.001)
PRIM60	0.0241	0.024	0.0239	0.024	0.0295
	(0.0081)	(0.0074)	(0.0786)	(0.0074)	(0.0063)
GOVCONS	−0.1575	−0.1322	−0.1651	−0.1318	−0.1244
	(0.0391)	(0.0406)	(0.0435)	(0.0492)	(0.0341)
REVCOUP	−0.0368	−0.0309	−0.0373	−0.0308	−0.0279
	(0.0066)	(0.007)	(0.0065)	(0.0067)	(0.0066)
DISTORT			0.0057	−0.0002	−0.0064
			(0.0097)	(0.0096)	(0.0047)
DISTY	−0.0009		−0.0009		
	(0.0003)		(0.0003)		
GINI		−0.0825		−0.0824	
		(0.0258)		(0.0257)	
Adjusted R^2	0.63	0.585	0.627	0.572	0.443
Standard error of the regression	0.011	0.01	0.011	0.01	0.014
Number of observations	45	41	45	41	98

Note: Standard error is in parentheses.

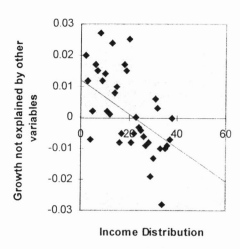

Fig. 4. Income distribution and growth unexplained by other variables

In regressions 3 and 4, the DISTORT variable is added. Practically, its inclusion does not affect the coefficients nor the significance of the parameters associated with our inequality variables. This DISTORT variable, a proxy of distortions in the economy, does not prove significant and furthermore has the wrong sign in regression 3. However, this variable does prove significant in other studies (Barro 1991). Our interpretation of this is given precisely by the introduction of the income distribution variable. In effect, according to our hypothesis, the greater the inequality in income distribution, the greater the economic instability. This, as discussed earlier, is reflected by heavy fluctuations in such key prices of the economy as the real exchange rate, the interest rate, and the price of capital goods. Therefore, the effect of distortions in the economy may be captured by the income distribution inequality variable.

Regression 5 supports this hypothesis. In effect, upon eliminating the income distribution variable from the regression, the significance of DISTORT increases remarkably (although, we must acknowledge, it does not manage to be significant at 10 percent) and the sign becomes negative, which is what would be expected a priori.[6]

Private investment as the dependent variable. Table 5 presents the regressions for private investment, using the same regressors as in the growth equations. In regression 1, it can be seen that all the regressors have the expected sign and are significant (although the GDP60 variable is significant at somewhat more than 10 percent). The income distribution variable appears with the right sign and is significant. Its coefficient (-0.002) indicates that for every 10 points of decrease in our inequality proxy (DISTY), all else remaining constant, the ratio of private investment to GDP increases by two percentage points. Thus, for example, the greater income distribution equality in Taiwan in relation to Brazil could explain (all else being constant) a higher rate of investment in Taiwan in the neighbourhood of 6 percent of GDP per annum.

Figure 5 shows the partial correlation between private investment and income distribution, which is obtained from the first regression in table 4. A distinct negative correlation between both variables can be observed.

Regression 2 uses the GINI variable as an income distribution proxy. It can be seen that this variable has, as expected a priori, a negative and significant coefficient (at somewhat more than 10 percent). As in the case of the growth regressions, the interpretation of its coefficient (-0.21) is very similar to the interpretation of the coefficient of the DISTY variable.

Regressions 3 and 4 include, as an additional explanatory variable, the distortion in the prices of capital goods (DISTORT). It has the right sign but is not significant, which again can be explained by its correlation with the inequality indicators, which indeed are significant. This is confirmed in regression 5, where, upon eliminating the inequality variable, the DISTORT variable becomes significant and has the right sign.

TABLE 5. Private Investment (percentage of GDP; dependent variable: private investment as percentage of GDP)

Variables	1	2	3	4	5
Constant	0.2322	0.2907	0.2258	0.2708	0.122
	(0.0547)	(0.0842)	(0.0543)	(0.0881)	(0.0307)
GDP60	−0.0073	−0.0055	−0.006	−0.0036	−0.0014
	(0.0048)	(0.0051)	(0.0053)	(0.0058)	(0.0039)
PRIM60	0.0797	0.0579	0.0784	0.0614	0.1081
	(0.479)	(0.0433)	(0.0472)	(0.0423)	(0.0293)
GOVCONS	−0.6207	−0.508	−0.5913	−0.4507	−0.2365
	(0.1692)	(0.1559)	(0.1849)	(0.1752)	(0.1352)
REVCOUP	−0.0877	−0.0727	−0.0806	−0.0623	−0.0676
	(0.0376)	(0.0403)	(0.0324)	(0.0325)	(0.0237)
DISTORT			−0.0341	−0.0394	−0.0521
			(0.0255)	(0.0281)	(0.0121)
DISTY	−0.0022		−0.0023		
	(0.0011)		(0.0011)		
GINI		−0.2138		−0.2059	
		(0.128)		(0.1287)	
Adjusted R^2	0.461	0.418	0.463	0.424	0.487
Standard error of the regression	0.044	0.043	0.044	0.043	0.49
Number of observations	39	35	39	35	76

Note: Standard error is in parentheses.

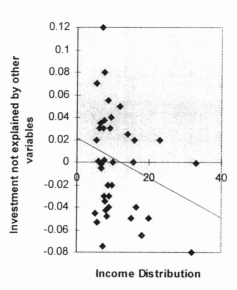

Income Distribution

Fig. 5. Income distribution and private investment unexplained by other variables

TABLE 6. Growth and Private Investment (dependent variable: per capita growth)

Variables	1	2	3	4
Constant	0.0258	0.0374	0.0255	0.0378
	(0.018)	(0.0194)	(0.0166)	(0.0194)
GDP60	−0.0056	−0.0056	−0.0059	−0.0057
	(0.0011)	(0.0013)	(0.0011)	(0.0013)
PRIM60	0.0118	0.0154	0.0115	0.015
	(0.0118)	(0.0108)	(0.0109)	(0.0108)
GOVCONS	−0.0768	−0.0524	−0.0789	−0.0544
	(0.0422)	(0.036)	(0.0423)	(0.0391)
REVCOUP	−0.0224	−0.0181	−0.0234	−0.0185
	(0.0088)	(0.0092)	(0.0074)	(0.0088)
DISTORT			0.0082	0.0023
			(0.0107)	(0.0106)
PRINV	0.1193	0.109	0.1273	0.1116
	(0.0348)	(0.0363)	(0.0318)	(0.038)
DISTY	−0.0007		−0.0006	
	(0.0003)		(0.0003)	
GINI		−0.0613		−0.0612
		(0.0241)		(0.0253)
Adjusted R^2	0.662	0.606	0.665	0.593
Standard error of the regression	0.01	0.009	0.01	0.009
Number of observations	39	35	39	35

Note: Standard error is in parentheses.

Economic growth and private investment.   Table 6 shows per capita growth regressions, which also include private investment (in percentage of GDP) as a regressor. It can be seen that the proxy variables of income distribution inequality keep their sign, magnitude, and significance. Moreover, the private investment variable is also significant and has the expected sign. This suggests that the explanatory variables other than private investment, among them income distribution, have an influence on economic growth beyond their influence on the level of investment. One interpretation of these results is that these variables have an influence not only on the level of investment but on its productivity. Thus, for example, more education has a positive effect on the productivity of investment and therefore on growth.

Estimation with two-stage least squares.   Table 7 shows the same regressions as table 4 but this time using least squares in two stages. This seeks to solve the problem derived from not having the income distribution variable at the beginning of the sample (1960), in other words, the simultaneity problem. Following Alesina and Rodrik (1994), several variables measured in 1960 are used as

TABLE 7. Per Capita Growth (least squares in two stages; dependent variable: per capita growth)

Variables	1	2	3	4
Constant	0.0756	0.1069	0.0801	0.1101
	(0.0138)	(0.0215)	(0.0147)	(0.0223)
GDP60	−0.0073	−0.0076	−0.0076	−0.0076
	(0.0012)	(0.0013)	(0.0012)	(0.0014)
PRIM60	0.0137	0.016	0.0126	0.0153
	(0.0079)	(0.0069)	(0.0078)	(0.0068)
GOVCONS	−0.1753	−0.1526	−0.187	−0.1581
	(0.042)	(0.0414)	(0.0448)	(0.0493)
REVCOUP	−0.0312	−0.0289	−0.0319	−0.0293
	(0.007)	(0.0075)	(0.0064)	(0.0072)
DISTORT			0.0829	0.0029
			(0.009)	(0.0097)
DISTY	−0.002		−0.0021	
	(0.0005)		(0.0005)	
GINI		−0.1468		−0.1508
		(0.0367)		(0.0365)
Adjusted R^2	0.621	0.584	0.625	0.574
Standard error of the regression	0.011	0.01	0.011	0.01
Number of observations	45	41	45	41

Note: Standard error is in parentheses.

instruments, such as per capita GDP, percentage of pupils in primary and secondary education, percentage of literacy, and quotient between pupils and teachers in primary education. The results indicate that the coefficients and the significance of the parameters remain much the same, with the exception of the coefficients of the primary school and income distribution variable.

Indeed, the coefficient of our income distribution proxy increases to somewhat more than double. This would appear to be indicating that the effect of distribution on growth is even stronger. We do not venture to draw a definitive conclusion as to whether the magnitude of the coefficient is closer to that indicated by table 4 or that indicated by table 7. What is clear, however, is that the greater the inequality, the more growth is affected negatively and in a significant manner, and this effect is probably somewhat greater than that shown in table 4.

Democracy and authoritarianism. Table 8 shows the results of the regressions carried out after eliminating from the sample those countries with nondemocratic governments during a significant part of the period considered. We seek thus to verify whether the story we are telling only applies to democracies,

TABLE 8. Growth in Democracies (dependent variable: per capita growth)

Variables	1	2
Constant	0.0285	0.0598
	(0.0173)	(0.0177)
GDP60	−0.0041	−0.0046
	(0.0011)	(0.0011)
PRIM60	0.0314	0.032
	(0.0127)	(0.0112)
GOVCONS	−0.0122	0.0066
	(0.0372)	(0.0356)
REVCOUP	−0.0397	−0.034
	(0.0162)	(0.0179)
DISTY	−0.002	
	(0.0004)	
GINI		−0.1412
		(0.0302)
Adjusted R^2	0.685	0.691
Standard error of the regression	0.007	0.007
Number of observations	23	23

Note: Standard error is in parentheses.

as suggested by Alesina and Rodrik (1994) and Persson and Tabellini (1991), or whether it applies to all the countries regardless of the political regime, as our hypothesis suggests.

On examining this table, it would appear that, indeed, the correlation between growth and income distribution is stronger for democracies. In effect, not only is the coefficient greater in absolute terms but it is also more significant. However, upon examining figure 6 the reason for this result becomes clear. There it can be distinctly appreciated that the negative correlation between both variables and its significance is heavily influenced by two observations that are clearly removed from the rest. These observations are those of Costa Rica and Venezuela, which during the estimation period have been democracies that present relatively unequal income distributions. The rest of the observations form a cloud of points that does not present any correlation whatsoever. In fact, if the same regression is run without including Costa Rica and Venezuela, a nonsignificant coefficient is obtained for the income distribution variable.[7]

Thus, the correlation between income distribution and growth appears much more robust in our first estimations, where all the countries for which information is available are included, not only the democracies. In point of fact, as can be seen in figure 4, when all the countries are included the result does not depend on one or two observations that are far removed from the rest.

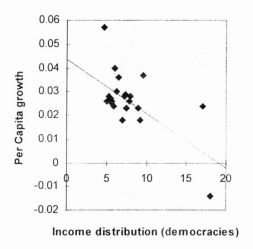

Income distribution (democracies)

Fig. 6.   Income distribution and growth in democracies

Unfortunately, the number of democracies is too low (23 in our sample) for definite conclusions to be drawn. Nevertheless, the evidence suggests that the median voter theory is not sufficient to explain the negative relation observed between income distribution and growth.

5.   Summary and Conclusions

This chapter has investigated the relation between income distribution and growth. The traditional approach in this area has been to study the causality that goes from growth to income distribution. It was only toward the end of the 1980s that the problem began to be formally studied in a different manner. In this new approach, economic growth depends upon certain structural characteristics of the economy such as income distribution.

A simple observation of the key variables reveals that there exist negative correlations between inequality and economic growth, on the one hand, and inequality and private investment on the other. This is borne out in a broad sample of 45 countries, which includes developed economies as well as developing ones. Moreover, there is a marked contrast between the Latin American experience and that of East Asia in this aspect. Over the last three decades, Latin America—which has severe distributive inequalities—presents meager results in terms of growth. At the same time, East Asia—a region with much greater distributive equality—has experienced spectacular economic growth. This evidence is most suggestive but not decisive. In order to draw conclusions, a rigorous analysis must be performed.

A formal empirical analysis bears out the preliminary impression. A regression with per capita growth as the dependent variable shows that the latter is influenced negatively by distributive inequality. Quantitatively, for every 10 points of increase in the DISTY coefficient (the income of the top quintile divided by that of the bottom quintile), per capita growth drops by 0.9 percent per annum. Thus, the distributive difference of 30 points in the DISTY index between Taiwan and Brazil—the two extreme countries of the sample—explains around 2.5 points of average annual growth.

The regression carried out with private investment as the dependent variable serves to corroborate the finding that distributive inequality affects it negatively. It also proves that income distribution has an effect on growth via channels other than its influence on private investment. This is borne out upon performing a regression between growth as an endogenous variable and private investment, income distribution, and other variables.

The results obtained apply adequately to the entire sample of countries, which includes democracies and authoritarian governments. This goes against the theory, based on the median voter theorem, that distribution affects growth only in a democracy. Furthermore, the results appear somewhat weaker when only democracies are included in the sample.

Another obstacle encountered was the lack of information on income distribution at the beginning of the sample (1960) for our group of countries. Therefore, the oldest available figure was used, which in general dated from the mid 1970s. Nevertheless, income distribution is fairly stable over time. And, on carrying out the regression using instrumental variables of 1960 for income distribution, the results are even more favorable to our hypothesis since the income distribution coefficient is even more significant.

In conclusion, a more equitable income distribution brings a "bonus" in investment and growth by moderating social conflicts and allowing greater stability in policies and key macroeconomic variables. It would be a mistake, however, to conclude from this work that a very aggressive redistributive program should be forced in order to attain greater growth. In the first place, the populist experiences warn against irresponsible expansions in fiscal and monetary policy. Second, to affect income distribution is a long-term process, even with the appropriate policies. The only way to obtain the growth bonus is with efficient redistributive policies within a process of accelerated economic development.

NOTES

We would like to express our gratitude for the valuable comments of Juan Andrés Fontaine, Andrés Solimano, an anonymous referee, and the participants in the conference The Determinants of Economic Growth, organized by the Instituto de Economía, Pontificia Universidad Católica de Chile. Any error or omission, however, is entirely our own responsibility.

1. This index is the ratio between the total income received by the richest 20 percent of the population of each country and the total income of the poorest 20 percent.

2. It may be argued, however, that a variant of this idea was of great importance in the macroeconomic policies implemented in some countries of Latin America in the late 1960s and early 1970s. According to this variant, the redistribution of income toward the poorer sectors of society would produce an increase in aggregate demand and a redirecting of this demand toward essential goods (where better use could be made of economies of scale) and would thereby step up growth. Not only did this idea fail in theory, by not considering supply-side factors, but in practice it resulted in disastrous experiences for the countries that implemented it. For an analysis of the Chilean case during the Unidad Popular (1970–73), a period of application of these policies, see Larraín and Meller 1991.

3. Instability (or volatility) is measured in both cases through the coefficient of variation.

4. In practice, what was done was to calculate the GINI coefficient using the figures for the five quintiles. For four of the 45 countries, only the figures for the extreme quintiles were available.

5. We do not have the GINI coefficient for Taiwan.

6. It could also be argued that distortions are simply not important for long-term growth and they become significant in some regressions due to errors of specification (e.g., due to the exclusion of the income distribution variable). Indeed, some authors suggest that "getting prices right" is much less important than other aspects of economic policy (Amsden 1989). Although this issue is still a matter of controversy, we think the available evidence supports the view that distortions matter for growth.

7. Although it is not significant, the coefficient continues to be negative, influenced mainly by another "far removed" observation, shown in the graph above and to the left, which pertains to Japan.

REFERENCES

Alesina, A., and D. Rodrik. 1994. "Distributive Politics and Economic Growth." *Quarterly Journal of Economics* 8 (May): 351–71.
Amsden, A. 1989. *Asia's Next Giant*. Oxford: Oxford University Press.
Banks, A. 1979. "Cross-National Time Series Data Archive." Center for Social Analysis, State University of New York at Binghampton. Mimeo.
Barro, R. 1991. "Economic Growth in a Cross Section of Countries." *Quarterly Journal of Economics* 106 (May): 407–43.
———, and H. Wolf. 1989. "Data Appendix for Economic Growth in a Cross Section of Countries." Mimeo.
Berg, A., and J. Sachs. 1988. "The Debt Crisis: Structural Explanations of Country Performance." NBER Working Paper 2,607. Mimeo.
Dornbusch, R., and S. Edwards. 1991. "The Macroeconomics of Populism." In *The Macroeconomics of Populism in Latin America,* edited by R. Dornbusch and S. Edwards. Chicago: University of Chicago Press.

Galor, O., and J. Zeira. 1993. "Income Distribution and Macroeconomics." *Review of Economic Studies* 60 (Jan.): 35–62.

Greenwood, J., and B. Jovanovich. 1990. "Financial Development, Growth, and the Distribution of Income." *Journal of Political Economy* 98 (Oct.): 1076–1107.

Kuznets, S. 1966. *Modern Economic Growth.* New Haven: Yale University Press.

Larraín, F., and P. Meller. 1991. "The Socialist Populist Chilean Experience: The Unidad Popular, 1970–73." In *The Macroeconomics of Populism in Latin America,* edited by R. Dornbusch and S. Edwards. Chicago: University of Chicago Press.

Larraín, F., and R. Vergara. 1993. "Investment and Macroeconomic Adjustment: The Case of East Asia." In *Striving for Growth after Adjustment: The Role of Capital Formation,* edited by L. Servén and A. Solimano. Washington, DC: World Bank.

Persson, T., and G. Tabellini. 1994. "Is Inequality Harmful for Growth? Theory and Evidence." *American Economic Review* 84 (June): 600–621.

Sachs, J. 1990. "Social Conflict and Populist Policies in Latin America." In *Labour Relations and Economic Performance,* edited by R. Brunetta and C. Dell'Aringa. New York: New York University Press.

Summers, R., and A. Heston. 1988. "A New Set of International Comparisons of Real Product and Price Levels: Estimates for 130 Countries." *Review of Income and Wealth* 34 (Mar.): 1–25.

World Bank. 1989, 1990. *World Development Report.* Oxford: Oxford University Press.

CHAPTER 8

Inequality, Poverty, and Development in Latin America

Oscar Altimir

1. Introduction

This chapter dwells upon two concerns of present economic debate: the relationship between inequality and growth—or, more comprehensively, development—and the effects of structural reforms on inequality. It attempts to link both by arguing that globalization and structural reforms are changing the style under which Latin American countries developed in the previous decades and therefore the structural framework in which both growth and inequality originate.

For that purpose, it reviews the trends and recent changes of income distribution in Latin America, setting them in the context of the style of development that prevailed in the region during the postwar period, of the crisis and adjustments of the 1980s, and of the "change of regime" involved in the present economic and institutional reforms. In doing so, it peruses available distributive data trying to disentangle observed changes with a view toward differentiating transient fluctuations of inequality from what may eventually become permanent shifts in the degree of inequality.

2. The Transformation of the Latin American Style of Development

2.1. The Postwar Style of Development

The style of development[1] that prevailed in Latin America after World War II was characterized by a growth dynamic based on: (1) the export of natural resources in which these countries had traditionally enjoyed absolute advantages, (2) industrialization protected from external competition and oriented to the domestic market, (3) expansion and diversification of private consumption, and (4) the sustained growth of public expenditure.

The expansion of public expenditure attended, first, to the progressive setting up of a sui generis welfare state, which protected and served emerging social strata. Second, it financed public investment considered to be strategic. Third, it involved various means of subsidizing private investment. Finally, it corresponded to the establishment of an extensive bureaucracy, required by the considerable state activism and also to absorb middle-class segments quickly emerging as a result of the dynamics of that style of growth.

That style of development implied a scheme of accumulation based on: (1) the appropriation of a significant part of the rents from the exploitation of natural resources by the state and the expanding urban sectors, (2) the appropriation of quasi rents originating in protection by the state and urban firms and workers, (3) transfers of resources to private investors by means of credit rationing and subsidies or tax exemptions, (4) reliance on foreign direct investment for developing technologically complex industries, and (5) the state as guarantor of investment in activities considered to be strategic (key natural resources, strategic supplies for industrialization, and defense and monopolistic utilities).

On the basis of this model, Latin American output grew 2.7 percent per capita per year between 1950 and 1980. At least for the major countries, average growth in this period was not very different from the rates they had experienced under the liberal order up to World War I and after the Great Depression. This rate of growth was similar to that of the United States, but it was not enough—during this "golden age" of the world economy—either to prevent the income gap relative to most of the advanced capitalist economies from widening or to keep pace with the relatively less developed but rapidly expanding economies of East Asia.

Capital accumulation was significant (over 6 percent a year) and in some countries (Brazil and Mexico) comparable to that of Japan, Korea, Germany, and Spain during the same period. The labor input also increased relatively rapidly, and the expansion of education caused the level of education of the labor force to increase faster than in the developed countries, although not as fast as in Korea and Taiwan. What made most of the difference between Latin America's growth performance and that of Western European or Asian countries was lagging productivity. The average[2] increase in joint factor productivity[3] (1.2 percent a year) was comparable to that of the laggards (the United States and the United Kingdom) among developed countries and was far behind the annual 3 to 4 percent of the other developed countries and even the Korean 2 percent.

In any case, postwar development in Latin America involved the dynamic creation of new jobs and an enormous transformation of the labor force. While this grew at a rate of 2.5 percent annually, rapid urbanization reduced the share of the agricultural labor force from 55 percent in 1950 to 32 percent in 1980. Employment in urban formal activities grew at about 4 percent a year, involving profound transformations of the occupational structure and a generalized social mobility. However, this was barely enough to absorb the increases in the urban labor force, which remained underutilized (i.e., unemployed or in informal activities) by about 30 percent (PREALC 1991).

The expansion of education was very significant. The net enrollment rate of children (6–11 years) reached 71 percent in 1970 and 82 percent in 1980. Secondary school enrollment reached 63 percent of youngsters in 1980 (vs. 15 percent in 1960), and 24 percent of the 18–23 age group (vs. 6 percent in 1960) were participating in higher education. However, the quality of education was increasingly deficient, mainly in terms of the poor quality of basic skills training, obsolete curricula in secondary education, and the questionable quality and productive irrelevance of much of higher education. On the other hand, the expansion of education took place in an increasingly inequitable style due to differential access to public education and segmentation according to quality (ECLAC/UNESCO 1992).

The change of production patterns—in terms of both activities and occupations—brought about sizable structural mobility, with a drastic reduction of agricultural strata and the rapid expansion of middle and upper urban strata. The expansion of education was consistent, in the first stages, with these structural changes, and therefore education became a basic vehicle of social mobility, enabling the enhancement of the middle class by incorporating strata emerging from the popular sectors. Among these, lack of education was one of the main factors pushing people into informal activities of low productivity. On the other hand, the rapid expansion of secondary and higher education and the emphasis on traditional curricula surpassed the requirements of production, leading to underutilization of the labor force and diminishing returns to higher education (Filgueira and Geneletti 1981).

2.2. Crisis, Adjustment, Reform, and the Transformation of the Style of Development

Eventually, in the 1980s, Latin American countries suffered a profound crisis comparable to that at the beginning of the 1930s. How long they could have continued to grow under the postwar style of development had it not been for the triple external shock that unleashed the crisis is an interesting but unanswerable counterfactual. The shocks dramatically exposed the external vulnerability and lack of structural flexibility of Latin American economies of all types, as well as their fiscal fragility.

In the 1970s, with the notable exception of Brazil, the dynamic forces behind the development model had passed their prime, as was revealed by flagging rates of productivity gains. International liquidity and the willingness of the banks to lend came as a blessed resource to fill the gap between productivity and expenditure. However, in too many instances the resources obtained through growing indebtedness were eventually diverted to private or public consumption instead of reinforcing investment, which—at 24 percent of GDP for the region as a whole—was increasingly less productive.

Inflows of capital came to represent a fourth of total payments capacity (in some countries, a third); under those circumstances, half of it was needed for the payment of interest and benefits to foreign capital. Either because they had high coefficients of indebtedness to exports or their external debt was growing faster than their exports, most countries in the region (with the remarkable exception of Colombia) faced external unsustainability of their growth (Altimir and Devlin 1994).

The generalized tendency toward overvaluation of national currencies, due to exchange rate policies devised to help maintain price stability, in many cases inconsistent with fiscal expansion, compounded the vulnerability of the economies to external shocks, aggravating them, in the event, by also stimulating capital flight.

Structural fiscal fragility, determined by the tendency—implicit in the style of development—to increase public expenditures beyond revenues, by the instability of these, and by the usual rigidity of most expenditures, was compounded by the debt crisis, which suspended the rollover of the service of external public debt, increased it by the assumption of private external debt, and significantly increased the burden of interest over total fiscal revenues.

In some countries, in which the state owned the main export commodity (oil, copper, or other minerals), necessary currency devaluation was beneficial for fiscal revenues and the "domestic transfer" problem for servicing the debt was easier to solve. In others, where that was not the case, devaluation had adverse fiscal effects and the domestic transfer to the government had to be effected by means of additional taxation (very difficult in recessionary contexts) or inflationary financing.

Thus, the "debt" crisis and its aftermath unveiled the structural fragilities of Latin American economies that had not been able to develop the capabilities and the flexibility to cope with the challenges of a rapidly changing international economy. Their external vulnerability, fiscal fragility, insufficient national savings, and slow technical progress were structurally interrelated results of the deployment of the postwar style of development beyond its ripening stage.

Latin American countries reacted to the abrupt reversal of foreign finance at the beginning of the 1980s with varied attempts at external adjustment. In most cases, such adjustments were unusually large, in accordance with the magnitude of the external shock. But, as a rule and like previous adjustments, they did not involve changing the main economic institutions. These had been previously reformed, with a market orientation, only in Argentina, Chile, and Uruguay, and in the first case they were reversed or suspended at the beginning of the crisis.

It was only later, as a second reaction to pervasive macroeconomic imbalances and attempting to set the foundations of future sustained growth, that a variety of reform packages were adopted in one country after another, in some of them very recently.

Although national reform processes are far from identical, they all pursue goals of macroeconomic stability and international competitiveness on the basis of fiscal discipline, freer trade, market mechanisms, and private investment. Opening up the economies to trade—to both the competition of imports and competion in export markets—privatizing state enterprises, and resorting to taxes for securing public revenues are the main pivots of the reform strategy, which also calls for the deregulation of markets. That involves a radical turnaround of the accumulation and growth model.

Capital accumulation turns out to be mainly the responsibility of private enterprises—whether these are domestic or foreign appears to be less relevant—in response to market signals and—at least in tradables—exposed to international prices. Even investment in utilities and other infrastructure comes under the aegis of the private sector, in some cases in association with the state, which retains regulatory power over monopolies. The scope for industrial policy is limited to the use of trade instruments recognized by the World Trade Organization (WTO) and to subsidies and tax expenditures, out of public revenues, intended to reinforce private investment and technological development.

Growth dynamics have changed in favor of exports and private investment and against public expenditure. Private consumption, however, has retained its key expansionary role, enhanced by the availability of imports and finance.

3. The Evolution of Inequality and Poverty

3.1. Inequality and Poverty in Postwar Development

Latin America has traditionally been a land of great income inequalities; most countries of the region have been among the more unequal societies of the developing world. Moreover, balancing spells of deterioration and improvement of the distribution of income, most of the bigger and medium-sized countries culminated, in 1980, the long period of postwar inward growth with a greater concentration of income almost irrespective of their average rate of growth. The only exceptions appear to be Colombia and perhaps Mexico and Venezuela (Altimir 1994a; see fig. 1 and table 1).

Multiple factors lie behind traditional Latin American inequality, many of them structurally interrelated. Among the statistically more significant are those related to agricultural underdevelopment—associated itself with great

Gini

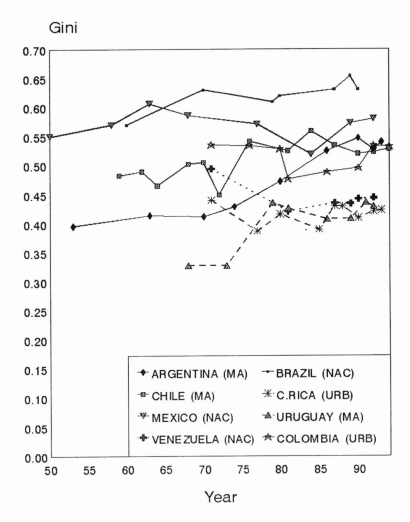

Fig. 1. Evolution of inequality in eight Latin American countries (Gini coefficients)

inequalities in land tenure or the access to land—the proportion of the labor force in agriculture, and the level of education of the labor force.[4] On the other hand, although it is difficult to measure, it is evident to any Latin American that the appropriation of quasi rents that originated in the style of development through oligopolistic or corporatist structures has added significantly to inequality, both of earnings and of income from property.

TABLE 1.   Latin American Countries: Inequality and Growth in the Long Term (% variation)

Countries	Periods	Recorded Changes of Income Concentration[a]		Annual Change	
		National	Urban	GDP[b]	GDP per Capita[b]
Argentina	1953–80	20	19	4.0	2.4
	1953–93	—	37	3.1	1.5
Brazil	1960–80	9	—	7.4	4.6
	1960–90	12	—	5.4	2.9
Chile	1960–68	—	9	4.6	2.2
	1960–80	—	15	3.4	1.4
	1960–92	—	17	3.4	1.6
Colombia	1964–78	− 13	− 5	5.5	2.9
	1964–88	− 14	—	4.8	2.4
	1964–92	—	− 9	4.6	2.3
Costa Rica	1971–77	7	7	6.1	3.3
	1971–93	4	6	3.9	1.1
Mexico	1950–84	− 6	—	5.9	2.9
	1950–92	5	—	5.2	2.3
Uruguay	1968–81	—	30	2.3	1.7
	1962–92	—	31	2.0	1.4
Venezuela	1971–81	− 10	—	3.8[c]	1.2[c]
	1971–92	− 6	—	2.3[c]	− 0.7[c]

[a]Results from comparing calculated Gini coefficients corresponding to pairs of comparable income distributions.
[b]For the 1950s and 1960s, at 1970 prices; for the 1970s and 1980s, at 1980 prices.
[c]At 1970 prices.

At the beginning of the 1970s, education by itself accounted for between 10 and 15 percent of total inequality, age by itself between 12 and 20 percent, and occupation alone between 3 and 17 percent, while the urban or rural location of earners and jobs with similar characteristics accounted only for between 2 and 7 percent of total inequality,[5] according to a decomposition exercise covering nine countries (Altimir and Piñera 1982). By themselves, personal characteristics (education, age, and sex) and employment characteristics (status, occupation, and kind of economic activity) accounted for roughly similar proportions of total inequality. However, education—in statistical association with the other variables—accounted for between 22 and 36 percent of total inequality.

But how were the *changes* of inequality related to the dynamics of the postwar style of development? A spell analysis of inequality and growth during the 1960s and 1970s (Altimir 1994a) shows that: (1) in a few instances, inequality decreased during periods of moderate growth (Mexico, 1968–77 and 1977–84) or rapid growth (Colombia, 1971–78, and Venezuela, 1971–81); (2) even in other spells of rapid growth (Brazil, 1970–80, and Mexico, 1963–68), it was only unchanged; while (3) inequality increased in most spells of moderate growth, low growth, or no growth (see table 2).

TABLE 2.   Latin America: Spell Analysis of Inequality and Growth

Change of inequality	No growth (up to 1%)	Growth 1.1%–2%	Growth 2.1%–3%	Growth >3%
Increased	Uruguay (62–68)		Argentina (53–61) Brazil (60–70) Chile (60–68) Mexico (50–58) Mexico (58–63)	
	Argentina (74–80) Chile (68–80) Peru (68/9–81)	Argentina (70–74)		Costa Rica (71–77) Uruguay (73–79)
Unchanged			Argentina (61–70) Colombia (64–71)	Mexico (63–68)
		Uruguay (68–73)		Brazil (70–80)
Decreased			Mexico (68–77) Mexico (77–84)	Colombia (71–78) Venezuela (71–81)

Source: Altimir 1994a.

[a]In terms of GDP per capita yearly growth, except for Venezuela (1971–81), for which real national income per capita was used.

Still open to question (and research) is the degree to which the human capital hypothesis can explain the recorded evolution of inequality in all those cases and in not so extended periods of time. The equalizing effects of the rapid expansion of education may be visible in the Colombian and Mexican cases of rapid growth. In the Brazilian case of rapid growth, it can be argued that the increase in the demand for higher skills offset the equalizing effect of the increasing supply of educated workers, given its small initial base (Birdsall, Ross, and Sabot 1995).

But why is it that more moderate growth, even with intense expansion of education, has almost always been accompanied by increases in inequality? A plausible hypothesis may be that at low and unstable growth rates institutional factors and labor market segmentation take precedence over human capital dynamics to keep or increase returns to education in the formal sector and keep even educated workers in informal activities underpaid.

Absolute poverty, which affected about 40 percent of Latin American households in 1970 (Altimir 1982), tended to decrease during the 1970s due to aggregate economic growth and the modernization of some segments of the agricultural sector. The incidence of poverty in rural areas showed a downward trend across the 1970s in almost all of the major countries, irrespective of the rate or stability of their growth, with the noticeable exception of Chile. Urban

TABLE 3.   Latin America: Changes in Income Distribution and Poverty in the 1970s

		Changes in Poverty Incidence		
Countries	Change in Income Concentration	National	Urban	Rural
Slow growth (≤1%)				
Argentina	I	M	I	D
Chile	I	I	I	I
Peru	I	D	I	D
Moderate growth (2–3%)				
Panama	—	M	I	D
Uruguay	I	—	I	—
Rapid growth (>3%)				
Brazil	M	D	M	D
Colombia	D	D	D	D
Costa Rica	D	D	D	D
Mexico	D	D	D	D
Venezuela	D	D	D	D

Source: Altimir 1994a.
Note: I = increased, M = maintained, D = decreased.

poverty decreased in those countries that attained high rates of per capita growth (Brazil, Colombia, Mexico, and Venezuela), but it tended to increase both in countries that experienced moderate growth and a widening of inequality (Costa Rica and Uruguay) and in countries (Argentina, Chile, and Peru) with increasing inequality and low and unstable growth during that last decade of the postwar period of inward development (Altimir 1994a; see table 3).

3.2.   The Distribution of Income through Crisis and Adjustment

Income concentration increased further during the crisis and adjustments of the 1980s. Almost all Latin American countries experienced acute redistributions of income during the decade of crisis, adjustment, and reforms, in most cases with regressive net outcomes at the end of the decade. Only Colombia and Uruguay have emerged in the 1990s with a similar or lesser income concentration than the one that existed before the onset of the crisis (see table 4).

In a previous essay (Altimir 1994b), I analyzed in detail the evolution of income concentration and poverty through the different macroeconomic phases that nine countries underwent during the 1980s and early 1990s. The results are summarized in table 5. The main highlights are as follows.[6]

1. Recessive adjustment to external shocks at the beginning of the decade in most cases had adverse effects on inequality. Colombia stands out as an exception due to the mild nature of its adjustment and increasing real wages. In

Brazil, inequality apparently remained invariant through the rapid adjustment of 1981–84, and this fact may also be associated with the rise in real wages. The small decline of inequality in Costa Rica during the 1980–83 period is less explicable, except for the possible influence of the drastic abatement of inflation.

2. Recovery after external adjustment only in some countries (Colombia, Chile, and Uruguay) brought improvement in the distribution of income. It is no wonder that inequality increased in Argentina (in 1983–86) and Venezuela (in 1986–89), where recovery was hesitant. But it is noteworthy that inequality increased in Brazil and Costa Rica amid vigorous increases in economic activity.

3. Those countries that again plunged into recession, after recovering from external adjustment, due to pervasive internal imbalances, additional external shocks, and accelerating inflation cum stabilization efforts, experienced even further increases of inequality. In Argentina and Peru, such imbalances drove the economies to hyperinflation; real incomes and wages went down and labor underutilization increased. In Mexico, external shocks, the acceleration of inflation, and stabilization efforts in 1985–87 determined a new recessionary spell, with an increase of informality and a drop of real wages, which suggests the possibility that part of the observed increase of inequality up to 1989 may have taken place during this period. The post-1986 acceleration of inflation in Brazil took place along with an almost stagnant level of activity and the eventual fall (in 1990) of real wages; this more gradual path was compatible, up to that point, with a slight decrease of concentration.

4. Two of the spells of stabilization and recovery from high inflation and recession (Argentina in 1990–93 and Mexico in 1987–89) resulted in different distributive outcomes. In the case of Argentina, a reduction in income concentration and in the high level of urban poverty was associated with getting out of hyperinflation and the improvement in employment. In the case of Mexico, on the contrary, there is some evidence that inequality may have increased.

5. In almost all of the observable instances of sustained—or even unsustainable—growth after recovery, such circumstances did not involve a further improvement in relative income distribution, although it naturally brought about decreases in urban poverty.

Among the countries that had already surpassed their precrisis levels of real income per capita, under relative macroeconomic stability—and had also presumably reached a stage of full-capacity growth—in the early 1990s, Colombia, Chile, and Uruguay also showed, at that stage, a similar or lower income concentration than before the crisis. In Colombia, labor underutilization was similar and real wages higher than the precrisis marks. The labor situation was also better in Chile, but there inequality was still somewhat higher than before the crisis (and quite a bit higher than before the structural reforms of the 1970s). In Mexico, by that time on a slow growth path, both the

TABLE 4. Income Distribution and Labor Situations before and after Adjustment and Reforms (indices, precrisis levels = 100)

Countries and Years[a]	Number of Years since Trade Reform	Real Per Capita Income	Urban Poverty	Income Concentration[b]	Labor Force Utilization[c]	Real Wages	Real Per Capita Social Expenditure
I. Growth at close to full capacity							
Chile 1968	—	91	43[e]	95[f]	—	104	—
1987	12	90	118[e]	104[f]	100	87	85
1990	15	104	103[e]	101	108	96	82
1992	17	116	87[e]	102	112	106	97[g]
1994	19	125	75[e]	103	108	114	105[g]
Colombia 1986	—	105	100	92	92	120	109
1990	—	112	97	94	99	116	117
1992	2	113	106	101	99	117	128
1994	4	123	—	101	100	124	—
Costa Rica 1990	5	89	138[d]	99	98	87	93
1992	7	95	156[d]	101	101	86	97[e]
Mexico 1989	2	83	122[h]	110[h]	86	75	59
1992	5	88	107[h]	112[h]	86	90	74[e]
Uruguay 1973	—	86	71	77	—	124	—
1989	14	90	133	96	—	93	101
1992	17	102	89	101	—	91	—

II. Underutilized productive capacity in early 1990s

Argentina	1970	—	90	71	87	78	98	—
	1990	—	72	320	116	88	79	75
	1992	2	85	200	112	87	82	89[i]
Brazil	1990	—	98	130	104	94	116	125[i]
Panama	1989	—	93	110	115	—	114	—
	1991	—	85	110	112	—	111	—
Peru	1990	—	72	190	—	—	44	40[i]
Venezuela	1990	1	75	183	105	91	44	65
	1992	3	78	178	106	95	43	—

[a]Base years: Argentina, Colombia, Costa Rica: 1980; Chile, Mexico, Panama, Uruguay, Venezuela: 1981; Brazil and Peru: 1979.

[b]Measured by the Gini coefficient. Income distribution: Brazil, Mexico, and Venezuela: national; Colombia, Costa Rica, and Panama: urban; Argentina, Chile, and Uruguay: metropolitan area.

[c]Percentage of the nonagricultural labor force employed in formal activities.

[d]Base: 1981 = 100.

[e]1991.

[f]Estimated on the basis of the average change of concentration in the employment and income and expenditure surveys for the greater Santiago area (see table 6).

[g]1993.

[h]Base: 1984 = 100.

[i]Base: 1980 = 100.

TABLE 5. Latin America (nine countries): Changes in Macroeconomic and Labor Variables and Distributive Changes in Different Macroeconomic Phases, 1980–93 (percentage over each period)

Periods and Countries	Years	Macroeconomic Variables[a]			Labor Market[b]			Distributive Changes[c]	
		RNI per Capita	RER	INF[d]	RW[e]	RMW	NALU	Concentration (Gini)	Urban Poverty
I. Recessive adjustment to external shocks									
Argentina	1980–83	−16	77	I	−8	53	10	I?	I+?
Brazil	1979–83	−11	22	I	10	−10	20	M	I
Chile	1981–83	−21	34	I	−11	−21	32	I	I
Colombia	1980–83	−6	−10	D	10	7	12	D	M?
Costa Rica	1980–83	−24	41	I/D	−22	−1	12	D	I+
Mexico	1981–84[f]	−12	40	I	−28	−32	12	I?	I?
Peru	1982–84	−13	12	I	−21	−20	45	—	I+
Uruguay	1981–86	−17	53	I	−13	−14	—	I	I+
Venezuela	1981–86	−29	48	—	—	6	24	I	I+
II. Recovery after external adjustment									
Argentina	1983–86	−2	−3	D	17	−28	10	I	I?
Brazil	1983–87	19	13	D/I	11	−26	−11	I	D
Chile	1983–87	14	74	—	−2	−26	−25	D	I?
Colombia	1983–86	12	64	I	9	6	3	D	M
Costa Rica	1983–88	12	14	I	8	16	−4	I	D?
Panama	1982–86	10	—	—	9	13	—	—	M?
Peru	1984–87	16	−2	D/I	25	−3	−15	I	D?
Uruguay	1986–89	12	10	M/I	6	−12	—	M	D
Venezuela	1986–89	−5	53	I	−43	−15	−5	I	I
III. Recession due to internal imbalances									
Argentina	1986–89	−13	43	I/H	−30	−62	14	I	I+
Brazil	1987–90	−7	−36	D/I	−5	−28	1	D	I
Mexico	1984–87	−7	42	I	−4	−17	21	I?	I

	Period			I/H				I/H	
Panama	1986–89	−25	—		—	−1	—	I?	I
Peru	1987–90	−29	−47		−64	−64	—	I?	I
IV. Disinflation and recovery									
Argentina	1990–93	25	−27	D	1	25	12	D	D
Mexico	1987–89	2	−24	D	8	−16	9	I?	I?
Panama	1989–91	−8	—		−3	−2	—	D	—
V. Growth beyond recovery									
Chile	1987–90	15	5	I	11	27	−15	D	D
	1990–92	12	−5	D	10	14	−7	M	D
	1992–94	8	—	D	8	9	8	M	D
Colombia	1986–90	6	30	I	−3	−7	−12	M	D
	1990–92	4	−10	D	1	−3	—	I	I
	1992–94	9	−16	D	6	1	−1	M	Ig
Costa Rica	1988–93	17	−5	D	12	−3	−6	M	D
Mexico	1989–92	6	−19	D	19	−18	—	I	D
Uruguay	1989–92	9	−5	D	−2	−24	—	I	D
Venezuela	1989–90	10	4	D	−6	−29	6	D	D
	1990–92	5	−11	D	−1	10	−8	M	D

Source: Changes in the macroeconomic and labor variables: ECLAC and ILO's Regional Employment Program for Latin America and the Caribbean; distributive changes: Altimir 1994b.

[a] RNIpc = real national income per capita, RER = real effective exchange rate, INF = inflation.

[b] RW = real urban or industrial wages, RMW = real minimum wage, NALU = nonagricultural labor force underemployed (per active person) equivalent to NALFIA + UU, NALFIA = nonagricultural labor force in informal activities (as defined by PREALC).

[c] I = increased, I+ = increased notably, D = decreased, M = maintained, ? = the most probable assumption for the phase (see text) on the direction of the changes observed during a longer period.

[d] I = increased, D = decreased, M = maintained inflation rate, H = entered into hyperinflation.

[e] Argentina: average wage in manufacturing; Brazil: industrial wage (average of Sao Paulo and Rio de Janeiro); Chile: average wage of nonagricultural workers; Colombia: wage of workers in manufacturing; Costa Rica: average remuneration declared to the social security; Mexico: average wage in manufacturing; Panama: average remuneration in manufacturing in Panama City; Peru: private sector workers' wage in Lima; Uruguay: average wage; Venezuela: average urban wage.

[f] This period includes a transitory recovery.

[g] 1988–92.

distributive situation and the labor indicators were worse than in the late 1970s (see table 4).

Different combinations of distributive changes during the 1980s and lagging per capita income made the incidence of urban poverty in 1990 higher than precrisis levels, with the exception of Colombia. By 1992, however, Chile and Uruguay had diminished poverty below those levels—in the first case, due to growth, and in the second also due to the improvement of income distribution. On the other hand, Colombia suffered a setback on the poverty front between 1990 and 1992.

The other countries in our sample offer a more discouraging picture, although none of them, at the time of the last observation, had yet regained a full-capacity growth path and some (like Brazil, Peru, and Venezuela) were still laboring under conditions of recession and instability. Income concentration and labor underutilization were in all cases significantly greater than before the crisis, income per capita was still lower than the precrisis marks, and consequently the incidence of urban poverty was considerably higher than it had been more than a decade before (see table 4).

4. Income Distribution in the Emerging Style of Development

4.1. Through the Looking Glass

In the last decade and a half, income distribution has been impacted by the multiple influences of: (1) external and internal shocks, (2) the effects of policy responses adopted to restabilize the economies, (3) the adoption of structural reforms that—along with the stabilization programs that formed part of their implementation—changed both the regulatory framework for economic activities and the system of incentives for microeconomic behavior, (4) economic recovery, (5) the underlying trends of structural transformation that were already at work before the crisis, and (6) the reinforcement or rectification of those trends as a consequence of reform.

These influences are intertwined behind the observed changes in the aggregate distribution of income and in the macroeconomic and labor market variables, upon which the preceding picture has been drawn. However, in order to at least partially disentangle the medley, we may consider for each country: (1) distributional change over the whole span of adjustment, recovery, and entry into sustained growth; and (2) inequality under the emerging style of development compared with the one prevalent under the previous style, before the outbreak of the crisis, in roughly similar situations of close to full utilization of productive capacity.

On the evolution of inequality in Latin America in the 1980s it has been concluded that "inequality in almost every case is strongly countercyclical" (Morley 1994) or "income inequality mirrored the economic cycle" (Psacharopoulos et al. 1995). However, as pointed out in Altimir 1994b and summarized earlier, observed changes in most cases are far from being symmetrical, fully correcting in the upturn the aggravation of inequality that came about during the downturn.

The interpretation that "the intense recessions put strong downward pressure on wages and employment levels, particularly for those at the bottom of the income pyramid and those living in the urban areas" (Psacharopoulos et al. 1995, 254) is confirmed by the data in table 5. In both recessions due to external shocks and the ensuing adjustment and recessions due to internal imbalances, increasing inequality is associated with deep falls of real wages and staggering increases in the underutilization of the urban labor force.[7]

But what about the distributive effects of recovery? In most cases, neither the previous level of the real wage nor the degree of productive (i.e., formal) employment was completely restored.[8] On the other hand, at the culmination of the recovery phase—for example, when the economies were back to full capacity—only in a few cases[9] was income concentration lower than before the recession. Even in those cases, urban poverty was similar or higher (see table 4). This points to the possible influence of factors in action beyond the mere fluctuation of real income.

First, the conditions under which stabilization and adjustment took place and the nature of the policy packages may have resulted in partially avoidable—and therefore not strictly "cyclical"—regressive outcomes. As suggested by the counterfactual simulation exercises surveyed by Bourguignon, de Melo, and Morrison (1991), "the social (i.e., for the poor) costs of adjustment could have been lower than those that were actually observed," although "in most cases, the gains would have been modest" (Morrison 1991, 1484).

On the other hand, "simulations of an alternative 'no adjustment' scenario . . . resulted in much higher social costs" (Morrison 1991, 1484). Actually, the postponement of adjustment (Peru) or its becoming unsustainable (Argentina, Brazil, Venezuela) and the ensuing acceleration of inflation aggravated the regressive outcomes (as can be seen in table 5).

The financial (as a result of investors' confidence) and political sustainability of eventually successful stabilization and adjustment programs may have determined their regressive bias. Taylor (1988) detects that in some cases (which include Chile) stabilization and liberalization were coupled with "apparently planned, regressive changes in income distribution" (109).

In fact, structural reforms may have been associated with "once and for all" regressive changes in the distribution of income, not only as a perceived requirement of the policy package for the stabilization and reform process to take hold but also as a short-term consequence of those reforms. Import liberalization—particularly when accompanied by currency appreciation—

hurt employment or wages in the import-substitution sectors. Formal or de facto deregulation of the labor market increased its flexibility, which in the restructuring phase meant layoffs or the reduction of real earnings (Garcia 1993). On the other hand, both the privatization of state enterprises and the reduction of the government's staff involved layoffs, while fiscal adjustment affected also the earnings of government employees and the real value of pensions.

Longer-term consequences of the structural reforms on income distribution have also to be distinguished from the distributive effects of stabilization and recovery, which were outlined previously. If these are counted out by looking only at situations of close to full utilization of productive (i.e., fixed capital) capacity and relative macroeconomic stability, the emerging picture is not only characterized by greater inequality than before the slump of the 1980s but also by worrisome indications that growth under the new economic order may be enhancing economic inequalities, at least for some time.

The analysis of the evolution of income distribution in the more mature case of a reformed economy in the region (Chile) by Marcel and Solimano (1994) confirms that the change of the style of development—or of the "economic regime"—after the mid-1970s market-oriented reforms[10] is very significant in explaining the permanent shift of the distribution of income in favor of the highest quintile.

Looking at that evolution through the discordant measurements available, it is nevertheless apparent that concentration increased in Chile after the structural reforms of the 1970s beyond the effects of the fluctuations in economic activity. It appears to have further increased in the 1980s (1987–88) after the second wave of reforms and the structural transformations fostered by the then long-standing reform process.

The University of Chile survey of Greater Santiago shows an increase (5 percent in the Gini coefficient) of income inequality between 1968 and 1978 or 1981 and a moderate further increase between 1981 and 1987. According to the published results of the Instituto Nacional de Estadisticas's (INE's) decennial income and expenditure surveys, the increase in income inequality in Greater Santiago has been substantially greater: between 1969 and 1978, the inequality of consumption expenditure (usually lower than that of income) increased a lot; in 1988—after the two waves of reforms—income inequality was 15 percent greater than in 1969. On the other hand, the significant deterioration of equity at the national level over the 20-year span that covers both reform phases is broadly corroborated by the results of INE's household income surveys, although these measurements are less comparable over time. Moreover, after recovery was completed around 1987, inequality remained approximately stable at the higher level it had attained under the new economic order (see table 6).

On the other hand, the long-term evolution depicted earlier is consistent

TABLE 6. Different Measurements of the Evolution of the Distribution of Household Income in Chile

Survey	Concept[a]	Coverage	1968	1969	1978	1981	1987	1988	1990	1992	1993	1994
Employment	YH	Greater Santiago	0.498	0.509	0.520	0.522	0.531					
Income (INE)	YH[b]	national	0.450		0.448			0.527				
	YHPC[c]	national							0.487	0.487	0.474	
Income and	YH[d]	Greater Santiago		0.44				0.507				
expenditure (INE)	GH[e]	Greater Santiago		0.33[f]	0.41[f]			0.45[f]				
CASEN (Mideplan)	YH[g]	national				0.534			0.530	0.526		0.533

[a]YH = household income, GH = household expenditure, YHPC = per capita household income.
[b]1968: CEPAL 1987; 1978 and 1988: Instituto Nacional de Estadísticas 1989.
[c]Instituto Nacional de Estadísticas 1995.
[d]1969: CEPAL 1987; 1988: Guardia 1995.
[e]Instituto Nacional de Estadísticas 1990.
[f]Interquintile Gini.
[g]Data processed by CEPAL.

with what Robbins (1994) found: that the relative wages of skilled (i.e., more educated) workers increased during the 1975–90 period due to within-industry upgrading of schooling and occupational shifts.

Uruguay was also an early, though gradual, reformer. In the mid-1970s, price deregulation and import liberalization was gradual; only the financial institutions were radically reformed.[11] Consistently, income distribution worsened significantly before the outbreak of the crisis of the 1980s. Since then, further reform—in particular, trade liberalization—has also proceeded gradually; on the other hand, in the new growth phase of the 1990s income concentration has been roughly similar to what it was before the crisis, although it is still much higher than the prereform levels (see table 4).

Colombia and Costa Rica were gradual reformers in the 1980s, and both processes have been accelerated in the 1990s (CEPAL 1995). Colombian income distribution emerged from the 1980s with a lower concentration than in 1980. However, between 1990 and 1992, when the reform process accelerated and was radicalized, income concentration deteriorated, slightly surpassing the 1980 level. In Costa Rica, income distribution in the early 1990s had nearly the same degree of concentration as before the crisis (see table 4).

In Argentina, Mexico, and Venezuela, inequality after the adjustments and reforms of the 1980s and early 1990s[12] was greater than before the crisis, in association with a significantly higher underutilization of the labor force and lower real wages (see table 4). However, neither of these economies was able to remain near the production frontier for long: first, Venezuela fell into recession, then the Mexican crisis and its effects on Argentina aggravated the underutilization of resources—and presumably inequality and poverty—underlining, by the way, the fact that consolidating the new style of development takes time in a process very exposed to external shocks.

Brazil and Peru had yet to recover from recession at the time (1990) of the last available observation on the distribution of income, so the income concentration and poverty levels these countries show in table 4 are still contaminated by cyclical circumstances. Moreover, at that time reforms in Brazil were gradual and partial, and in Peru they were just beginning.

4.2. Increasing Productivity Disparities

Another way of looking at trends underlying increased inequality in reformed economies is through the evolution of productivity and employment in different segments of the production systems.

During the period of expansion under relative stability in the early 1990s, restructuring economies such as Argentina, Brazil, Mexico, and Peru increased their productivity in formal manufacturing with reductions of employment, while gradual reformers Colombia and Costa Rica attained (lesser) increases in output per worker in manufacturing with net creation of employment. In this period, Chile expanded its manufacturing output more on the basis of greater

Increase of VA/Worker (%)

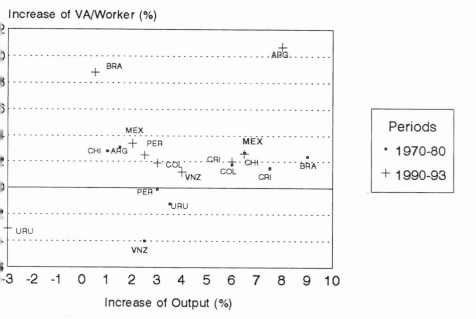

Periods
- 1970-80
+ 1990-93

Increase of Output (%)

Fig. 2. Output and productivity growth in Latin American manufacturing. (Data from ECLAC 1996a.)

employment than productivity increases, quite opposite to what had happened in the 1970s, when restructuring was associated with net job destruction, as in recently reformed economies (see fig. 2).

Moreover, during this period the rise of productivity in formal manufacturing (and, within manufacturing, in larger firms) has been greater than in all secondary activities, implying that output per worker has decreased in small manufacturing firms and the construction sector. On the other hand, the rapid modernization of large-scale mining contrasts with the increasing backwardness of lesser mining activities, and the restructuring of modern services makes them diverge from the lagging productivity of the huge pockets of small and informal services. Even allowing for the many instances of productivity catching up in traditionally backward peasant and subsistence agriculture, all this compounds a panorama of widely increasing disparities of productivity, which may be at the root of correspondingly widening income disparities (ECLAC 1996a).

5. The Long-Term View

The quest for a universal relationship between growth (or the level of development) and equity has frequently taken the form of asserting a causal relationship from growth to the distribution of income, going back to Kuznets (1955). More recently, findings of a positive correlation across countries between a better distribution and higher growth rates (Alesina and Rodrik 1992; Persson and Tabellini 1994; Birdsall, Ross, and Sabot 1995) have led to emphasizing the positive growth effects of falling inequality, as some of the contributors to this volume do. However, as soon as we view the causality as reciprocal or simultaneous,[13] more than unidimensional, the analytical problem becomes more complex, particularly if we recognize the polity in the background, which points to at least a three-way relationship.

One way to incorporate that complexity into the analysis is to recognize that, at least in principle, the relationship between growth and inequality may be different (and evolve differently) under different styles of development. If, by "style of development," we mean the dynamics of functioning of a country characterized by a distinct configuration of the forces and pattern of growth, the articulation with the international economy, the institutional framework of incentives and regulation (the "policy regime"), and the mechanisms for the appropriation of economic rents and the accumulation of capital, then the style of development implies a particular set of relationships between the mechanisms of growth and those distributing incomes.

If that is so, the relationship between growth and inequality would evolve according to the "logic" of the style of development and to the consequences of its progressive deployment and its eventual blight. Such a perspective would recast the analysis of the apparently (synchronic) different evolution of growth and inequality in the postwar period in, for example, Colombia and Mexico, on the one side, and Argentina and Chile on the other.

But it would also imply that the change of the style of development involved in the rapidly changing relationship with the international economy, institutional reforms, and the change of the policy regime would be expected to transform the bases on which growth, structural change, and inequality are related. Furthermore, even the transition from the previous to the new style of development may bring about a "quantum" jump or discontinuity of aggregate inequality. We have to wait for the accumulation of evidence under the new style of development to investigate the former hypothesis, but there is mounting evidence to illustrate the latter, as is done in section 4.

As indicated earlier, growth in the last phases of deployment of the postwar style of development had two different types of distributive outcome: when moderate or disrupted, it was accompanied by increasing inequality; when rapid, it frequently involved distributive improvement (more marked at the national than at the urban level), the notable exception in this second instance being Brazil (see table 1).

In the 1960s, moderate growth was accompanied by increasing or, at most, unchanged inequality. Rapid growth was not the norm in this phase; where it happened (Mexico, 1963–68), it was associated with unchanged inequality (see table 2).

In the 1970s, most cases of moderate to high growth involved decreases in inequality, except for Brazil, Costa Rica, and reforming Uruguay. Slow or disrupted growth involved increases in inequality; in Argentina and Chile, both circumstances were contemporary with adjustment and structural reforms, although only in the second case did they eventually stick, giving rise to a transformation of the style of development (see table 2).

As already discussed, on the one hand the crisis of the 1980s disturbed both growth and the distribution of income across the region, and, on the other hand, the transformation of the style of development brought about by reforms created a new structural framework within which the relationship between both is evolving.

Looking at the instances in which somehow recovery has turned into growth under the new economic order, as we did earlier, and comparing them with equivalent situations of full-capacity performance before the change of the economic order, there are indications that the Kuznets-type, long-term relationship between the level of per capita income and inequality—whatever it had been in each country under the previous style of development—has shifted upward (see fig. 3).

In fact, as far as we associate the transformation of the style of development with structural reform, such a shift can be identified in the cases of Argentina, Chile, and Uruguay in the 1970s and again in Argentina, Colombia (after an as yet unexplained downward shift in 1981), Mexico, and eventually Venezuela in the 1990s, as can be seen from the solid lines in figure 3, where recessionary points have been excluded. On the contrary, there is no such shift in the 1980s in gradual reformer Costa Rica, and some shift is observed in the late 1980s in unreformed Brazil.

This would imply that—in fact more than in theory—the emerging style of development is characterized by a more unequal distribution of income than was the previous one, corresponding in each country a greater degree of inequality to a similar level of real per capita income.

6. Conclusions

The previous discussion attempted to unravel from the available evidence indications of changes in inequality associated with structural reforms and the ensuing transformation of the style of development that remain after stabilization and recovery from the shocks and adjustments of the 1980s.

That such changes occurred is by no means surprising, given the fact that structural reform involved radical changes in the mechanisms of accumulation and the system of incentives. To the extent that the reform process has been quick and drastic (as it was in Chile in the past and more recently in Argentina and Mexico), the "capitalist shock," represented by the switch of the accumula-

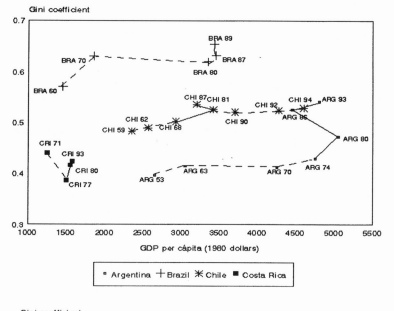

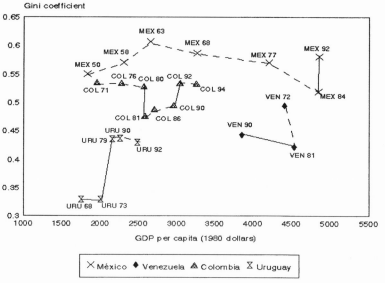

Fig. 3. Inequality changes in eight Latin American countries

tion process to private hands, had abruptly opened new investment opportunities. On the other hand, the sequels of recession, cum liberalization and privatization of state monopolies, involve abnormally low asset prices, which offer wide opportunities for speculation in real state, equity, and monopolistic rents. As a relatively small number of firms and people is in a position to take advantage of these sudden opportunities, all this gives rise to a rapid concentration of wealth[14] when sustained growth and the consolidation of the reform process create a boom in asset prices.

Reform of labor relations and changes in the functioning of the labor market also have a bearing on the hysteresis of inequality beyond wage containment for stabilization purposes and cyclical recovery. The effects of labor deregulation on job and wages vulnerability are immediate, while the corresponding incentives to the private sector may give place to job-creating investment later.

The effects of fiscal adjustment on public sector employment and wages and on pensions may turn out to be even more permanent, as long as fiscal austerity is maintained on the basis of these expenditures and the reform of the pension system restricts its redistributive component.

Whether the recorded increases in inequality will be permanent or may be either reversed or enhanced with the full deployment of the emerging style of development, it is in most cases too soon to say. However, the case of Chile, where the change of style has matured beyond the crisis and adjustment and into now long-standing sustained growth, gives some grounds for thinking that such changes may be permanent.

In the longer run, the question is open as to whether the emerging style of development will generate some sort of equitable growth or will tend to maintain or even enhance present inequalities, thus hampering the long-term sustainability of growth. For the first scenario to be realized, rapid and sustained growth is a necessary condition. Macroeconomic sustainability is essential both to avoid further social costs and to maintain the momentum of investment. Rapid growth—quite a bit higher than the moderate rates of recent performance in most countries of the region—is needed to both enhance and maintain international competitiveness and increase the likelihood of creating enough productive jobs and making a significant dent in poverty. Rapid and sustained growth will require higher levels of investment, financed mainly through increased domestic savings, for which purpose present saving functions have to be shifted upward by means of vigorous policies for financial development (ECLAC 1996b).

Sufficient conditions for rapid growth to be equitable hopefully are: (1) that domestic and external savings are channeled into reproductive investment, involving significant gains in productivity across the whole of the productive system; (2) that small and medium enterprises have sufficient access to capital and technology to fully participate in the modernization process; (3) that investment in human capital matches or even surpasses fixed investment, as a vehicle both of incorporating technological knowledge in production and of enabling people to fully participate in the growth process and benefit from productivity gains; and (4) that universal access to high-quality education and training set the basis for human capital accumulation to be equalizing.

But the improvement and enhancement of social equity is needed, in turn, for the long-term sustainability of growth on at least two counts. On the one hand, a certain degree of equity in the multiple dimensions of the social structure—along with social mobility—is required for the maintenance of social stability, which appears to be required if higher and stable levels of saving and investment are to be attained. On the other hand, the sustained incorporation and diffusion of modern technology in the productive system calls not only for the appropriate formation of human capital but also for the widest spread of capabilities and creativity among the population, which should therefore be able to satisfy basic needs and develop using the objects, codes, and values of modernity.

Behind the idealized picture of the functioning of the emerging syle of development lie, however, some difficult trade-offs, which have to be overcome in order to attain equitable growth. The main ones are rooted in the accumulation process itself. First, gearing the system of incentives toward promoting accelerated investment and massive savings naturally tends to prize the synergy of big conglomerates and the ubiquity of important savers; the ensuing tendency toward the concentration of market power and wealth has to be counterbalanced with deliberate efforts to develop institutions and instruments that will enable small and medium entrepreneurs to compete for dynamic markets and enable workers to participate significantly in the accumulation of financial assets. Second, for human capital accumulation to become equalizing, the spectrum of demand for skills has to be wide and dynamic, the unskilled able to upgrade, and those with medium and higher skills abundant enough, relative to demand, to achieve a mobile, productive, and affluent labor force.

Latin America shares with the developed countries the challenges of social integration under the new techno-productive paradigm and economic and financial globalization, but it bears its own particular burden of underdeveloped structures and sources of extraordinary inequalities. It has to find its own way in the universally difficult task of reconciling capitalist growth with social equity.

NOTES

The author is director of the *CEPAL Review.* The views expressed are his sole responsibility and do not necessarily reflect those of the organization. Thanks are due to Ricardo

Carciofi and Andrés Solimano for their comments on an earlier draft, which were very useful in improving it, and to an anonymous referee, whose pointed comments obliged me to state more clearly the methodological stance of the analysis.

1. The notion of "style of development" is used here in its positive sense, as the (stylized) configuration of actual processes of growth and change systemically inter-related in a given society—as used by Pinto (1976) and Altimir (1990)—and not in the normative sense in which it has sometimes been used (Wolfe 1976), referring to the characteristics of development "preferred" by different social groups and rep-resenting optative patterns of development (and types of society) attainable by means of appropriate strategies and policies. On the other hand, "style of development," in that sense, is preferred here to the related notion of "development model" because of its wider—societal beyond the economic—focus, its more empirical than para-digmatic characterization, and thereby its more "open" (or less deterministic) im-plications.

2. The magnitudes commented on here correspond with the simple arithmetic average of the six major countries (Argentina, Brazil, Chile, Colombia, Mexico, and Venezuela) covered in Economic Commission for Latin America and the Caribbean (ECLAC's) growth accounting exercise for 1950–94 (Hofman 1995).

3. Labor-adjusted joint factor productivity, that is, the portion of growth "unex-plained" by the accumulation of factors or by the increase of "labor quality" (in the present case, represented by the weighted average of years of education of the labor force). See Hofman 1995.

4. These factors are, at least, significantly associated with the differences of income concentration between Latin American countries. In 1970, the following Spear-man rank correlation coefficients were calculated between inequality and: per capita product (.5), share of the labor force in agriculture (.96), underemployment in agricul-ture (.97), relative productivity of agriculture with respect to manufacturing (.75), and years of education of the labor force (.7). See Altimir 1992.

5. These are the ranges of variation of the marginal contribution of each variable (i.e., controlling for other variables) to total inequality—as measured by the Theil index—in 14 surveys corresponding to nine Latin American countries. Joint contribu-tions of all variables considered in this exercise "explained" between 68 and 88 percent of total inequality of individual earnings, which were not adjusted for underreporting (Altimir and Piñera 1982).

6. The availability of income distribution measurements and their (approximate) correspondence with different macroeconomic phases, in each country, determined the periods selected in table 5.

7. The exceptions are Colombia, where the mildness of the recession and the attenuation of inflation allowed for an increase of real wages, and Brazil, where during recessionary adjustment real wages increased, during 1987–89 they fell moderately, and labor underutilization increased very little. In both cases, the labor regime and labor policies prevented downward pressures from being strongly exerted.

8. Exceptions are Brazil, Colombia, and Panama, regarding real wages, and Chile and Costa Rica regarding employment. There were no exceptions regarding both variables (see table 4).

9. These were Colombia and Uruguay.

10. That damage was represented by a "post-1974" dummy variable in their

econometric analysis of the factors affecting each quintile's income share through the 1960–92 period (Marcel and Solimano 1994, 239, 241).

11. Capital flows were liberalized, along with the domestic interest rate, and foreign currency deposits were authorized.

12. Argentina had previously (in the 1970s) undergone structural reforms and adjustment, and at the culmination of which process it exhibited a higher degree of inequality and poverty than at the beginning of that decade (see table 4). In the early 1980s, most of those reforms were reversed or suspended.

13. See (in ECLAC 1990) a discussion of the complex interrelationships between social equity, technical progress, international competitiveness, growth, institutions, and education.

14. The likelihood that a good portion of the incomes associated with this additional wealth (when actually realized) may not be captured by the household survey measurements we are using to assess inequality only underlines the fact that they probably underestimate the distributive worsening taking place during these phases of the reform process.

REFERENCES

Alesina, A., and D. Rodrik. 1992. "Distribution, Political Conflict, and Economic Growth: A Simple Theory and Some Empirical Evidence." In *Political Economy, Growth, and Business Cycles,* edited by A. Cukierman, Z. Herkowitz, and L. Leiderman. Cambridge: MIT Press.

Altimir, O. 1982. *The Extent of Poverty in Latin America.* World Bank Staff Working Paper 522. Washington, DC: World Bank.

———. 1990. "Development, Crises and Equity." *CEPAL Review* 40:7–27.

———. 1992. "Crecimiento, distribución del ingreso y pobreza en América Latina." Paper presented to a seminar organized by the Inter-American Development Bank, Washington, DC, March.

———. 1994a. "Cambios de la desigualdad y la pobreza en la América Latina." *El Trimestre Económico* 61 (241): 85–133.

———. 1994b. "Income Distribution and Poverty through Crisis and Adjustment." *CEPAL Review* 52:7–32.

———, and R. Devlin. 1994. *Moratoria de la deuda en América Latina.* Buenos Aires: Fondo de Cultura Económica.

———, and S. Piñera. 1982. "Análisis de descomposición de las desigualdades de ingreso en la América Latina." *El Trimestre Económico* 49 (196): 813–60.

Birdsall, N., D. Ross, and R. Sabot. 1995. "Inequality and Growth Reconsidered: Lessons from East Asia." *World Bank Economic Review* 9 (3): 477–508.

Bourguignon, F., J. de Melo, and C. Morrison. 1991. "Poverty and Income Distribution during Adjustment: Issues and Evidence from the OECD Project." In "Adjustment with Growth and Equity," edited by F. Bourguignon, J. de Melo, and C. Morrison. *World Development* 19 (11): 1485–1509.

CEPAL. 1987. *Antecedentes estadísticos de la distribución del ingreso: Chile, 1940– 1982.* Serie Distribución del Ingreso 3. Santiago: United Nations.

————. 1995. *Reformas económicas en América Latina: Una síntesis de la experiencia en once países.* UN publication no. LC/R.1606.

ECLAC. 1990. *Changing Production Patterns with Social Equity.* UN publication no. LC/G 1601-P. Sales no. E.90.II.G.6. Santiago: United Nations.

ECLAC. 1996a. *The Economic Experience of the Last Fifteen Years: Latin America and the Caribbean, 1980–1995.* UN publication no. LC/G.1925. Santiago: United Nations.

ECLAC. 1996b. *Strengthening Development: Interaction between Macro and Micro-economics.* UN publication no. LC/G,1898. Santiago: United Nations.

ECLAC/UNESCO. 1992. *Education and Knowledge: Basic Pillars of Changing Production Patterns with Social Equity.* Sales no. E.92.II.G.6. Santiago: United Nations.

Filgueira, C., and C. Geneletti. 1981. *Estratificación y movilidad ocupacional en América Latina.* Cuadernos de la CEPAL 39. Sales no. S.81.II.G.60. Santiago: United Nations.

Garcia, N. E. 1993. *Ajuste, reformas y mercado laboral.* Santiago: OIT.

Guardia, A. 1995. *Distribución del ingreso en Chile, 1990–1993, según la Encuesta de Hogares.* Estadística y Economía 10. Santiago: INE.

Hofman, A. 1995. "Economic Growth and Fluctuations in Latin America: The Long Run." Paper presented at the conference Development Strategy after Neoliberal Economic Restructuring in Latin America, University of Miami, March 24–25.

Instituto Nacional de Estadísticas. 1989. "Resultados Encuesta Suplementaria de Ingresos. Press release, September. Santiago.

————. 1990. "Resultados de la Encuesta de Presupuestos Familiares." Press release, May. Santiago.

————. 1995. "Ingresos 1990–1993 de Hogares y Personas, Encuesta Suplementaria de Ingresos." Santiago. Mimeo.

Kuznets, S. 1955. "Economic Growth and Income Inequality." *American Economic Review* 45 (March): 18–30.

Marcel, M., and A. Solimano. 1994. "The Distribution of Income and Economic Adjustment." In *The Chilean Economy: Policy Lessons and Challenges,* edited by B. P. Bosworth, R. Dornbusch, and R. Labán. Washington, DC: Brookings Institution.

Morley, S. 1994. "Poverty and Inequality in Latin America: Past Evidence, Future Prospects." Policy Essays 13. Overseas Development Council, Washington, DC. Mimeo.

Morrison, C. 1991. Foreword to *Adjustment with Growth and Equity,* edited by F. Bourguignon, J. de Melo, and C. Morrison. *World Development* 19 (11): 1483–84.

Persson, T., and G. Tabellini. 1994. "Is Inequality Harmful to Growth?" *American Economic Review* 84 (3): 600–621.

Pinto, A. 1976. "Notas sobre estilos de desarrollo en América Latina." *Revista de la CEPAL* no. 1 (Primer semestre de 1976): 97–128.

PREALC. 1991. *Empleo y equidad: el desafío de los moventa.* Santiago: OIT.

Psacharopoulos, G., et al. 1995. "Poverty and Income Distribution in Latin America during the 1980s." *Review of Income and Wealth* A1 (3): 245–64.

Robbins, D. 1994. *Relative Wage Structure in Chile, 1957–1992: Changes in the Structure of Demand for Schooling.* Estudios de Economía 21 (número especial).

Departamento de Economía de la Facultad de Ciencias Económicas y Administrativas de la Universidad de Chile. Santiago.

Taylor, L. 1988. *Varieties of Stabilization Experience: Towards Sensible Macroeconomics in the Third World.* Oxford: Clarendon.

Wolfe, M. 1976. *El desarrollo esquivo: Exploraciones en la política social y la realidad sociopolítica.* Mexico City: CEPAL/Fondo de Cultura Económica.

PART III

The State, History, and Reform

CHAPTER 9

The Growth of Government and the Reform of the State in Industrial Countries

Vito Tanzi and Ludger Schuknecht

1. Introduction

What should governments do and how big should they be? These questions
have been discussed vigorously and frequently for years. However, the discussion has often been confined to developments after World War II. Not much is
effectively known about the long-term trends in the overall economic involvement of government and about the composition of government expenditure.
More importantly, there is little evidence on (or even discussion of) what
countries gained, in terms of economic or social objectives, from the increasing
involvement of the state in the economy. These issues are important, however,
in determining how the state should be reformed and what can be learned from
the experiences of countries that have attempted to reform the state in recent
years.

This chapter documents a rapid expansion in the size of government
among today's industrialized countries during the past 125 years. This expansion was caused largely by expenditures normally associated with the "welfare
state." Thus, it was not technical factors that caused most of the growth of
government.[1] Over the years, prevalent attitudes vis-à-vis the role of the state
have been changing, and political institutions have been changing as well to
accommodate the demands for more state involvement in the economy. We
will argue that this trend, in conjunction with special interest politics, also
facilitated the expansion of expenditure that was less productive in terms of
social or economic objectives.

What lessons does this teach us for the reform of the state? The conclusion
of this chapter is that there is considerable scope for scaling back current
government activities *without sacrificing much in terms of social economic
objectives.* We argue that, in fact, governments may not need to be bigger than
they were 30 to 40 years ago. However, to make governments smaller than they
are today, it will be important to have strong legal and institutional controls on
public expenditure. Countries with overly large governments should introduce

bold and radical institutional reforms to make possible a reduction of less productive government activities. If this were done, the future could, indeed, witness the return of smaller public sectors without significant loss in terms of social welfare. Of course, during the transition to a smaller state, some groups would gain or lose more than others. Furthermore, such a transition would necessarily be politically difficult because of the resistance on the part of those groups that would experience losses of benefits in the short run.[2]

The chapter is organized as follows: section 2 describes the growth in the level of government expenditure for several industrial countries over the past 125 years. It also attempts to show how this correlates with changes in attitudes toward the role of the state and with changes in political institutions. Section 3 looks at the composition of government expenditure and revenue, while section 4 assesses the gains, in terms of identifiable economic and social objectives, that may have accompanied government growth. Section 5 looks at the scope for and political implications of major fiscal reform, evaluates progress in a few reform-oriented countries, and discusses trends in the future role of the state. Section 6 provides some concluding remarks.

2. The Growth of Government from a Historical Perspective

2.1. The Period up to World War II

Economists' and societies' views of the role of the state have changed considerably over the last two centuries. In the nineteenth century, classical economists and political philosophers generally advocated the minimal state in part as a reaction to the distorting role that governments had played in the eighteenth century.[3] Perhaps this reflected the view that: "Almost everything which the State did in the eighteenth century in excess of its minimum functions was, or seemed, injurious or unsuccessful" (Keynes 1926, 12). They saw the government's role limited to national defense, police, and administration because government "cannot have any other national function but the legitimate defense of individual rights" (Bastiat 1944–45). In 1776, Adam Smith had anticipated the role of the state in providing public goods or, in his words, "erecting and maintaining those public institutions and those public works, which, though they may be in the highest degree advantageous to a great society, are however, of such a nature, that the profit could never repay the expense to any individual or small number of individuals. . . . [These public works are mainly] those for facilitating the commerce of the society, and those for promoting the instructions of the people."[4]

For classical economists, the government role should be small and limited to the allocation of resources. The countries' institutional frameworks, such as the U.S. Constitution, did not specify any other economic role for the state. Consequently, in the last century, government involvement in the economy of a number of industrialized countries, for which we could determine the level of spending for 1870, was minimal (table 1).[5] Average public expenditure amounted to only 8.3 percent of GDP. In the United States, government expenditure was less than 4 percent of GDP, and in most newly industrialized European countries of the period, such as Germany and the Netherlands, expenditure did not exceed 10 percent of GDP. By the standard of classical economists, France's government share of 12.6 percent was considered to be heavy state involvement in the economy.[6]

In the latter part of the nineteenth century, however, classical economists were challenged by Marxist thinking, which strongly influenced the socialist movement in Europe. Toward the end of the century, the German economists Schmoller and Wagner added redistribution to the list of legitimate government functions, demanding some state-induced redistribution of wealth from the rich to the less fortunate. By that time, public *primary* education was already predominant (Connell 1980) and the first social security system, albeit with minimal eligibility and benefits, was introduced in Germany in the 1880s (Altenstetter 1986). "By the end of the nineteenth century, the setting was prepared for the modern concepts of social protection" (Rimlinger 1971).

Nevertheless, laissez-faire attitudes continued to predominate, and the role of the government remained limited. The average share of public expenditure in GDP increased slowly between the 1870s and World War I, growing from 8.3 percent in 1870 to 9.1 percent in 1913. The arming of Germany, France, and the United Kingdom, in anticipation of World War I, is reflected in these countries' higher public expenditure levels, while expenditure in Japan, Sweden, Spain, Norway, Switzerland, and the United States was still below 10 percent of GDP. In a few countries, the share of government expenditure in GDP even declined over this period. It should be recalled that this was a period when much of Europe became "modern" and many large public works (railroads, metros) were completed.[7]

World War I brought about a considerable increase in average levels of government expenditure. This increase was largely a result of military spending. Governments had expanded their revenue bases to finance at least part of their war efforts, and they were able to maintain higher expenditure levels after the war (Peacock and Wiseman 1961). In part, they also had to pay back their war-related debt or reparations. By 1920, or a little thereafter, public expenditure had increased to an average of 15.4 percent, with only Spain, Sweden, Switzerland, and the United States staying below 10 percent of GDP. In France, Germany, and the United Kingdom, the countries most affected by the war, expenditure exceeded 25 percent of GDP. Austria, Canada, Japan, the Netherlands, and Norway belonged to the group of "medium-sized" governments with expenditure levels between 10 and 15 percent of GDP.

TABLE 1. The Growth of Government Expenditure, 1870–1994 (as a percentage of GDP)

	Later Nineteenth Century (about 1870)[a]	Pre–World War I (about 1913)[a]	Post–World War I (about 1920)[a]	Pre–World War II (about 1937)[a]	Post–World War II (1960)	1980	1990	1994
Austria	—	—	14.7	15.2	35.7	48.1	48.6	51.5
Belgium	—	—	—	21.8	30.3	58.6	54.8	54.8
Canada	—	—	13.3	18.6	28.6	38.8	46.0	47.4
France	12.6	17.0	27.6	29.0	34.6	46.1	49.8	54.9
Germany	10.0	14.8	25.0	42.4	32.4	47.9	45.1	49.0
Italy	11.9	11.1	22.5	24.5	30.1	41.9	53.2	53.9
Japan	8.8	8.3	14.8	25.4	17.5	32.0	31.7	35.8
Netherlands	9.1	9.0	13.5	19.0	33.7	55.2	54.0	54.4
Norway	3.7	8.3	13.7	—	29.9	37.5	53.8	55.6
Spain	—	8.3	9.3	18.4	18.8	32.2	42.0	45.6
Sweden	5.7	6.3	8.1	10.4	31.0	60.1	59.1	68.8
Switzerland	—	2.7	4.6	6.1	17.2	32.8	33.5	37.6[b]
United Kingdom	9.4	12.7	26.2	30.0	32.2	43.0	39.9	42.9
United States	3.9	1.8	7.0	8.6	27.0	31.8	33.3	33.5
Average	8.3	9.1	15.4	18.3[c]	28.5	43.3	46.1	49.0
Australia	—	—	—	—	21.2	31.6	34.7	37.5
Ireland	—	—	—	—	28.0	48.9	41.2	43.8
New Zealand[d]	—	—	—	—	26.9	38.1	41.3	35.7
Average	—	—	—	—	25.4	39.5	39.1	39.0
Total average	8.3	9.1	15.4	20.7	27.9	42.6	44.8	47.2

Source: Organization for Economic Cooperation and Development 1994a and 1995a; Mitchell 1983, 1992, and 1995; Tanzi and Fanizza 1995; Fernandez 1976; *Bureau of Census Historical Statistics of the USA,* 1975; International Monetary Fund, *Government Finance Statistics.*

[a]Or nearest available year after 1870, before 1913, after 1920, and before 1937.
[b]1992.
[c]Average; computed without Germany, Japan, and Spain (all undergoing war or war preparations at this time).
[d]GFS data, data available for 1960 is 1970, central government data only.

After World War I, attitudes toward the role of the government started changing, as reflected in the title of Keynes's 1926 book, *The End of Laissez-Faire*. In that book, Keynes wrote: "The important thing for government is not to do things which individuals are doing already, and to do them a little better or a little worse; but to do those things which at present are not done at all" (46–47). Keynes implied that many things were not being done at the time.

By the late 1920s many European countries had introduced rudimentary social security systems, and the Great Depression resulted in a wave of expansionary government expenditure policies, including social programs (Ashford and Kelley 1986). The Great Depression was seen by many as a great failure of laissez-faire, one that justified governmental intervention. The United States introduced its first major public expenditure program with the New Deal. By 1937, public expenditure had increased to an average of 20.7 percent, or of 18.3 percent when excluding Germany, Japan, and Spain, which were in a state of war or war preparation.[8] Expenditure had increased in all countries and had increased by over 40 percent in Canada, Germany, Japan, the Netherlands, and Spain. With the exception of Sweden, Switzerland, and the United States, public expenditure exceeded 15 percent of GDP in all countries. By 1937, the "minimal state" committed to "laissez-faire" policies had largely disappeared. The ground was becoming fertile for the future growth of the welfare state.

2.2. The Post–World War II Period

The post–World War II period, and particularly the period between 1960 and 1980, saw an unprecedented enthusiasm for activist expenditure policies coupled with rapid growth in the involvement of government in the economy. In his influential book, Richard Musgrave (1959) described the allocative, stabilizing, and redistributive functions of modern government. The development of the theory of public goods and externalities suggested a growing allocative role for the state. Keynes's *General Theory* (1936/47) provided the tools for stabilization and another powerful reason for governmental intervention.[9] And the popularity of socialism made the redistributive role progressively more important. It was believed at the time that progressive taxation, presumably with a stable base and no serious disincentive effects, could provide the financing for expenditure policies. Furthermore, it was believed that these expenditure policies could identify and target potential beneficiaries with low administrative and efficiency costs (Tanzi 1986). It is remarkable that most studies, at the time, did not find any negative impact on the economy associated with very high marginal tax rates.

This intellectual belief in the role and power of the state was also embedded in the legal-institutional framework for countries' policy-making. Some erosion of constraints on government expenditure policies had begun in the late nineteenth century and continued until World War II (Moser 1994). However, after World War II this process accelerated. Several countries made strong legal provisions for interventionist policies in their constitutions (e.g., Germany and Switzerland) or through their legislatures (e.g., the United States) and supreme courts supported such policies when interpreting the consistency of activist legislation with the existing legal framework (Moser 1994).

In Germany, the new postwar constitution stressed the role of the state in shaping the "social market economy." In the late 1960s, macroeconomic stabilization was also embedded in the constitution as a government objective. After the first oil crisis, the German Supreme Court exempted the government budget from the constitutional deficit limit. In Switzerland, the farthest reaching revision of federal powers was introduced in 1947 and included the subsidization of industry and agriculture. In 1971, the Swiss court permitted state intervention for social policy motives. The U.S. Constitution has no strong provisions against economic and social legislation and is very difficult to change. The Supreme Court of the United States de facto helped in changing constitutional rules by permitting, first, the New Deal legislation and later postwar activist legislation such as the 1946 Employment Act (Moser 1994). The Employment Act of 1946 declared that the federal government was responsible for promoting "maximum employment, production, and purchasing power" (see Okun 1970, 37). This was indeed a major departure from laissez-faire.[10]

The growth of government was also facilitated by the dynamics of the political process in democratic societies. Expenditure growth was furthered by interest group lobbying for spending programs and by bureaucrats demanding larger budgets. Monetary financing of government deficits weakened expenditure control. Additional institutional factors led to asymmetries in the political costs of taxing and spending. In democracies, legislators typically have an incentive to enhance their political support by voting for spending projects in their districts because wealth is transferred to their voters while the costs are borne by all voters in the country. By the same token, they are reluctant to increase taxes that will affect their constituencies. In some countries, certain changes in the federalist decision-making processes have increased expansionary pressures on the budget.[11]

It is important to keep this historical and institutional perspective in mind when assessing the expansion of public expenditure since World War II. Between 1937 and 1960, public expenditure, as a share of GDP, only declined in Germany and Japan. It increased considerably in Austria, Canada, the Netherlands, Sweden, Switzerland, and the United States. The average expenditure level increased from 20.7 percent of GDP to 27.9 percent.

The rapid expansion of public expenditure between 1960 and 1980 is remarkable because it occurred when most countries were not engaged in war efforts. Public expenditure as a share of GDP increased from an average of 27.9 percent of GDP in 1960 to 42.6 percent in 1980. It about doubled in Belgium, Ireland, Japan, Spain, Sweden, and Switzerland and increased very rapidly in the other industrialized countries. By 1980, public expenditure exceeded 50 percent of GDP in Belgium and Sweden. No industrial country kept public expenditure below 30 percent of GDP, and only Australia, Japan, Spain, Switzerland, and the United States stayed close to this level.

Skepticism about the role of government emerged in the late 1960s and 1970s when shortcomings in the underlying theoretical models favoring activist government policies and problems with their implementation became apparent. The failure of expenditure policies to allocate resources efficiently, redistribute in a well-targeted manner, and stabilize the economy during the stagflation of the 1970s was coupled with newly discovered disincentive effects of high taxes and growing underground economies. With Margaret Thatcher as prime minister in the United Kingdom and Ronald Reagan as president in the United States, two forceful and articulate opponents of big government came to power. From their powerful positions, they carried out a determined political attack on large government.[12]

Few countries, however, accompanied their antigovernment rhetoric with actual shifts in their policy regimes.[13] In part because of the tyranny of past commitments, and because of the power of interest groups, on average, public expenditure levels continued to increase, albeit at a slower pace. In 1990, public expenditure reached 44.8 percent of GDP. In 1994, it reached 47.2 percent. Over the 1980–94 period, the share of public expenditure in GDP declined only in Belgium, Ireland, New Zealand, and, marginally, the Netherlands. It increased significantly in Canada, France, Italy, Norway, Spain, and Sweden.

When comparing overall developments between the late nineteenth and late twentieth centuries, it is noticed that half of government expenditure growth—from 8 percent of GDP around 1870 to 28 percent in 1960—occurred during the two World Wars. Expenditure growth to 47 percent of GDP in the 34 years after 1960 equalled expenditure growth in the century before.

The most striking change in the size of government took place in Sweden and Norway, which had two of the smallest governments of the nineteenth and the early twentieth centuries and now have two of the "biggest." The next section looks at changes in the composition of government expenditure in order to shed more light on the changing role of the state over the past 125 years.

3. The Composition of Government Expenditure from a Historical Perspective

3.1. Government Consumption

Government consumption[14] has grown considerably over the past 125 years. At the end of the nineteenth century, government consumption ranged between 2.5 and 6.7 percent of GDP for the six countries for which data are available

TABLE 2. Government Consumption, 1870–1994 (as a percentage of GDP)

	About 1870	About 1937	1960	1980	1990	1994
France	5.4	15.0	14.2	18.1	18.0	19.5
Japan[a]	—	—	8.0	9.8	9.1	9.8
Netherlands	6.7	12.3	12.6	17.9	14.5	14.4
Norway	2.6	3.2	12.9	18.8	21.0	20.8
Spain	4.9	10.7	8.3	12.5	15.5	17.0
Sweden	5.5	10.4	16.0	29.3	27.4	27.3
United States	2.5	6.5	16.6	17.6	18.1	16.4
Average	4.6	9.7	12.7	17.7	17.7	17.9
Australia	—	—	11.2	17.6	17.1	17.2
Austria	—	—	13.0	18.0	17.8	19.0
Belgium	—	—	12.4	17.8	14.5	15.3
Canada	—	—	13.4	19.2	19.8	20.2
Germany	—	—	13.4	20.2	18.4	19.3
Ireland	—	—	12.5	19.2	15.1	15.8
Italy	—	—	12.0	14.7	17.4	17.1
New Zealand	—	—	10.5	17.9	16.7	15.4
Switzerland	—	—	8.8	12.7	13.3	14.3
United Kingdom	—	—	16.4	21.6	20.6	21.6
Average	—	—	12.4	17.9	17.1	17.5
Total average	4.6	9.7	12.5	17.8	17.3	17.7

Source: Commission of the European Communities 1995; Organization for Economic Cooperation and Development 1995c; Mitchell 1983, 1992, and 1995; Delorme and Andre 1983; Foster and Stewart 1969; Okawa 1979, 172–73; International Monetary Fund, *Government Finance Statistics.*

[a]Government consumption and interest were 5.2 percent of GDP in 1885 and 19.3 percent in 1937.

(table 2). Comparing these numbers to overall expenditure (table 1), it is evident that at that time between half and two-thirds of total expenditure fell into this category. The very low level of expenditure also suggests that governments provided just a minimum in services beyond "the administration of justice" and defense. Public education and spending for infrastructures were probably the other main expenditure categories in the late nineteenth century.

Government consumption increased from an average of 4.6 percent in 1870 to 9.7 percent of GDP in 1937. In France, it almost tripled, from 5.4 to 15 percent of GDP. In the other countries, the increases were more modest. Over this period, government consumption as a share of overall public expenditure hardly changed and ranged between 50 percent for France and two-thirds for the Netherlands and the United States.

By 1960, government consumption had increased to 12.5 percent of GDP. The average increase was moderated by the decline in government consumption in France and Spain, which, in 1937, had been at war or in preparation for it. Norway, Sweden, and the United States expanded government consumption considerably during this period. Surprisingly, the highest share of government consumption in 1960 can be observed in the United States (16.6 percent) and the lowest one in Japan (8.0 percent).[15] By 1960, on average, government consumption had fallen below 50 percent of total expenditure.

The next two decades saw further increases in government consumption, with the average increasing to 17.8 percent of GDP. By 1980, only Japan, Spain, and Switzerland stayed around the 10 percent threshold; on the other hand, Sweden's, Germany's, and the United Kingdom's government consumption exceeded 20 percent of GDP.

This increase in public consumption can explain only part of the growth of total government expenditure in this period. The share of public consumption fell from almost 50 percent in 1960 to about 40 percent of total public expenditure in 1980. In addition, productivity growth in the public sector seems to have been much slower than in the private sector. For example, Levitt and Joyce (1987) have argued that, although government consumption in the United Kingdom increased from 16.5 percent of GDP in 1964 to 21.8 percent in 1984, the real increase was negligible. At 1980 prices, government consumption only increased from 20.7 to 20.8 percent.[16]

Since 1980, government consumption has remained broadly constant within the 17 to 18 percent of GDP range and has even declined in Belgium, Ireland, New Zealand, the Netherlands, and Sweden. The main reason for this decline may lie in the declining involvement of government in the production of goods and services due to privatization or subcontracting of services to the private sector.

3.2. Transfers and Subsidies

The most dramatic change in the composition of government expenditure can be observed for transfers and subsidies (table 3), indicating that policy decisions rather than technological factors have played the greatest role in the growth of public spending. In the late nineteenth century, the average level of subsidies and transfers was less than 1 percent of GDP. At that time, the United Kingdom was the leader in this category, with 2.2 percent of GDP, while France and Japan hardly reached the 1 percent mark. Transfers in Spain or Norway were negligible.

By 1937, the Great Depression coupled with emerging social security systems had resulted in an increase in average expenditure on subsidies and transfers to 3.8 percent of GDP. France, Norway, and especially the United Kingdom had experienced the largest transfers. While in the late nineteenth century transfers and subsidies amounted to only about 10 percent of public expenditure, by 1937 this share had risen to almost 20 percent.

Transfers and subsidies continued to increase until 1960, when they reached 8.3 percent of GDP or about 30 percent of total public expenditure. The United Kingdom continued to be found at the top of the list. Canada, France, and Norway exhibited the strongest increase, to around 10 percent of

TABLE 3.   Government Expenditure on Subsidies and Transfers, 1870–1992 (as a percentage of GDP)

	About 1870	About 1937	1960[a]	1970[ab]	1980[ab]	1992[ab]
Canada	0.5	1.6	9.7	12.4	13.2	14.9
France	1.1	4.2	11.4	21.0	24.6	28.9
Japan	1.1	1.4	3.9	6.1	9.8	8.5
Norway	0.2	4.4	12.1	24.4	27.0	35.3
Spain	0.1	2.5	1.0	6.7	12.9	21.0
United Kingdom	2.2	10.3	14.0	15.3	20.2	24.2
United States	—	2.1	5.7	9.8	12.2	13.4
Average	0.9	3.8	8.3	13.7	17.1	20.9
Australia	—	—	—	10.5	16.7	18.5
Austria	—	—	—	16.6	22.4	22.6
Belgium	—	—	—	20.7	30.0	29.0
Germany	—	—	—	12.7	16.8	19.2
Ireland	—	—	—	18.8	26.9	23.4
Italy	—	—	—	17.9	26.0	29.1
Netherlands	—	—	—	29.0	38.5	38.5
New Zealand	—	—	—	11.5	20.8	16.5
Sweden	—	—	—	16.2	30.4	34.4
Switzerland	—	—	—	7.5	12.8	13.3
Average	—	—	—	16.1	24.1	24.5
Total average	0.9	3.8	8.3	15.1	21.2	23.0

Source: Organization for Economic Cooperation and Development 1995a; Mitchell 1992; Delorme and Andre 1983; Foster and Stewart 1969; Peacock and Wiseman 1961; Okawa 1979; International Monetary Fund, *Government Finance Statistics.*
[a]Or closest year available.
[b]Central government.

GDP, but Japan and the United States also expanded their transfer and subsidy provisions considerably. Only Spain reduced expenditure in this category.

Between 1960 and 1980, the earlier social policies became today's welfare state. Consequently, subsidies and transfers as a share of GDP more than doubled, to more than 20 percent of GDP or about 50 percent of government expenditure.[17] In Belgium, France, Ireland, Italy, the Netherlands, Norway, and Sweden, expenditure in this category exceeded or approached one-quarter of GDP, with a share of 38.5 percent of GDP as a maximum in the Netherlands. Japan was the only country where transfers and subsidies stayed below 10 percent of GDP. Over the post-1980 period, the expansionary trend continued but at a slower pace. Expenditure on transfers and subsidies increased to almost one-quarter of GDP, still roughly half of total government expenditure. However, there were marked differences among countries, as a few, such as Ireland and New Zealand, began to curtail the role of the state, while some others, especially Spain, continued expanding their welfare expenditures.

TABLE 4.   Social Expenditure Components, OECD Countries, 1960–90 (as a percentage of GDP)

	1960	1970	1980		1990	
			Non-EC	EC	Non-EC	EC
Health	2.6	4.0	5.6	5.5	6.0	5.2
Pensions	—	—	6.6	8.0	7.5	9.0
Other	7.5	10.0	6.0	7.2	7.6	7.5
Total Social Expenditure	10.1	14.0	21.6	21.6	21.2	21.7

Source: Organization for Economic Cooperation and Development 1994b, table 1.

The development of social expenditure between 1960 and 1990 tells a similar story (table 4). Social expenditure as a share of GDP more than doubled between 1960 and 1980, from 10 percent to more than 20 percent of GDP, and was largely unchanged over the next decade. The share of expenditure for education (not indicated) and health were roughly constant at one-quarter of social expenditure each over the period. Forecasts made on the basis of the aging of the population suggest that the share of social expenditure, especially on pensions and publicly financed health care, will continue to increase over the next several decades in the absence of changes in underlying policies.

3.3.   Interest Payments

In recent years, interest payments have emerged as an important component of public expenditure. Historically, interest payments were only high during post-war periods, to service war-related debt. Interest payments in the United States, for example, exceeded one-third of government expenditure during the post–Civil War period and increased from less than 1 percent of GDP before World War II to more than 2 percent in the postwar years.[18] After the 1960s, however, the rapid rise in public expenditure and subsequent public debt accumulation in most industrialized countries was not war related. Government expenditure on interest increased rapidly, from an average of 1.4 percent of GDP in 1970 to more than 4 percent in 1992 (table 5). In Belgium and Italy, interest payments now exceed 10 percent of GDP, or about 20 percent of total government expenditure, a serious burden on the countries' government finances.[19] Only few countries have escaped this trend. For the majority, the ratio of public debt to GDP continues its upward trend.

Another disturbing development in fiscal expenditure patterns is the decline in government gross fixed capital formation in recent decades. In the European Union (EU), for example, expenditure in this category declined from an average of 4.3 percent in 1970 to 3.2 percent in 1985 (Tanzi 1986). In fact, there seems to be a negative correlation between expenditure for interest payments and expenditure for public sector capital formation (Tanzi and Lutz 1993).

TABLE 5.   Government Expenditure on Interest, 1870–1992 (as a percentage of GDP)

	About 1870	About 1937	1960[a]	1970[ab]	1980[b]	1992[ab]
France	5.2	5.4	1.7	0.5	1.5	2.5
Netherlands	2.4	4.8	3.2	1.3	3.7	4.7
Spain	3.3	3.9	0.9	0.5	0.7	3.4
United States	1.4	1.0	1.7	1.3	2.3	3.7
Average	3.1	3.8	1.9	0.9	2.1	3.6
Australia	—	—	—	1.7	1.8	1.5
Austria	—	—	—	0.8	2.5	3.9
Belgium	—	—	—	2.8	6.2	10.1
Canada	—	—	—	1.2	2.5	4.6
Germany	—	—	—	0.4	1.0	1.7
Ireland	—	—	—	3.5	6.3	7.5
Italy	—	—	—	1.8	5.4	11.4
Japan	—	—	—	0.4	2.4	3.0
New Zealand	—	—	—	2.6	3.9	5.7
Norway	—	—	—	1.0	2.7	2.6
Sweden	—	—	—	1.0	4.1	4.2
Switzerland	—	—	—	0.3	0.5	0.5
United Kingdom	—	—	—	2.7	4.7	2.7
Average	—	—	—	1.6	3.4	4.6
Total average	3.1	3.8	1.9	1.4	3.1	4.3

Source: Mitchell 1992; Delorme and Andre 1983; Peacock and Wiseman 1961; International Monetary Fund, *Government Finance Statistics,* various issues.
[a]Or closest available year.
[b]Central government only.

3.4. Revenue

The growth of public expenditure needs to be financed. Until two decades ago, this had been achieved mainly through increased revenue collection (see table 6). In 1960, total government revenue averaged 28.2 percent of GDP, almost equal to the total expenditure of 27.9 percent. Balanced budgets predominated, and the "big spenders" of that time—Austria, France, Germany, the Netherlands, Sweden, and the United Kingdom—also had the highest revenue to GDP ratios. By 1970, revenue had increased to 32.4 percent of GDP, still roughly in balance with expenditure. The oil shock of the mid-1970s caused the first major divergence between public expenditure and public revenue, as governments attempted to maintain real incomes through increased spending.

By 1994, the picture had changed considerably. Revenue had increased to more than 43 percent of GDP but expenditure had grown even faster. Countries with high expenditure levels still had the highest revenue to GDP ratios. In Belgium, the Netherlands, Norway, and Sweden, the revenue to GDP ratio exceeded 50 percent. On the other hand, Australia, Japan, Switzerland, and the

TABLE 6.   Government Revenue, 1960–94 (as a percentage of GDP)

	Total Revenue				Indirect Taxes		Direct Taxes		Social Security Contributions		Other	
	1960	1970	1990	1994	1970	1990	1970	1990	1970	1990	1970	1990
Australia	24.4	24.2	30.6	32.9	7.7	8.5	13.2	17.5	0.0	0.0	3.3	4.6
Austria	34.4	35.7	47.2	48.2	13.3	16.0	9.0	13.3	9.1	14.8	4.3	3.1
Belgium	27.5	37.0	48.8	50.3	13.1	12.2	11.2	17.1	10.4	17.2	2.3	2.2
Canada	25.7	31.3	41.9	42.2	9.9	9.4	14.0	17.7	3.0	5.2	4.4	9.6
France	34.9	39.3	49.0	49.4	15.0	15.1	7.1	8.9	14.4	21.0	2.8	4.0
Germany	35.0	38.9	43.8	46.8	13.2	12.4	10.8	11.5	12.6	16.8	2.4	3.1
Italy	28.8	28.8	42.2	45.1	10.5	10.6	5.1	14.4	11.2	14.4	2.0	2.8
Ireland	24.8	33.2	37.9	38.8	18.8	16.4	8.5	13.8	2.5	5.2	3.4	2.4
Japan	18.8	19.7	31.4	32.7	4.4	4.1	9.4	15.2	4.4	9.2	1.5	2.9
Netherlands	33.9	41.1	49.9	52.1	10.8	12.3	13.0	15.5	13.8	17.0	3.5	5.0
New Zealand[a]	—	27.4	39.7	35.9	7.5	12.5	16.7	21.6	0.0	0.0	3.2	5.6
Norway	33.1	39.3	56.3	55.3	16.8	16.4	15.1	16.1	6.3	12.1	1.1	11.7
Spain	18.1	22.8	39.5	41.2	7.9	10.7	3.4	12.0	6.4	13.0	5.4	3.8
Sweden	32.1	39.8	64.9	60.1	11.2	17.2	21.6	23.4	5.9	15.6	1.1	8.7
Switzerland	23.3	23.8	33.4	34.2[b]	6.4	5.8	9.7	12.9	5.6	10.4	2.1	4.3
United Kingdom	29.9	39.8	38.8	36.31	16.2	15.8	14.4	14.0	5.1	6.3	4.1	2.7
United States	26.3	29.2	29.4	31.2	5.6	4.8	14.0	12.7	5.6	8.7	4.0	3.2
Total average	28.2	32.4	42.6	43.1	11.1	11.8	11.5	15.2	6.8	11.0	3.0	4.7

Source: Tanzi and Fanizza 1995; Organization for Economic Cooperation and Development 1992; Commission of the European Communities 1995; International Monetary Fund, *Government Finance Statistics*, various issues.
[a]Central government data only for 1990 and 1994.
[b]1992.

United States had revenue levels of "only" around 30 percent of GDP, reflecting their lower expenditure levels. However, unlike the situation in 1960, revenue had fallen considerably behind expenditure and most countries had a fiscal deficit.

Between 1970 and 1994, revenue increases were largely the result of higher direct taxes and social security contributions while revenue as a share of GDP did not change much for indirect taxes and other revenue. In 1970, direct and indirect taxes each yielded about one-third of total revenue.[20] Social security contributions of 6.8 percent of GDP and other revenue of 3.0 percent of GDP contributed the remainder. In 1990, revenue from direct taxes had increased to 15 percent of GDP and exceeded 20 percent of GDP in New Zealand and Sweden. Social security contributions averaged about 11 percent and exceeded 15 percent in Belgium, France, Germany, the Netherlands, and Sweden. These figures suggest high marginal tax and contribution rates and high cumulative tax rates in many countries.

In summary, the growth of government in today's industrialized countries reflects largely the growth in the provision of goods and services over two world wars and, more importantly, the rapid growth of the welfare state since 1960. Recently, interest payments have also been rising because the revenue increases did not keep pace with expenditure growth, leading to the rapid accumulation of government debt. The next section looks at the question of which countries have gained in terms of social and economic objectives from the growth in government spending.

4. What Have Countries Gained from the Growth in Public Spending?

Do improvements in social and economic objectives justify the fact that governments now allocate and redistribute between one-third and two-thirds of their resources in the economy? Today, many observers might answer this question in the negative. Many now argue that the public production of goods and services is inefficient and that social objectives are not achieved, or at least not achieved in a cost-effective manner. Government production of goods and services has frequently been identified as inferior or more costly than private sector production.[21] As regards the welfare state and income transfers, social safety nets have, in many countries, been transformed into universal benefits with widespread free-riding behavior, and social insurance has frequently become an income support system, with special interests making any effective reform very difficult (Roberti 1989). The social policies of the OECD countries often appear inefficient, if not ineffective, in achieving their stated objectives, and they have been found to undermine self-reliance (Organization for Economic Cooperation and Development 1994b).[22] To shed some light on these claims, it is useful to look at historical developments in some social and economic indicators to see how these may have changed in response to the growth of public spending. We also compare the social "performance" of country groups with different levels of public spending.

4.1. Historical Developments in Social Indicators

In the period between the 1870s and World War I, social indicators reflected reliance on the market mechanism and limited government involvement in the economy. In the late nineteenth century, unemployment was mostly below 5 percent. At that time, public primary education was generally fairly widespread, and by 1900 universal primary education with five or more years of presumably compulsory schooling was well established in Western Europe, North America, Australia, and New Zealand (Connell 1980).[23] In 1870, average years of schooling exceeded five, but countries such as Austria, Italy, Ireland, Japan, the Netherlands, and the United Kingdom lagged behind (table 7). In Canada, France, Switzerland, and the United States, average school attendance exceeded seven years. However, death rates and infant mortality were very high, reflecting limited progress in medical techniques and services or little use of the medical progress made. In this period, one has to agree with Keynes that there was need for the government to play a larger role "to do things which . . . [were] not done at all."

By 1937, social indicators had improved markedly, except for unemployment as most countries were still suffering from the Great Depression. Infant mortality had declined considerably, from an average of 176 per 1,000 births in 1870 to 68 in 1937. Some countries exhibited almost modern levels of infant mortality of well below 50. The death rate had come down, from an average of 21.3 per 1,000 in 1870 to 12.5 in 1937. Some countries showed death rates below 10. In addition to the impact of governmental action, these changes reflect technical progress in the health sector as well as increases in per capita income. Average primary school attendance had increased to more than seven years, with no country showing less than five.

By 1960, health indicators had improved further. Infant mortality had fallen to 27, with much less variance among countries. The death rate had also fallen further, to about 10, and it did not deviate much among the countries listed. In addition, unemployment had virtually disappeared, suggesting relatively well-functioning labor markets and little disincentive to work. It seems that by 1960 several basic social problems had been successfully tackled. For the period up to 1960, a reasonable claim can be made that the increased public sector spending (on education, health, training, etc.) had led to measurable improvements in social indicators.

TABLE 7.   Social Indicators before World War I until 1960 (as a percentage of GDP)

	Unemployment rate (in %)			Infant mortality (per 1000 births)			Death rate (per 1000/population)			Years of primary schooling (average years)	
	About 1870[a]	About 1937	1960	About 1870	About 1937	1960	About 1870	About 1937	1960	About 1870	About 1937
Australia	3.9	8.8	2.4	111	38	20	14.2	9.4	8.6	6.2	9.2
Austria	—	—	3.5	253	92	38	29.4	13.3	12.7	3.6	7.3
Belgium	—	13.8	5.4	145	83	31	23.6	12.5	12.4	5.0	8.0
Canada	—	9.1	7.0	187	77	27	16.2	10.4	7.8	7.5	10.0
France	7.0	—	—	101	70	27	28.4	15.0	11.3	7.2	7.9
Germany	0.2	4.6	1.3[b]	298	64	34[b]	27.4	11.7	11.6[b]	—	7.4
Ireland	—	—	6.7	95	73	29	17.2	15.3	11.5	2.9	7.3
Italy	—	4.6	4.2	230	109	44	—	14.3	9.5	2.9	5.7
Japan	2.5	3.7	1.1	—	106	31	18.9	17.1	7.6	4.3	7.1
Netherlands	—	26.9	1.2	211	38	18	11.1	8.8	7.7	4.7	7.1
New Zealand	3.9	—	—	93	39	23	—	9.6	8.8	6.4	9.3
Norway	—	20.0	2.5	101	42	19	16.2	10.4	9.1	5.9	6.3
Spain	—	—	—	203	130	36	31.6	18.9	8.7	5.5	5.0
Sweden	—	10.8	1.4	132	45	17	19.8	12.0	10.0	6.3	5.7
Switzerland	—	10.0	—	222	47	21	25.8	11.3	9.7	8.0	7.0
United Kingdom	3.7	7.8	1.7	160	58	22	22.9	12.4	11.5	2.6	6.8
United States	4.0	14.3	5.5	—	50[c]	23[c]	17.0	10.8[c]	9.5[c]	7.9	8.4
Total average	3.6	11.2	3.4	176	68	27	21.3	12.5	9.9	5.7	7.4

Source: Mitchell 1983, 1992, and 1995.
[a]Or earliest before 1913.
[b]West Germany only for 1960.
[c]Data is for white population only.

4.2. Government Performance, Social Indicators, and Government Spending after 1960

Though the evidence available is limited, various government performance indicators suggest that the growth in spending after 1960 may not have brought about significantly improved economic performance or greater social progress. In a sense, this growth in spending was less socially productive than that before this period.[24] The group of countries with "big governments"—those that increased spending the most—did not "perform" better than the ones with "small governments," for example, the countries that had increased their spending the least. As mentioned before, between 1960 and 1990, public expenditure increased in all countries. But today's "big governments" grew faster than the others. By 1990, their share of public expenditure in GDP had increased from an average of 31 percent in 1960 to 55 percent in 1990 (table 8). By way of comparison, the size of "small governments" had increased from 23 to 35 percent.[25]

Looking at expenditure composition, public expenditure on subsidies and transfers (or, from a functional perspective, social security) had increased the most. By 1990, subsidies and transfers comprised 55 percent of total spending for big governments, 50 percent for medium-sized governments, and about 40 percent for small governments.[26] Interest obligations had also developed very differently between country groups: by 1990, interest payments by "big governments," at over 6 percent of GDP, were more than twice as high as those for "small governments." Other expenditure components, including investment, education, and health, did not differ much between country groups.

Improvements in economic and social indicators after 1960 have been quite limited, and countries with small governments generally have not fared worse than those with big governments (table 9). Real economic growth declined somewhat between 1960 and 1990. Average growth for the preceding five-year period, however, was higher in countries with small governments in both periods. Gross fixed capital formation and inflation did not change significantly between 1960 and 1990, and by 1990 they did not differ much between country groups. The unemployment rate, the share of the shadow economy, and the number of registered patents suggest that small governments exhibit more regulatory efficiency and inhibit less the functioning of labor markets, participation in the formal economy, and the innovativeness of the private sector. The worsening of the unemployment rate and the growing shadow economy since 1960 may also reflect interventionist policies and rising taxes during this period, particularly in countries with large state sectors.

Social indicators, such as income distribution, literacy, secondary school enrollment, life expectancy, and infant mortality, improved modestly between 1960 and 1990 in all three country groups. At the same time, emigration, an indicator of the hope for a better life in another country, declined, except in

TABLE 8. The Size of Government and Public Expenditure—Composition in Different Country Groups (as a percentage of GDP)

| | Industrialized Countries | | | | | | Newly Industrialized Countries[d] |
| | "Big" Governments[a] | | "Medium-sized" Governments[b] | | "Small" Governments[c] | | |
	1960	1990	1960	1990	1960	1990	1990
Total expenditure	31.0	55.1	29.3	44.9	23.0	34.6	18.2
Consumption	13.2	18.9	12.2	17.4	12.2	15.5	5.0
Transfers and subsidies[e]	22.3	30.6	15.2	21.5	10.2	14.0	5.7
Interest[e]	1.5	6.4	1.3	4.2	1.3	2.9	1.5
Investment[e]	3.1	2.4	3.2	2.0	2.2	2.2	3.4
Expenditure by function							
Health[f]	2.6	6.6	3.0	5.9	2.3	5.2	3.3
Education	4.5	6.4	2.9	5.6	3.4	5.0	3.4
Social security[e]	13.5	19.5	9.6	13.9	6.2	7.9	1.0
Research & development[g]	—	2.0	—	1.6	—	2.0	—

Source: Organization for Economic Cooperation and Development 1994a and 1994d; UNESCO 1993, vols. 1 and 2; United Nations Development Programme 1993, table 12; International Monetary Fund, *Government Finance Statistics*, various issues.

[a]Belgium, Italy, Netherlands, Norway, Sweden (public expenditure more than 50 percent of GDP in 1990).

[b]Austria, Canada, France, Germany, Ireland, New Zealand, Spain (public expenditure between 40–50 percent of GDP in 1990).

[c]Australia, Japan, Switzerland, United Kingdom, United States (public expenditure less than 40 percent of GDP in 1990).

[d]Chile, Hong Kong, Korea, Singapore; 1990 or nearest available year.

[e]Central government, 1972.

[f]1991 data for 1990.

[g]Annual average for 1989–91.

countries with medium-sized governments. However, in 1990, differences between country groups were small. Only certain social cohesion indicators, such as the number of prisoners and the divorce rate, were less favorable for countries with small governments, mostly an account of unfavorable data for the United States, and income distribution was somewhat more equal in countries with big governments than in countries with small ones.[27] In conclusion, the evidence available, while limited, suggests that small governments did not "produce" less desirable social indicators than big governments did. Furthermore, they have had better economic and regulatory efficiency indicators.

4.3. Newly Industrialized Economies

Public spending in today's newly industrialized economies is much lower than in the industrialized countries.[28] Average total expenditure amounts to only 18.2 percent of GDP (table 8), with the main difference from the industrialized countries being lower expenditure on subsidies and transfers. However, expenditure on health, education, and public investment in newly industrialized economies is relatively high. Public investment expenditure of 3.4 percent of GDP exceeds the average share for industrialized countries.

Again, we find that small government does not seem to produce unfavorable economic performance or less desirable social indicators (table 9): school enrollment, life expectancy, and infant mortality in these economies do not differ significantly from those of the more advanced industrialized countries. The unemployment rate is considerably lower, and the income distribution is not much more unfavorable either.

Comparing public expenditure and social indicators in some newly industrialized countries of Asia and in Chile in 1992 or 1993 with those of selected industrialized countries during a roughly comparable period of per capita GDP (1960–70) confirms the favorable picture for today's newly industrialized countries (table 10). In 1960, total public expenditure and expenditure composition in Japan were similar to those of Chile, Korea, and Singapore today. At the same time, in 1960, public expenditure on government consumption and social security was already higher in Italy than it is today in the newly industrialized economies.

The similarities in social indicators between industrialized countries of 1960 and newly industrialized countries of 1992 are striking. Unemployment, income distribution, literacy, schooling, life expectancy, and infant mortality are all quite similar, with a few exceptions such as Italy's low secondary school enrollment in 1960 and Singapore's relatively high illiteracy rate in 1992.

In summary, we conclude that social indicators improved the most between 1870 and 1960 when the welfare state was still in its infancy. The expansion of public expenditure and the welfare state during the last three decades has yielded limited gains in terms of social objectives while possibly

TABLE 9. The Size of Government and Government Performance Indicators in Different Country Groups

	Industrialized Countries						Newly Industrialized Countries[d]
	"Big" Governments[a]		"Medium-sized" Governments[b]		"Small" Governments[c]		
	1960	1990	1960	1990	1960	1990	1990
Economic and regulatory efficiency indicators							
Real GDP growth (in percent)[e]	3.2	2.6	4.0	3.3	4.6	3.3	6.2
Gross fixed capital formation (in percent of GDP)	23.4	20.5	21.1	21.3	19.6	20.7	31.2
Inflation (in percent)	1.7	5.4	1.6	4.3	2.3	6.1	15.3
Unemployment rate (in percent)	2.9	6.1	4.6	9.2	2.7	4.2	2.9
Size of shadow economy (in percent of GDP)[f]	4.9	11.1	3.8	8.2	3.5	6.2	—
Patents/10,000 population (inventiveness coefficient)	—	2.0	—	2.3	—	8.6	—
Social indicators							
Rank in UN human development[g]	—	11.0	—	13.0	—	6.0	—
Income share of lowest 40 percent	15.6	24.1	16.4	21.6	17.4	20.8	17.0
Illiterate population as percent of population 15 +	9.3	2.9	13.3	4.6	2.2	0.5[h]	9.2
Secondary school enrollment (in percent)	55.0	93.0	51.0	99.0	61.0	89.0	81.0

Life expectancy	72.0	77.0	70.0	77.0	71.0	77.0	74.0
Infant mortality/1,000 births	23.0	6.7	29.0	7.1	22.4	6.4	9.8
Prisoners/100,000 people	—	38.0	—	68.0	—	154.0[i]	—
Divorces (in percent of marriages contracted, 1987–91)	—	33.0	—	33.0	—	36.0	—
Emigration (in percent of total population)[j]	0.6	0.2	0.3	0.8	0.2	0.1	0.1

Source: Organization for Economic Growth and Development 1995b; Organization for Economic Growth and Development 1994c; World Bank 1993a and 1994b; United Nations Development Programme 1994; Mitchell 1983, 1992, and 1995; Weck-Hannemann, Pommerehne, and Frey 1984, table 7, p. 67; International Monetary Fund, *Government Finance Statistics*, various issues; International Monetary Fund, *International Finance Statistics*, various issues.

[a] Belgium, Italy, Netherlands, Norway, Sweden (public expenditure more than 50 percent of GDP in 1990).

[b] Austria, Canada, France, Germany, Ireland, New Zealand, Spain (public expenditure between 40–50 percent of GDP in 1990).

[c] Australia, Japan, Switzerland, United Kingdom, United States (public expenditure less than 40 percent of GDP in 1990).

[d] Chile, Hong Kong, Korea, Singapore.

[e] Average of preceding five years, 1956–1960 or 1986–1990.

[f] Most recent data available is 1978, used in 1990 column.

[g] 1992.

[h] US only. Others below 5 percent, UNESCO statistics.

[i] Excluding United States, average is 64.

[j] Data available for 1960 is 1970, data for 1990 may include 1993 in some countries. Newly industrialized countries data, only Korea is available (1993).

TABLE 10. The Size of Government and Economic and Social Indicators at Comparable Levels of Development, Selected Countries (as a percentage of GDP, unless otherwise indicated)

	Industrialized Countries			Newly Industrialized Economics		
	Italy 1960	Japan 1960	United States 1960	Chile 1993[a]	Korea 1992[a]	Singapore 1992[a]
Public Expenditure						
Total Expenditure	30.1	17.5	27.0	21.8	17.0	19.0
Consumption	12.0	8.0	16.6	6.2	5.7	9.9
Transfers and subsidies	—	3.9	5.7	11.1	8.4	2.7
Interest[b]	1.8	0.5	1.3	1.3	0.6	2.4
Investment[b]	2.5	3.2	1.2	3.2	2.2	4.5
Health	3.4	1.9	1.3	2.9	4.4	3.4
Education	3.6	4.1	4.0	3.7	3.6	3.4
Social Security	9.8	3.8	5.0	7.3	1.7	0.4
Economic and social indicators						
Real GDP growth (in percent)	8.0	13.1	2.2	6.6	9.5	8.8
Inflation (in percent)	1.4	3.6	1.5	12.7	6.2	2.3
Unemployment rate	4.2	1.1	5.5	4.6	2.4	2.7
Income share of the lowest 40 percent	15.6	15.3	15.9	17.0	19.7	15.0
Illiterate population as percent of population +15	9.3	2.2	2.2	6.6	3.7	13.9
Secondary school enrollment (in percent)	34.0	74.0	86.0	72.0	90.0	70.0
Life expectancy	70.0	69.0	70.0	72.0	71.0	75.0
Infant mortality/'000 births	40.0	25.0	25.0	17.0	11.0	6.0

Source: World Bank 1993a and 1994b; United Nations Development Programme 1993; UNESCO 1993; Organization for Economic Cooperation and Development 1992 and 1994d; International Monetary Fund, Government Finance Statistics, various issues; International Monetary Fund, International Financial Statistics, various issues.

[a]Or nearest available year.

[b]1972 for Italy, Japan, and United States, central government data.

damaging the countries' economic performance. Today, countries with small governments and the newly industrialized countries show similar levels of social indicators, but these are achieved with lower expenditure, lower taxes, and higher growth than in countries with big governments.

The next section looks at the potential scope for government reform, experiences in reform countries, and possible developments in the future role of the state.

5. Reforming Government

5.1. The Scope for Reform

If one accepts the conclusion that: (1) by 1960, most industrialized countries had reached adequate levels of social welfare; (2) the growth of government over the last 35 years has not contributed much to the achievement of social and economic objectives; and (3) today's newly industrialized economies show favorable social indicators in spite of low public spending, there may indeed be considerable scope for reducing the size of the state, especially for the "big government" countries.

A convenient benchmark to use in assessing the scope for reducing the current size of government is the level of public spending in 1960—and, perhaps, in today's newly industrialized economies. In Japan and Switzerland in 1960, the level of public expenditure was less than 20 percent of GDP, almost identical to the level in the newly industrialized economies today. Public expenditure in other countries did not exceed 30 percent of GDP. Over the long run, total public expenditure could be reduced to, perhaps, less than 30 percent of GDP without sacrificing much in terms of social and economic objectives.

It is important to consider how the composition of government expenditure should change to accommodate the decline in total expenditure. In Japan and Switzerland in 1960, public consumption absorbed less than 10 percent of GDP. This is about half of today's average expenditure on public consumption for industrialized countries (table 2). Hence, there should be considerable scope for cuts in public consumption in many countries.

Because most of the historical increase in expenditure originated with subsidies and transfers, many expenditure reductions would have to take place in this category. Subsidies and transfers amounted to less than 4 percent of GDP in Japan in 1960 and had increased to around 10 percent in Japan and Switzerland by 1992 (table 3). This level is similar to that prevailing in some of today's newly industrialized economies (table 10). It is only half of the average of more than 20 percent of GDP in all industrialized countries in 1992. Cutting back the welfare state in a careful and well-planned way that preserves basic social and economic objectives could yield significant budgetary savings while still providing essential social safety nets and basic social insurance.

A major rethinking of public expenditure policies is therefore necessary. Some fundamental and radical reforms will be unavoidable if the objective of much lower public expenditure is to be achieved. The experience of countries that have attempted to reduce public spending confirms this view.

There is no precise road map for reform, but scaling down the welfare state is of prime importance. In the long run, pension and health systems reform would yield considerable budgetary savings in most countries. One could argue that there is no compelling economic reason for far-reaching state involvement in these areas beyond basic social assistance, for example, in the form of a basic allowance for the poor or the unemployed and of insurance against catastrophic events such as major illnesses or accidents for everyone. With proper reforms, most pension, health, and social insurance needs could be satisfied by the private sector, thus reducing the need for public spending. However, this drastic change would require a major departure from the present way of doing things.[29] It would also require an expanded regulatory role for the public sector.

There is little controversy over the need for free public *primary* education. There is some controversy as to the role of the public sector for *secondary* education. At the level of tertiary or university education, however, fully or partly privately financed universities could replace costly public university systems.[30] In the United States, for example, university education is largely private. Some countries have also experimented with privatizing the government production or even the provision of many goods and services. The private building and operation of roads, prisons, airports, railroads, and municipal services could be extended considerably in many countries.[31] Once again, this would require a relatively well working private market and an efficient regulatory role for the government.

The question of where to draw the line between government and private sector activities, however, cannot be answered universally. Where to draw the line changes with time and across countries. The better working is the market economy, the less extended can be the role of the public sector. Of course, the more efficient is public administration and the less important are rent-seeking activities, the greater could be the role assigned to the public sector. Technical considerations such as cost-benefit analysis should complement the political process in deciding on who should perform which function in an economy. Thus, it is important to create institutions (such as the Congressional Budget Office in the United States) that are capable of doing such analyses.

Reducing public expenditure will free up resources for private use and reduce the demands on the tax system. The overly strong reliance on direct taxes and social security contributions in many industrial countries could be reduced. Marginal tax and contribution rates could, thus, become more modest.

This would reduce the disincentive effects of taxation and stimulate growth. The tax base could be broadened as the incentive to leave the formal economy or seek tax exemptions declines. Budget surpluses could be generated to retire part of the accumulated public debt and thereby reduce the interest burden on the budget. In summary, *public expenditure as a share of GDP could be lowered considerably without necessarily compromising social welfare.*

5.2. The Implementation of Reforms

Arguing for a reduced role of the state in the economy raises important questions: how can reforms be implemented politically and what time frame should be expected? Again, there is no precise road map. Reforms aimed at changing the basic economic policy regime of countries cannot ignore the fact that in the short run some groups will inevitably be hurt by the reforms. The political opposition that this will generate guarantees that their full implementation may take decades rather than a few years.

Reforming government and reducing public expenditure can generate considerable long-term benefits if they result in higher economic growth. However, reforms will stimulate growth mainly when they alter the expectations of the private sector about the future investment climate for both real and human capital. Such a change in expectations may require not just the application of operational policy instruments but a shift in the policy regime or the rules of the game that constrain policymakers (Brennan and Buchanan 1985; Solimano 1994).[32] If existing rules have resulted in expansionary expenditure policies, a reversal in such policies will not happen automatically (Forte and Peacock 1985). The rules have to change so that policymakers' incentives for fiscal policy-making will also change.

This rather abstract argumentation has been translated by some economists into various practical policy recommendations and policy platforms aimed at controlling the forces that result in public expenditure growth. A prominent approach for controlling expenditure is through constitutional rules. For example, in the United States the idea of a balanced budget amendment has been proposed by some and rejected by others for some years. In some countries, constitutional rules now guarantee the independence of their central banks, rendering the monetization of fiscal deficits more difficult. It has been argued that direct democracy as a constitutional principle has slowed the expansion of public expenditure in Switzerland (Pommerehne and Schneider 1982).

Constitutional rules have the advantage that they tie a government's hands more firmly than does simple legislation because they are more difficult to reverse. However, they are no panacea for fiscal problems because they require strong implementation and enforcement mechanisms.[33] In some countries where they exist, they are disregarded or circumvented. Consensus building and strengthening of interest groups and agencies with an interest in the new rules may increase their chances of implementation and may assure their longevity.

The expected long-term benefits that may derive from less state involvement are not enough to guarantee the required political support for the change. Reforms will inevitably be painful, especially in the short run, for groups that gain from public spending. These groups will oppose the reforms and will make the introduction and implementation of the reforms more difficult. The detrimental short-run effects of the reforms on some groups need to be addressed by policymakers. As a basic principle, compensation for large losses and insurance against catastrophic events should be considered as a means of gaining political support for the reforms. If reforms contain sunset clauses or are implemented with a time lag, this can facilitate adjustment to the new economic environment (Buchanan 1994).[34]

5.3. Experiences with Government Reform

Recent experiences with government reform in a number of countries have one common feature: countries that successfully reversed expansionary trends in public expenditure and revitalized their economies did so through fundamental changes in the underlying policy regime. The country experiences also confirm what we argued before: major government reforms take a long time to implement. We will briefly look at four countries that have attempted to reform the state in the past 15 years, for example, Chile, New Zealand, Ireland, and Belgium, and will discuss major changes in expenditure policies and the underlying policy regime.

Chile. The most impressive reduction in public expenditure has been achieved in Chile. Total expenditure declined from a maximum of 34.1 percent of GDP in 1982 to 21.8 percent in 1993 (table 11).[35] Transfers and subsidies were halved, to 11 percent of GDP, while government consumption also declined considerably, from 10.8 to 6.2 percent of GDP. By 1993, total investment had increased from 14.6 to 25.6 percent of GDP, growth was high, and unemployment low. A pioneering reform of the pension system sharply reduced the role of the government in this area.[36] Chile undertook also "dramatic reforms of its health sector by decentralizing the government-run health system and by creating private health insurance institutions" (see World Bank 1993b, 162).

The impressive results have been achieved with a mixture of constitutional and quasi-constitutional reforms that fundamentally altered the character of the Chilean government and economy. The new 1980 constitution guarantees property rights and limits the role of government as a discretionary regulator. Social security and most public enterprises were privatized, and the central bank became independent. Budgetary procedures were reformed, and many

TABLE 11. Public Expenditure Development and Government Reform (as a percentage of GDP)

	Belgium		Chile		Ireland		New Zealand		United Kingdom		
	1983	1994	1982	1993	1983	1994	1988	1994	1983	1989	1994
Total expenditure	63.9	54.8	34.1	21.8	53.2	43.8	45.6	35.7	44.7	37.5	42.9
Government consumption	17.5	15.3	10.8	6.2	19.3	15.8	11.5	15.4	21.7	19.4	21.6
Interest[ab]	8.2	10.1	0.5	1.3	9.1	7.5	7.2	5.7	3.9	3.3	2.7
Transfers and subsidies[abc]	33.0	29.0	20.6	11.1	30.9	23.4	24.8	13.2	21.9	17.3	24.2
Capital expenditure[ab]	4.4	2.5	2.2	3.2	3.8	2.6	2.1	1.3	2.0	2.1	3.7
Health[b]	6.2	7.0	2.3[a]	2.5[a]	6.8	5.0	3.0	5.6	5.4	4.9	5.5
Education[b]	7.5	6.2	5.0	2.9	6.2	5.1	5.7	5.7	5.6	4.7	—
Social security[ab]	23.5	21.3	14.3	7.3	13.1	11.4	14.8	14.0	11.6	10.2	12.8

Source: Poullier 1993, vol. 2, tab. 4; UNESCO 1993; Organization for Economic Cooperation and Development 1994a and 1995a; International Monetary Fund, *Government Finance Statistics,* various issues.

Note: The table compares the year of maximum public expenditure with the most recent available data.

[a]Central government data.

[b]Or nearest available year.

[c]Includes transfers to other levels of government. Therefore, some double counting may occur in the government consumption and transfers and subsidies categories.

government procedures were subjected to stricter rules and accountability. All this reduced the scope of lobbying for preferential tax treatment, social benefits, or favorable regulation by special interests. It replaced a "clientelistic state" with "a more autonomous state" where "the costs of government transfers and interventions are (at least partially) internalized, and therefore sound fiscal policy becomes achievable" (Velasco 1994).[37]

New Zealand. New Zealand is another country that has reduced the role of state through far-reaching changes in its economic policy rules. In 1988, public expenditure amounted to 45.6 percent of GDP, but by 1994 it had declined to 35.7 percent. This reduction was achieved almost exclusively in the area of transfers and subsidies, which were reduced from 24.8 percent in 1988 to 13.2 percent in 1994. Interest expenditure also came down, from 7.2 percent in 1988 to 5.7 percent in 1994. As the transmission of reforms in the economy takes some time, these consolidation efforts have only recently resulted in a revitalization of the economy and an increase in the growth rate.

In New Zealand, the reform process started in 1984. Most state enterprises were privatized, and subsidies and price supports for agriculture were abolished. The tax system was simplified, marginal rates were sharply reduced, and the tax bases were broadened (New Zealand, Department of Finance 1986). The central bank was made independent, with an inflation ceiling its only objective. In 1990–91, social policy reform replaced universal entitlements with a modest safety net with means testing. Significant structural changes in public administration gave rise to output-oriented administrative performance evaluation, and changes in the budgetary process facilitated the implementation of fiscal policy objectives (Scott 1995). Although New Zealand does not have a formal constitutional tradition, these changes altered the economic policy regime in a fundamental way. As with Chile, rent-seeking opportunities were reduced through privatization, transfer and subsidy reductions, tax reform, and the reorientation of administrative incentive structures. In addition, the government invested in social consensus building and strengthened vested interests in the new policy regime (e.g., it introduced a privatization ministry) (New Zealand, Treasury Department 1990).

Reform in New Zealand was achieved mainly through a strong executive controlling Parliament, which is typical for a Westminster-style governance structure. Fortunately for New Zealand, so far both main political parties have supported the reform effort.[38] However, the United Kingdom itself illustrates a possible weakness of the Westminster system: reforms are relatively easy to reverse. Although public expenditure in Britain had declined from almost 45 percent in 1983 to 37.5 percent in 1989, by 1994 this reduction had been largely reversed (table 11). Transfers and subsidies were higher in 1994 than at the beginning of the Thatcher reforms in 1983. But as of now there is no evidence that the reforms in New Zealand are in danger of being reversed.

Ireland. Ireland also achieved an impressive reduction in public expenditure between 1983 and 1994. Total expenditure declined from 53.2 to 43.8 percent of GDP. Reducing subsidy and transfer payments has been the driving force, and such expenditure declined from more than 30 percent of GDP to 23.4 percent. Fiscal consolidation has also translated into declining outlays for interest on public debt of more than 3 percent of GDP.

In Ireland, a public debt level of 130 percent of GDP is considered one of the main reasons why public consensus on fiscal consolidation emerged in the mid-1980s.[39] In addition, Ireland is economically and politically oriented toward the European Union. The Common Market project, and more recently the Maastricht Treaty and its convergence criteria, have provided a strong outside incentive for Ireland to get its fiscal house in order.

Belgium. Although Belgium achieved a considerable adjustment in public expenditure between 1983 and 1992, the changes were less fundamental than in the other countries examined here, and the picture is not quite as positive. Total public expenditure declined from 63.9 to 54.8 percent. However, since 1990 there has been no further progress in reducing public expenditure. In Belgium, the outside constraints of the Common Market and Maastricht as well as a heavy public debt burden also appear to have driven the adjustment of public expenditure. However, the reform package has consisted of a number of marginal policy adjustments rather than bold changes in the country's policy regime. Recent changes in the federalist structure could make expenditure control even more difficult.

5.4. Trends in the Role of the State

Economic thinking has come a long way from classical political economy and the minimal state, via Marxist or Keynesian interventionism, to today's emphasis on rules and accountability in making state activity more productive. However, at the political level this emphasis has so far changed policy regimes in only a few countries. An important reason is that interest groups oppose the curtailment of their rent-seeking opportunities or the reduction in their benefits.

There are, however, a number of reasons why reform of the state might progress in an increasing number of countries. These reasons include the lagged impact of economic thinking on policy-making, easier access to information about successful reforms, and stronger international competition between countries. Changes in economic thinking and better understanding of what governments should do take time to affect decision makers. The impact of ideas is certainly very powerful, as Keynes pointed out, but that impact is felt only after a period that can be very long. For example, Keynesian writings of the 1930s did not have a strong influence on policy-making until the 1960s. Similarly, modern thinking about the role of the state is likely to have its full influence on policy-making only at some future time. For the time being, it has affected only a few countries, but there is evidence that it is beginning to influence many, including the EU countries and the United States (even though the latter already ranks as a "small government" country in our definition).

More easily available information about international "success stories" cannot fail to affect other countries and influence the actions of their policy-makers.[40] The success of the newly industrialized Asian economies and some Latin American countries has been well documented, and interest in their policy strategies is widespread. These are countries with small governments.

As the international economy becomes more competitive and capital and labor become more mobile, countries with big, and especially inefficient, governments risk falling behind in terms of growth and welfare. When voters and industries recognize the long-term benefits of reform in such an environment, they and their representatives may push their governments toward reform. Under these circumstances, policymakers will find it easier to overcome the resistance of special interest groups. The constraint of international competition may be particularly important for countries in which international agreements such as the Maastricht Treaty eliminate undesirable alternatives to adjustment such as protectionism and competitive devaluation.[41] The successful reforms of Ireland, New Zealand, and Chile may spread to more countries.

6. Concluding Remarks

This broad and wide-ranging chapter has shown how public expenditure as a share of GDP grew, over more than a century in all the industrialized countries, to reach its recent high levels. Over the past century, the ratio of public expenditure to GDP grew as much as five times. It is difficult for us today to visualize a world with countries in which governments spent only 10 percent of GDP. However, the ones that did so a century ago were not backward countries but vibrant and modernizing economies. For example, much of the Paris that we admire today was built at a time when France was spending only about 12 to 13 percent of its GDP on public sector activities. However, these countries did not yet have public health care, public pensions for almost everyone, free education at all levels, unemployment compensation, subsidies to families and households, and so on.

Modern societies have accepted the view that governments must play a larger role in the economy and must pursue modern objectives such as income redistribution and maintenance. The clock cannot be turned back, and in fact it should not be. For the majority of citizens, the current world is certainly more welcoming than the one that existed a century ago. However, we have argued that most of the important social and economic gains can be achieved with a drastically lower level of public spending than what prevails today. Perhaps the level of public spending does not need to be much higher than, say, 30 percent of GDP to achieve most of the important social and economic objectives that justify governmental intervention. However, this would require radical reforms, a well-functioning, private market, and an efficient regulatory role for the government.

The radical reforms must *aim at maintaining public sector objectives while reducing the level of public spending.* They will require much privatization of higher education and health care. They will require the privatization of some pensions and many other changes. In this process, the role of the government will change from provider to overseer or regulator of activities. Its role will be mainly to set the "rules of the game" in the economy.

This chapter has shown that some movement in the direction indicated earlier is noticeable. In many countries, there is general disillusionment with high levels of taxation and public spending. However, there is still strong opposition from the specific groups that benefit from the spending to having their benefits reduced. The argument that the reforms would make most citizens better off in the long run will not allay concerns in the short run. Besides, in the shrinking of the spending cake some will lose more than others. Furthermore, some still question whether governments will be able to play their new, and perhaps more demanding, roles with the necessary degree of efficiency to guarantee that fundamental objectives will be achieved with drastically reduced spending.[42] Still, from the discussion in this chapter, we predict that over the next few decades we shall see some important reductions in the share of public spending in GDP in industrialized countries.

NOTES

1. These technical factors are often behind the so-called Wagner's Law and Baumol's disease, which attempt to explain why government expenditure tends to grow over time in response to economic development.

2. The promise that most would gain over the long run is not likely to make those who lose in the short run refrain from attempting to prevent the changes.

3. See on this a little-known book by Keynes (1926).

4. Smith 1937, 681. By the beginning of the nineteenth century, private charity was already considered inadequate, and public relief and punishment programs for the poor were introduced, mainly to maintain law and order (Rimlinger 1971).

5. In a recent essay, one of the authors has warned that the role of government is not limited to spending but that it can be pursued through quasi-fiscal activities and regulations (see Tanzi 1995). In this chapter, we focus on spending and taxing and thus largely ignore that warning.

6. See Leroy-Beaulieu (1888) for such an attitude and for an anticipation of the Laffer curve.

7. Perhaps a note of warning on the data is necessary. Obviously, there are problems of comparability of data, but these problems are not likely to change the basic trends reported here.

8. Part of this increase in the ratio of spending to GDP was the result of the fall in GDP rather than the increase in real spending.

9. In 1966, Walter Heller wrote about "Lord Keynes' spectacular rescue of economics from the wilderness of classical equilibrium" (4).

10. However, during the so-called Lochner era, from 1905 to the late 1930s, the U.S. Supreme Court interpreted the due process clause of the U.S. Constitution (Fourteenth Amendment) as protecting freedom of contract and thus imposed quite strict limits on the state's power to regulate market activity.

11. For a number of theoretical and empirical articles on this subject, see Forte and Peacock 1985; Mueller 1986; and Buchanan, Rowley, and Tollison 1987. For a survey of the literature on budget deficits, see also Alesina and Perotti 1995.

12. Reagan popularized the view that, far from being a solution to problems, the government could be a cause of them.

13. Section 4 looks in more detail at experiences with government reform.

14. Government consumption is defined as the sum of wages, salaries, materials, and supplies. This is the part of government spending that absorbs or uses *directly* economic resources. It is an economic definition that does not identify the function of the expenditure. It may thus include social spending provided in kind (e.g., public housing) rather than cash.

15. In the United States, this increase was largely due to defense spending, which in 1960 was much higher than in 1937. In fact, the difference between these two countries in 1960 is explained almost entirely by the difference in defense spending.

16. This divergence in productivity growth between the public and the private sector is sometimes referred to as Baumol's disease (see Baumol 1967).

17. Before World War II, social security was largely fragmented and decentralized, while postwar expansion of the welfare state coincided with the widespread nationalization of social security.

18. After World War II, in the United States, the share of public debt to GDP was about twice what it is today. However, the level of real interest rates was very low or even negative, thus reducing the burden of the debt.

19. Large interest payments can potentially lead to an explosive situation when they result in larger deficits and in growing debt-to-GDP ratios.

20. Earlier data were not readily available.

21. This is mainly due to noneconomic objectives being added to economic objectives of government production. For a survey of this issue, see Borcherding, Pommerehne, and Schneider 1982 and World Bank 1995. The recent enthusiasm over privatization indicates that many policymakers share this view.

22. There are also growing concerns that countries are approaching the limit of revenue collection as political resistance increases and disincentives depress activity and drive people into the underground economy (Peacock 1986; Tanzi 1986).

23. By 1900, the extension of public secondary education was under consideration in many of these countries (Connell 1980). In practice, however, persons who completed primary education were still a minority in several of these countries.

24. At that time, there was much optimism that governments could solve many social and economic problems through higher spending. With the benefit of hindsight, many now agree that that optimism was unjustified.

25. For the classification of countries into these groups, see notes to table 8.

26. Of course, as shares of GDP, the differences were much greater.

27. Whether a two to three percentage point difference in the income share of the lowest 40 percent of households is worth allocating 20 percent of GDP to public expenditure and taxes is debatable.

28. Our sample of newly industrialized economies includes Chile, Hong Kong, Korea, and Singapore. We refer to these as economies rather than countries because of the inclusion of Hong Kong.

29. For proposals for fundamental reforms in this area, see World Bank 1994a. For an analysis of such a possibility for the United States, see Kotlikoff 1995.

30. Scholarships or access to credit could help students from poor families to acquire university educations.

31. There is by now a considerable body of literature discussing the private provision of infrastructure, especially utilities and transportation (World Bank 1994a), roads (Gomes-Ibañes and Meyer 1993), health (Young 1990), and education (see Walford 1989 or James 1984 on the experiences of the Netherlands). See also Van der Gaag 1995 on private and public sector activities in developing countries.

32. On the operational level, expenditure control can be strengthened with the help of improved accounting procedures. The introduction of market-simulating incentive schemes in the "production process" of the public sector can also improve expenditure control and efficiency (Peacock 1986).

33. The importance of credibility for policy commitments is discussed in Borner, Brunetti, and Weder 1995.

34. This strategy benefited the implementation of the Common Market in the EU. The adjustments of all parties involved, including opponents to free trade, were facilitated considerably by the fact that announcing and advertising the reforms planned for the end of 1992 began as early as 1986, after an agreement on the Single European Act had been reached (Schuknecht 1992).

35. The table compares expenditure policies during the year in which total expenditure was at a historic maximum with the most recent year available.

36. The Chilean pension reform is having, and is likely to continue having, a profound effect on the pension systems of other countries.

37. Although this new policy regime was achieved under an autocratic regime, so far it has remained unaltered under the new democratic regime.

38. The same thing has occurred in Chile, proving that over the medium term fundamental reform may not be political suicide.

39. For "An Irish Overview" of the situation in the mid-1980s, see the intervention by Alan Dukes, then minister of finance of Ireland, in Bristow and McDonagh 1986, 127–38.

40. A virtuous contagion effect may be at work in this area. The IMF and the World Bank are likely to help promote this effect.

41. The conclusion of the Uruguay Round and the strengthening of GATT

through the forming of the World Trade Organization (WTO) also have increased international competition and, indirectly, pressure for fiscal reform.

42. If the reduction in public spending is accompanied by a proliferation of inefficient regulations, then the advantages of the change will be limited. On this possibility, see Tanzi 1995.

REFERENCES

Alesina, Alberto, and Roberto Perotti. 1995. "The Political Economy of Budget Deficits." *Staff Papers* (International Monetary Fund) 42 (March): 1–31.

Altenstetter, Christa. 1986. "German Social Security Programs: An Interpretation of Their Development, 1883–1985." In *Nationalizing Social Security in Europe and America,* edited by Douglas E. Ashford and E. W. Kelley. Greenwich, CT: JAI.

Ashford, Douglas E., and E. W. Kelley. 1986. *Nationalizing Social Security in Europe and America.* Greenwich, CT: JAI.

Bastiat, Frederic. 1944–45. *Harmonies of Political Economy.* 2 vols. Santa Ana, CA: Register.

Baumol, William J. 1967. "Macroeconomics of Unbalanced Growth: The Anatomy of Urban Crisis." *American Economic Review* 57 (June): 415–26.

Borcherding, Thomas E., Werner W. Pommerehne, and Friedrich Schneider. 1982. "Comparing the Efficiency of Private and Public Production: The Evidence from Five Countries." *Zeitschrift für Nationalokonomie,* suppl. 2: 127–56.

Borner, Silvio, Aymo Brunetti, and Beatrice Weder. 1995. *Political Credibility and Economic Development.* New York: St. Martin's.

Boston, Jonathan. 1993. "Reshaping Social Policy in New Zealand." *Fiscal Studies* 14 (3): 64–85.

Brennan, Geoffrey, and James M. Buchanan. 1985. *The Reason of Rules: Constitutional Political Economy.* Cambridge: Cambridge University Press.

Bristow, John A., and Declan McDonagh, eds. 1986. *Public Expenditure: The Key Issues.* Dublin: Institute of Public Administration.

Buchanan, James M. 1994. "Lagged Implementation as an Element in Constitutional Strategy." *European Journal of Political Economy* 10 (May): 11–26.

———, Charles K. Rowley, and Robert D. Tollison, eds. 1987. *Deficits.* New York: Basil Blackwell.

Comin, Francisco. 1985. *Fuentes Cuantitativas para el estudio del Sector Público en España, 1801–1980.* Madrid: Instituto de Estudios Fiscales.

Commission of the European Communities. 1995. *General Government Receipts, Expenditures, and Gross Debts.* Brussels: Commission of the European Communities.

Connell, W. F. 1980. *A History of Education in the Twentieth Century World.* New York: Teachers College Press.

Delorme, Robert, and Christine Andre. 1983. *L'Etat et l'Economie: Un Essai d'Explication de l'Evolution des Dépenses Publiques en France, 1870–1980.* Paris: Seuil.

Fernández Acha, Valentin. 1976. *Datos Básicos para la Historia Financiera de España (1850–1975).* Madrid: Ministerio de Hacienda, Instituto de Estudios Fiscales.

Forte, Francesco, and Alan T. Peacock. 1985. *Public Expenditure and Government Growth*. Oxford: Basil Blackwell.

Foster, R. A., and S. E. Stewart. 1991. *Australian Economic Statistics, 1949–50 to 1989–90*. Sydney: Reserve Bank of Australia.

Gomez-Ibañez, Jose, and John R. Meyer. 1993. *Going Private: The International Experience with Transport Privatization*. Washington, DC: The Brookings Institution.

Heller, Walter W. 1966. *New Dimensions of Political Economy*. Cambridge: Harvard University Press.

International Monetary Fund. Various issues. *Government Finance Statistics*. Washington, DC: International Monetary Fund.

————. Various issues. *International Financial Statistics*. Washington, DC: International Monetary Fund.

James, Estelle. 1984. "Benefits and Costs of Privatized Public Services: Lessons from the Dutch Educational System." *Comparative Education Review* 28:605–24.

Keynes, John Maynard. 1926. *The End of Laissez-Faire*. London: Hogarth.

————. 1936/47. *The General Theory of Employment, Interest and Money*. London: Macmillan.

Kotlikoff, Laurence J. 1995. "Privatization of Social Security: How It Works and Why It Matters." In *Tax Policy and the Economy*, edited by James M. Poterba. NBER Conference Report. Cambridge: MIT Press.

Leroy-Beaulieu, Paul. 1888. *Traité de la Science des Finances*. Paris: Guillaumin.

Levitt, M. S., and M. A. S. Joyce. 1987. *The Growth and Efficiency of Public Spending*. Cambridge: Cambridge University Press.

Mitchell, Brian R. 1983. *International Historical Statistics: The Americas and Australasia*. Detroit: Gale.

————. 1992. *International Historical Statistics: Europe, 1750–1988*. 3d ed. New York: Stockton.

————. 1995. *International Historical Statistics: Africa, Asia, and Oceania, 1750–1988*. 2d rev. ed. New York: Stockton.

Moser, Peter. 1994. "Constitutional Protection of Economic Rights: The Swiss and U.S. Experience in Comparison." *Constitutional Political Economy* 5 (Winter): 61–79.

Mueller, Dennis C. 1986. *The Growth of Government: A Public Choice Perspective*. DM/86/33. Washington, DC: International Monetary Fund.

Musgrave, Richard A. 1959. *The Theory of Public Finance: A Study in Public Economy*. New York: McGraw-Hill.

New Zealand, Department of Finance. 1986. *Statement on Government Expenditure Reform*. Wellington: Government Printer.

————. Treasury Department. 1990. *Briefing to the Incoming Government*. Wellington: Treasury Department.

Okawa, Kazushi. 1979. *Estimates of Long-Term Economic Statistics of Japan since 1868*. Tokyo: Toyo Keizai Shinpo Sha.

Okun, Arthur M. 1970. *The Political Economy of Prosperity*. Washington, DC: Brookings Institution.

Organization for Economic Cooperation and Development. 1992. *Historical Statistics, 1960–1990*. Paris: OECD.

————. 1994a. *Economic Outlook*. No. 55. Paris: OECD.

————. 1994b. *New Orientations for Social Policy*. Paris: OECD.

————. 1994c. *Trends in International Migration: Continuous Reporting System on Migration.* Paris: OECD.

————. 1994d. *The Reforms of Health Care Systems: A Review of Seventeen OECD Countries.* Paris: OECD.

————. 1995a. *Economic Outlook.* No. 56. Paris: OECD.

————. 1995b. *Main Science and Technology Indicators: Issues for 1994.* Paris: OECD.

————. 1995c. *Main Economic Indicator.* Paris: OECD.

Peacock, Alan. 1985. "Macro-economic Controls of Spending as a Device for Improving Efficiency in Government." In *Public Expenditure and Government Growth,* edited by Francesco Forte and Alan Peacock. Oxford: Basil Blackwell.

————. 1986. "The Political Economy of the Public Expenditure." In *Public Expenditure: The Key Issues,* edited by John A. Bristow and Declan McDonagh. Dublin: Institute of Public Administration.

————. 1992. *Public Choice Analysis in Historical Perspective.* Cambridge: Cambridge University Press.

————, and Jack Wiseman. 1961. *The Growth of Public Expenditure in the United Kingdom.* Princeton: Princeton University Press.

Pommerehne, Werner W., and Friedrich Schneider. 1982. "Unbalanced Growth between Public and Private Sectors: An Empirical Examination." In *Public Finance and Public Employment,* edited by Robert H. Haveman. Detroit: Wayne State University Press.

Rimlinger, Gaston V. 1971. *Welfare Policy and Industrialization in Europe, America, and Russia.* New York: Wiley.

Roberti, Paolo. 1989. "Some Critical Reflections on the Principles and Instruments of the Welfare State." *Labour: Review of Labour Economics and Industrial Relations* 3:95–125.

Schuknecht, Ludger. 1992. *Trade Protection in the European Community.* Chur: Harwood Academic.

Scott, Graham. 1995. "Government Reform in New Zealand." International Monetary Fund. Mimeo.

Smith, Adam. 1937. *An Inquiry into the Nature and Causes of the Wealth of Nations.* Rpt. New York: Modern Library.

Solimano, Andrés. 1994. "After Socialism and Dirigisme: Which Way Now?" In *Rebuilding Capitalism: Alternative Roads after Socialism and Dirigisme,* edited by Andrés Solimano, Osvaldo Sunkel, and Mario I. Blejer. Ann Arbor: University of Michigan Press.

Tanzi, Vito. 1985. "Monetary Policy and Control of Public Expenditure." In *Public Expenditure and Government Growth,* edited by Francesco Forte and Alan Peacock. Oxford: Basil Blackwell.

————. 1986. "Public Expenditure and Public Debt." In *Public Expenditure: The Key Issues,* edited by John Bristow and Declan McDonagh. Dublin: Institute of Public Administration.

————. 1995. *Government Role and the Efficiency of Policy Instruments.* IMF Working Paper 95/100. Washington, DC: International Monetary Fund.

————, and Domenico Fanizza. 1995. "Fiscal Deficit and Public Debt in Industrial

Countries, 1970–1994." IMF Working Paper 95/49. Washington, DC: International Monetary Fund.

———, and Mark Lutz. 1993. "Interest Rates and Government Debt: Are the Linkages Global Rather Than National?" In *The Political Economy of Government Debt,* edited by H. A. A. Verbon and F. A. A. M. van Winden. Amsterdam: North-Holland.

UNESCO. 1993. *World Education Report, 1993.* Paris: UNESCO.

United Nations Development Programme. 1993. *Human Development Report, 1993.* New York: Oxford University Press for the UNDP.

———. 1994. *Human Development Report, 1994.* New York: Oxford University Press for the UNDP.

U.S. Bureau of the Census. 1975. *Historical Statistics of the United States: Colonial Times to 1970.* Washington, DC: Government Printing Office.

Van der Gaag, J. 1995. *Private and Public Initiatives: Working Together for Health and Education.* Washington, DC: World Bank.

Velasco, Andres. 1994. "The State and Economic Policy: Chile, 1952–92." In *The Chilean Economy: Policy Lessons and Challenges,* edited by Barry Bosworth, Rudiger Dornbush, and Paul Laban. Washington, DC: Brookings Institution.

Walford, Geoffrey. 1989. *Private Schools in Ten Countries: Policy and Practice.* London: Routledge.

Weck-Hannemann, Hannelore, Werner W. Pommerehne, and Bruno S. Frey. 1984. *Schattenwirtschaft.* Munich: Vahlen.

World Bank. 1993a. *Social Indicators of Development, 1993.* Washington, DC: World Bank.

———. 1993b. *World Development Report, 1993.* New York: Oxford University Press.

———. 1994a. *Averting the Old Age Crisis.* Oxford: Oxford University Press.

———. 1994b. *Social Indicators of Development, 1994.* Washington, DC: World Bank.

———. 1995. *Bureaucrats in Business: The Economics and Politics of Government.* World Bank Policy Research Report 1020–0851. Washington, DC: World Bank.

———. Various issues. *World Tables.* Washington, DC: World Bank.

Young, David W. 1990. "Privatizing Health Care: Caveat Emptor." *International Journal of Health Planning and Management* 5:237–70.

CHAPTER 10

Reforming the State: Political Accountability and Economic Intervention

Adam Przeworski

If markets efficiently allocate all resources to uses, then any state intervention is a source of inefficiency. If efficiency is the goal, the goal of state reform is obvious: the state must be prevented from intervening in the economy. But, if there are ways in which market allocations can be improved, then the institutional question becomes more complex: how to enable the state to do what it should while preventing it from doing what it should not?

To satisfy these constraints, governments must know what to do, have instruments for effective intervention in the economy, have incentives to intervene well, and be punishable when they do not. The design problem is to find institutional arrangements that support these conditions, given that economic agents have information governments do not observe and public officials have information citizens do not observe. If such institutions can be and are well designed, an economy subject to state intervention is superior to one with no role for the state. If they are not, the welfare consequences of an interventionist state cannot be unambiguously assessed.

What one thinks about the proper role of the state depends on one's model of the economy as well as of the state itself. One question is: "What is there for the state to do?" The other is: "What kind of a state will do all and only what it should?" My argument is that the quality of state intervention in the economy depends to a large extent on the effectiveness of mechanisms by which governments are forced to account to the public for their actions. Governments may fail to regulate effectively because they do not know how to or because they have no incentives to do so. The specter of self-interested politicians and bureaucrats haunts the theory of regulation: there is no reason, we are told, to expect government officials to be motivated by something other than everyone else, namely, private self-interest. Yet, even if government officials have no sense of public service, and many do, under democracy they are subject not only to the rule of law but to mechanisms of accountability, primarily but not exclusively elections. Well-designed political institutions would cause governments to engage mostly in socially desirable economic interventions regardless of their motives. Hence, in my view, the reform of the state should be oriented not toward limiting the role of governments in the economy but toward equipping them for this role and making them accountable to citizens.

I proceed as follows. In section 1, I briefly review controversies concerning the relation between the state and the economy. In section 2, I draw consequences of the economic theory of incomplete markets and imperfect information for our understanding of this relation. In section 3, I argue that well-designed institutions would allow and induce governments to intervene in the economy in a way that would be constrained Pareto superior to an economy with a noninterventionist state. In section 4, which is the only original contribution of this chapter, I discuss how citizens can control governments. In section 5, I propose the limits of state intervention and contrast my argument with alternative projects of state reform.

These notes are but a preliminary sketch. I deliberately abstain from two subjects that are directly relevant to the topic: the economic content of desirable state interventions and any details of implementation theory. My purpose is only to formulate an agenda, not to provide operational answers.

1. The State and the Economy:
Contrasting Perspectives

Debates about the proper role of the state in the economy run around in circles in which arguments about market failures are countered with claims about regulatory failures.

In a Walrasian economy, markets are complete, information is perfect, and there are no public goods, externalities, transaction costs, or increasing returns. Since under these assumptions the market generates the first-best allocation of resources, there is no place for the state in this framework. State intervention, in any form or fashion, is but a transfer of income, and, in turn, transfers of income, by making rates of return diverge from the competitive allocation, reduce incentives and misinform about opportunities. This conclusion follows directly from the model of the economy: since the state has nothing to contribute, anything it does is pernicious. The function that relates consumer surplus (or, as Morey [1984] points out, often confusedly in this literature, welfare) to government intervention is thus monotonically downward sloping. Yet this is an assumption, not a conclusion.[1]

Yet the very fact that this model has to be characterized at least in part negatively—by the absences of public goods, externalities, transaction costs, and increasing returns—indicates an immediate problem. In the presence of these "failures," markets no longer allocate efficiently. This is the observation that underlay the doctrine of state intervention enshrined in the 1959 Bad Godesberg Programme of the German Social Democratic Party (SPD): "markets whenever possible, the state when necessary." The general prescription that emerged from this observation was that markets should be left alone to do what they do well, that is, allocate private goods in those cases in which the private rate of return does not deviate from the social rate, while the state should provide goods nonrival in consumption, facilitate transactions, correct externalities, and regulate monopolies due to increasing returns. As Arrow (1971, 137) optimistically put it, "when the market fails to achieve an optimal state, society will, to some extent at least, recognize the gap, and nonmarket social institutions will arise attempting to bridge it."

Neoliberals attacked this view in several ways: (1) by arguing that, in the absence of transaction costs, market imperfections can be efficiently dealt with by the market under a suitable reassignment of property rights (Coase 1960); (2) by pointing out that the notion of market imperfections, including public goods, is unclear and no theory specifies them ex ante (Stigler 1975, 110); (3) by remarking that even if the market fails to act efficiently there is no guarantee that the state would do any better (Stigler 1975, chap. 7; for a classification of "public failures," see Wolf 1979); and (4) by claiming that public goods are produced not because they are beneficial to the public that demands them but because they are profitable to the special interests that supply them (Stigler 1975; Shepsle 1979; Shepsle and Weingast 1981).

Neoliberals maintain that prescriptions for state intervention are based on a naive model of an omniscient and benevolent state.[2] They claim that the reason the state intervenes is the same as that for any other economic action: the private self-interest of someone. Hence, while the state is necessary for an economy to function, it can and does damage the economy. Here lies the fundamental dilemma of economic liberalism: "The economist recognizes that government can do some things better than the free market can do but he has no reason to believe that democratic processes will keep government from exceeding the limits of optimal intervention" (Posner 1987, 21). Indeed, analyses of the downfall of Keynesianism presented in the middle 1970s, whether from the left (Habermas 1975), the center (Skidelsky 1977), or the right (Stigler 1975), were almost identical: the state became powerful, and for this reason it offered an attractive target for rent seeking by private interests. As a result, the state was permeated with special interests, private logic prevailed, and the internal cohesion of state interventions disintegrated.

Thus, the goal of "constitutional" economics became to disable state interventions, particularly those that discriminate among private projects, respond to current economic conditions, or directly transfer incomes. Thus, for example, in Posner's (1987, 28) view, "a government strong enough to maintain law and order, but too weak to launch and implement ambitious schemes of economic regulation or to engage in extensive redistribution, is probably the optimal government for economic growth." The neoliberal institutional prescription is to prevent the state from being able to intervene because the very potential that the state could do something is sufficient, in that view, to cause economic damage.[3]

The institutional technology for limiting the state includes (1) reducing the size of public administration, (2) reducing the size of the public sector, (3) insulating the state from private pressures, (4) relying on rules rather than allowing discretionary decisions, and (5) delegating decisions subject to dynamic inconsistency to independent bodies that have no incentives to yield to political pressures. Public administration should be reduced by layoffs because the state is "bloated" and the productivity of public services is allegedly lower than that of the private sector.[4] The public sector should be privatized because governments are supposed to be more responsive to political pressures from public than from private firms. The state should be "insulated" from political pressures so that it will not fall prey to rent seeking by private interests.[5] Economic policy should be governed by rules, such as the gold rule or the balanced budget amendment in the United States, that would eliminate discretion and thus overcome the suboptimality due to dynamic inconsistencies (Kydland and Prescott 1977). Finally, an alternative to rules is to delegate important policy decisions, particularly in the monetary realm, to institutions that are independent of political pressures and thus have no incentives to yield to dynamic inconsistencies (Cukierman 1992).

Whether or not one finds these arguments against state intervention persuasive, the view that, even in the absence of these "traditional" failures, markets are efficient now appears dead or at least moribund. The inefficiencies originating from the absence of some markets and from imperfect (more accurately, endogenous) information[6] are both more profound and more devastating than the imperfections that blemish the Walrasian market. In a recent summary, Stiglitz (1994, 13) put it bluntly: "The standard neoclassical model—the formal articulation of Adam Smith's invisible hand, the contention that market economies will ensure economic efficiency—provides little guidance for the choice of economic systems, since once information imperfections (and the fact that markets are incomplete) are brought into the analysis, as surely they must be, there is no presumption that markets are efficient." When some markets are missing, as they inevitably are, and information is endogenous, as it inescapably is, markets need not clear in equilibrium, prices do not uniquely summarize opportunity costs and can even misinform, externalities result from most individual actions, information is often asymmetric, market power is ubiquitous, and "rents" abound.[7] These are no longer "imperfections": there is nothing out there to be blemished, no unique "market," but alternative institutional arrangements, each with different consequences.

Moreover, some forms of state intervention are inevitable. As Stiglitz (1993, 27) observed: "Governments cannot sit idly by when faced with the impending collapse of a major financial institution. Moreover, both banks and investors know that the government will step in because it cannot commit itself *not* to intervene in the economy. . . . The government thus performs the role of an insurer, whether or not it has explicitly issued a policy." Cui (1992) has shown that the economy can function only if the state insures investors (limited liability), firms (bankruptcy), and depositors (the two-tier banking system). But this kind of state involvement inevitably induces a soft budget constraint. The state cannot simultaneously insure private agents and not pay the claims, even if they result from moral hazard. Hence, if markets are incomplete and information imperfect, moral hazard and adverse selection render first-best allocations unreachable.

Even the most ardent neoliberals think that governments should provide law and order, safeguard property rights, enforce contracts, and defend the country from external threats. And already, even if only these minimal functions are treated as providing utility to individuals or inputs to private production, the entire framework of analysis becomes transformed: there is something governments can do to improve market allocations. The economics of incomplete markets and imperfect information opens a space for a much greater role for the state. The neoclassical complacency about markets is untenable: markets simply do not allocate efficiently.[8] Even if governments have only the same information as the private economy, some interventions by governments would be unambiguously constrained Pareto improving (Stiglitz 1994).

Thus, the state has a positive role to play: the aim of reforming the state must be to build institutions that simultaneously allow governments to fulfill this role and prevent them from abusing their power. This is not a new program: the question of which institutions would enable and provide incentives for governments to do what they should, but would render governments unable or unwilling to do what they should not, has been the constitutional engineering problem since the end of the eighteenth century. But the perspective implied by the new economics of information changes fundamentally our understanding of what is entailed in pursuing the program of state reform.

2. The Economy as a Network of Principal-Agent Relations

Once we understand that markets are inevitably incomplete and economic agents have access to different information, we discover that there is no such thing as "the" market, only differently organized economic systems. The very language of "the market," subject to interventions by "the state" is misleading. The problem we face is not of "the market" versus "the state" but of specific institutional mechanisms that would induce individual agents to behave in a collectively beneficial manner.

When some markets, particularly risk markets, are missing and when particular individuals have access to different information, relations between some classes of actors are those of principals and agents tied by explicit or implicit contracts. In a world with many contingent states of nature, such contracts cannot specify all the eventualities, and principals may, but not always would want to, retain residual control: the right to make decisions when conditions not covered under the contract arise. *Ownership* may thus refer separately to the claim to residual income and the claim to residual control.

The generic problem of principal-agent relations is the following. Agents have some information, which principals do not directly observe: they know their own preferences, they have a privileged knowledge of their capacities, and they may have a chance to observe some states of the world that principals cannot. The principal may be able to costlessly observe actions of agents, or may be able to infer these actions from the outcomes, or may decide to bear of the costs of monitoring these actions. The principal must induce the agent to act in his or her interest while meeting the "participation" constraint—that is, providing the agent with income (or utility) above the next-best opportunity—and the "incentive compatibility" constraint that allows the agent to act in his or her self-interest. An important aspect of this arrangement is the allocation of risks, which may be borne exclusively by either of the parties or shared, depending on their risk postures.

The "economy" is a network of multifarious and differentiated relations between particular classes of principals and agents: managers and employees, owners and managers, and investors and entrepreneurs, but also citizens and politicians, and politicians and bureaucrats. The performance of firms, governments, and the economy as a whole depends on the design of institutions that regulate these relations. What matters is whether employees have incentives to maximize effort, whether managers have incentives to maximize profits, whether entrepreneurs have incentives to take only good risks, whether politicians have incentives to promote public welfare, and whether bureaucrats have incentives to implement goals set by politicians.

Institutions organize all these relations: those that are purely "economic," such as between employers and employees, owners and managers, or investors and entrepreneurs; those that are purely "political," such as between citizens and governments or politicians and bureaucrats, as well as those that structure state "intervention"; and those between governments and private economic agents. The state is thus not the only institution that needs to be "reformed": if the economy is to operate efficiently, all these principal-agent relations must be structured appropriately.

Yet the role of the state is unique since the state sets the incentive structures confronting private agents in their relations by mandating or prohibiting some actions by law, changing relative prices via the tax system, facilitating transactions, and coercing participation.[9]

Let me provide just one example. Suppose that I buy car theft insurance. I drive to my destination and have the choice of parking a few blocks away from where I am going, in a place where the car is unlikely to be stolen, or parking right in front, in a place where the car is more likely to be stolen. Given that I am insured, I take the risk and park in the more dangerous place. Now the state comes in: it taxes me and uses the tax revenue to place a policeman in the dangerous place. As a result, car theft is less likely, the insurance company loses less money, and my premium goes down, more than compensating for the increased tax. This "intervention" is constrained-Pareto superior to the status quo. The state is inextricably present in my relation with the insurer: although our relation is strictly "private," it is shaped by the state. The state permeates the entire economy; it is a constitutive factor of all private relations. Problems of institutional design cannot be avoided by throwing the state out of the economy. They must be confronted as such.

3. Institutional Design for Effective Interventions

It is not my topic to discuss the purely "economic" relations extensively studied elsewhere. Conceived more narrowly, a reform of the state should focus on three classes of mechanisms: those that relate the state to private economic agents, those that relate citizens to the state, and those that relate different state agents (in particular elected politicians) to career bureaucrats. My central thesis is that the efficiency of an economic system depends on the design of these three principal-agent relations.

One way to state conditions for effective state intervention is that governments must be able to control economic actions of private actors and citizens must be able to control governments.[10] Private agents must benefit by behaving in the public interest and must suffer when they do not, and so must governments. These conditions must be fulfilled simultaneously: a government that has the power to intervene in the economy may, and is likely to, act in its own self-interest unless it is accountable to citizens. In turn, if citizens fully control a government that can do nothing to affect their welfare, democracy is impotent.

To provide a full-fledged example of how political accountability affects the quality of state economic intervention, I summarize a model of Laffont and Tirole (1994, chap. 16), as follows.

There are two periods. In period 1, a firm that is a natural monopoly has either high costs or low costs with some probabilities. These costs are observed by the government but not by the public. A firm with high costs can invest to lower them. This investment is socially beneficial.

A good intervention is, then, one in which the government subsidizes investment if the firm has high costs in period 1 and the government does not pay for investment otherwise. A bad intervention is one in which the government fails to subsidize investment by a firm with high costs or the government subsidizes a firm with low costs and splits the rents with the firm.

Laffont and Tirole (1994) investigate the welfare consequences of two constitutional mechanisms: one that allows the period-1 government to commit the period-2 government to not confiscating the income from investment by the firm ("commitment constitution") and one that prohibits this kind of a commitment ("noncommitment constitution"). As one would expect, they find that commitment encourages investment. But commitment is not always superior to discretion: while commitment induces socially beneficial investment, it also allows a dishonest period-1 government to enter into a rent-generating long-term contract. As Laffont and Tirole (1994, 620) observe: "The cost of commitment is that the government may identify with the firm and bind the nation to a bad outcome over the long run."[11] Noncommitment is better if investment brings relatively little gain, if the firm is likely to be efficient to begin with, if collusion between the firm and government is costly, and if the government is neither clearly honest nor clearly dishonest. Obviously, if the period-1 government is dishonest, discretion is better.[12] Hence, different mechanisms of "intervention," that is, actions of government directed at private agents, induce different behaviors of the government and the firm, with consequences for public welfare.

In turn, different public reactions to government behavior affect the quality of intervention. Laffont and Tirole assume that governments want to be reelected. They show that the concern with reelection reduces the proclivity of dishonest governments to collude with the firm. While some dishonest governments will collude (noncollusion is not an equilibrium), by voting appropriately citizens can reduce the probability of collusion. Accountable governments intervene better than those that are not.

In the Laffont-Tirole story, the government regulates a monopoly. Yet this example is generic. In the light of recent research (summarized in Grossman 1990), the state should engage in infrastructural investments not supplied efficiently by private agents and it should pursue measures that increase the rate of return to private projects. This role includes a selective industrial policy that would comprise preferential credit rates for high-technology industries, in which the market rate of return is much lower than the social rate, for projects that suffer from high costs of entry, substantial economies of scale, or steep learning curves, projects that have potential spillovers across firms due to externalities and asymmetries of information between suppliers and buyers. In all these situations, an appropriate state intervention improves on the efficiency of market allocations.

Hence, state intervention can be superior to nonintervention when the institutional design allows governments to intervene in the economy and citizens to control governments. At the risk of repetition, it bears emphasis that both are necessary: governments must be able to tell when their interventions would increase social rates of return, and they must have instruments for effective intervention. But governments themselves must have incentives to intervene well and must be subject to sanctions when they do not act in the public interest. Citizens must be able to discern good from bad governments and be able to sanction them appropriately, so that those incumbents who act well win reelection and those who do not lose them. Finally, the elected politicians must want and be able to control bureaucracies, which are not subject to direct popular sanctions.

These conditions are stringent, and they can never be fully satisfied. The intervention mechanisms may not reach the first-best allocation: if agents are risk averse, tradeoffs must be made between providing agents with incentives and insuring them against the vicissitudes of luck. As Rasmusen (1989, 152) observed, "incentive compatibility and insurance work in opposite directions," and the cost is some inefficiency. Hence, there are some pooling equilibria in which the state cannot distinguish good from bad private behavior and makes mistakes by rewarding inefficiency or punishing efficiency. As I argue later, the political accountability mechanism may fail to support full citizen control over governments. Finally, political institutions may fail to establish effective oversight over the bureaucracy: as Niskanen (1971) and others have argued, bureaucrats can escape the control of politicians and aggrandize their interests.

But institutional design matters. As the experience of the airline industry seems to indicate, regulation must be tailored to fit industries with different characteristics. As empirical studies of government accountability indicate, the ability of citizens to control politicians is contingent on specific institutional arrangements as well as the structure of the party system. As analyses of administrative oversight show, minute institutional arrangements affect the ability of legislators to control bureaucrats (Miller and Moe 1983). In all these relations, properly designed mechanisms can improve on market allocation: regulation can be better crafted and political institutions can better support government accountability and effective administrative oversight.

4. Accountability and Representation

Given Laffont and Tirole's (1994) magisterial treatise, it would be presumptuous of me to delve into mechanisms of effective state intervention in the economy. In turn, I will examine the conditions under which voters can control politicians.

While the language is arbitrary, two distinct questions are entailed: (1) are citizens able to retain governments that act in their best interest and throw out governments that do not and (2) is the threat of being thrown out sufficient to induce governments to behave well? To stipulate a terminological distinction, I will say that governments are "accountable" if citizens can discern whether governments are acting in their best interest and sanction them appropriately, so that those incumbents who act in the best interest of citizens win reelection and those who do not lose them.[13] Yet accountability is not a sufficient condition for making governments act in the best interest of citizens. Even if citizens are able to make governments account for their actions, governments may fail to do everything possible to further their interests: incumbents may accept the possibility of defeat and dedicate themselves to the pursuit of their own interests rather than those of the electorate. Hence, governments may be accountable but not representative. And, in the end, it is representation that matters.

Representation is problematic because politicians have interests of their own as well as some private information, not observed by citizens, about their own motives, some states of the world, and causal relations between policies and outcomes.[14] Politicians pursue their interests subject to sanctions by citizens, which are implemented by means of a variety of mechanisms but most centrally by elections.

The problem of citizens is thus to induce governments to act to enhance their welfare rather than pursue self-interest, often in collusion with private parties. To induce representation, citizens must set up institutions and choose a voting rule that (1) meet politicians' participation ("self-selection") constraint, that is, make it at least minimally attractive for people who have other opportunities to want to be politicians and painful for them to lose jobs;[15] and (2) meet the incentive compatibility constraint, that is, make it in the interest of politicians to do what citizens would want them to do.

The form of the latter constraint depends on politicians' objectives. While politicians may have multiple objectives, we need to distinguish those who care only about getting reelected (the "Chicago" model: Stigler 1975; Peltzman 1976; Becker 1983) from those who seek private rents (the "Virginia" model).

If politicians are only reelection oriented, then they choose policies that maximize the expected vote (or the probability of reelection). If voters are ignorant, rationally or not, then politicians can sell some policies to special interests and use the resources raised in this way to make themselves visible to voters or dupe them into a belief that they are acting representatively. The equilibrium that maximizes votes is therefore associated with suboptimal regulation and a loss of consumer surplus.[16]

Thus, to the extent to which politicians raise resources from private agents to finance parties and campaigns, voters should be particularly sensitive to the evidence of campaign contributions. Contributions by special interests offer prima facie evidence that politicians are not acting representatively. Citizens, therefore, would want to make political financing as transparent as possible.[17]

This model, however, ignores two issues. One is that if voters are rationally ignorant, that is, if they do not acquire information only about matters of little consequence to them, the loss of consumer surplus cannot add up to much: Stigler's (1975) jump from rational ignorance to a picture of a regulatory nightmare is a nonsequitur. If voters are irrational, as Becker (1983) seems to assume, then there are no limits to the damage politicians can do. But Becker's claim that public opinion can be manipulated and votes bought with money is not based on any story as to why people would be so gullible.[18]

The second issue that the Chicago model overlooks is the role of the opposition. Citizens have two agents, not one: the incumbent government, which chooses policies; and the opposition, which wants to become the government. The opposition is an agent of citizens since it wants to win office, and in order to win office it must also anticipate the retrospective judgments that voters will make about the incumbents at election time. Anticipating these judgments, the opposition has incentives to monitor the government and inform citizens (truly or not) about the bad performance of the incumbents.[19] It can win elections if it persuades voters that the incumbent government is not representative. Even if, to begin with, citizens care only about outcomes, not about the policies that generated them, the opposition can induce voters to care about policies if it succeeds in persuading them that different policies would have led to better outcomes (Arnold 1993). And if opposition parties inform citizens about the misdeeds of the government or just about the sources of their money, they lower the cost of information to voters.

Yet the existence of an opposition that wants to and can monitor government performance should not be taken for granted. If all parties are hostage to the same interests, they will collude in hiding it. Under some electoral systems, incumbents of both parties may prefer to collude against all challengers rather than compete with one another (Crain 1977). The opposition can be so divided that it expends most of its efforts on internal fights rather than focusing attention on the incumbents. The opposition may see no chance of winning and do something else rather than monitor the government (see Pasquino 1994 with regard to the Partito Comunista Italiano). And it may or may not have resources to do so.

To summarize, if politicians are interested exclusively in being (re)-elected, then they will behave representatively unless (1) voters are gullible or (2) parties derive financing from the same interest groups or collude for other reasons. Rational ignorance is not sufficient to generate much damage, and gullibility can be reduced by exposure to conflicting sources of information. The institutional design called for to meet the incentive compatibility constraint of (re)election-seeking politicians includes transparency of campaign contributions and a facilitation of conditions for a vigorous opposition, perhaps including preferential public financing for new parties.[20]

The incentive compatibility constraint has a different form when politicians are self-interested, that is, to the extent that their objective is to maximize the present value of the future flow of some private benefits ("rents" above the opportunity cost) costly to citizens. These rents may entail simple theft, a cushy job once out of office, private perks while in office, or shirking on the job. Governments then have a one-electoral-period utility function that increases directly in current rents but also in the probability of reelection, which is, in turn, a decreasing function of rents.[21]

Citizens' problem is then to set up a trade-off for politicians—between extracting rents and losing office or not extracting rents and staying in office— that will induce them to keep rents low. The difficulty, however, is that citizens may not observe rents. Neither do they observe some states of nature that governments do observe. Moreover, citizens have limited knowledge of the causal relations between policies and outcomes (Salmon 1993). Citizens care only about outcomes, but they want to know whether they are as well off as possible under conditions that they do not observe. Hence, they must make inferences about the types of governments they face from what they do observe. And such inferences are easier to draw under some conditions than under others.

To illustrate what is entailed, examine a simple model. Suppose that citizens are not certain whether the conditions are "good" or "bad." Governments observe these conditions, but citizens do not. For example, governments know whether the state coffers are full or empty and whether the negotiating posture of international financial institutions is accommodating or belligerent, while citizens observe neither. Governments decide whether to follow a policy A, which is better for citizens when conditions are good, or a policy B, which is better when conditions are bad. Suppose further that under either condition the rents for the government are higher when they pursue B rather than A, so that governments always have an incentive to choose B. Finally, assume that reelection gives a bonus, V, to the incumbent. To make this analysis less abstract, let me use numerical examples in which always $V > 2$.

Now, suppose that the structure of payoffs is as follows (the first number in each pair is government rents, but remember that citizens observe only their welfare, which is the second number):

		Government	
		A	B
Nature	Good	0,5	2,2
	Bad	0,2	1,3

Under these conditions, citizens are ex post certain that the government is representative if it generates an outcome of at least 3. And they can enforce representation by a simple retrospective rule: vote Yes (retain incumbents) if welfare is at least 3, vote No otherwise. Since outcomes for citizens are uniquely mapped on government actions, the standard retrospective voting will enforce representation.[22]

Things are more complicated when the observational situation is as follows:

		Government	
		A	B
Nature	Good	0,5	1,4
	Bad	0,2	1,3

Now the same simple retrospective rule (vote "for" if the outcome is at least 3) will no longer enforce representation. Under this rule, governments will choose B under good conditions, and citizens will get 4 and will vote for the incumbent, but they would have gotten 5 had the incumbent chosen A. True, citizens can still make unique inferences from their welfare to government policies: they know that the government is representative if the outcome is either 5 or 3. Hence, they can set up a retrospective rule that would induce representation: vote "for" if the outcome is 5 or 3, vote "against" if it is 4 or 2.[23] But this rule demands highly sophisticated knowledge: citizens must know which policy yields which outcome under each set of conditions.

Yet, even if citizens have good theories, if they know the effects of policies on outcomes as well as the government does, they may be still unable to judge whether the government is representative. Suppose that the observational structure is the following:

		Government	
		A	B
Nature	Good	0,5	2,3
	Bad	0,2	1,3

Now citizens do not know if they got 3 because conditions were good but the government unrepresentative or because conditions were bad and the government representative. While the mechanism of accountability is necessarily retrospective, representation cannot be always enforced by retrospective voting, by judgments based on the observed outcomes alone.[24]

Under such conditions, citizens must base their voting decisions on something other than the past record of the incumbent. The data available to citizens comprise the past record of the incumbent in altering individual and general welfare, promises of the incumbent about the future, information by challenger(s) about government actions, promises of the challenger(s), and some guesses about types of politicians conditioned by this information as well as other clues such as identities, symbols, and personal characteristics. Citizens must use whatever information they can get.

Hence, when citizens cannot infer government behavior directly from observing the outcomes of government policies, they are forced to make inferences from whatever information they have. To induce representative behavior, citizens must punish some governments that in fact are acting in good faith. Nor will they avoid rewarding some governments that are acting in bad faith. Complete accountability is not possible.

Yet accountability can be enhanced by a number of institutional conditions:

1. Voters must be able to assign clearly the responsibility for government performance. Empirical research shows that the relation between economic performance of the incumbent and the share of the vote the incumbent obtains is stronger when political parties are stable (Paldam 1991) and the responsibility for the particular policies can be clearly assigned (Powell and Whitten 1993).

2. Voters must be able to vote out of office parties responsible for bad performance. This may appear to be a universal feature of democracy, but under some electoral systems it becomes next to impossible (witness the continued tenure of the Christian Democrats in Italy or of the Liberal Democratic Party in Japan). As Pasquino (1994, 25) put it with regard to Italy, "governing parties seemed to expropriate the voters of the political influence by making and unmaking governments at all levels with very little respect for electoral results."

3. Politicians must have incentives to want to be reelected. This condition becomes problematic when there are limitations on reeligibility and, particularly, when political parties are not continuing, bureaucratic organizations that offer its militants career patterns.

4. While some advantage may accrue to incumbency,[25] so that incumbents have incentives to promote representative policies, it cannot be exploited to assure the chances of reelection.

5. There must be an opposition that monitors the performance of the government and informs the citizens. Indeed, any reasonable understanding of control over politicians must focus on the role of the opposition.

6. Mechanisms of accountability must not only be "vertical"—from elected politicians to voters—but also "horizontal"—from different branches of the government to each other (O'Donnell 1991). The legislature must play an active role in deliberating and formulating policies.[26] Persson, Roland, and Tabellini (1996) show that governments will be induced to act representatively even when voters are ignorant if the separation of powers between the executive and the legislature is appropriately designed.[27]

7. The executive must be able to control the bureaucracy.[28] This control can be enhanced by "fire alarm oversight" (McCubbins and Schwartz 1984): institutional mechanisms through which citizens can directly monitor the functioning of the bureaucracy and inform politicians.

8. There must be institutions, independent of other organs of the government, that will provide citizens with the information needed to improve their posterior evaluation of governmental actions, not only outcomes. Such institutions may include: (1) some kind of a body that will ensure the transparency of campaign contributions; (2) an independent auditing branch of the state, an auditor general (World Bank 1994, 32) in the vein of the Chilean *contraloria;* and (3) an office of the ombudsman that can serve as a vehicle for popular control over the bureaucracy. These are, in the language of an Australian commission, "accountability agencies" (Dunn and Uhr 1993).

The sum of these conditions appears formidable, but they show that citizens' control over governments can be enhanced by an appropriate institutional design: a clear party system with stable parties, vigorous opposition, and limitations on incumbents; an effective system of checks and balances; a decent level of information; and nonelectoral mechanisms for control over specific policy realms or particular organs of the government.

5. Conclusion

The reform of the state should be conceived in terms of institutional mechanisms by which governments can control the behavior of private economic agents and citizens can control governments. The question of whether or not a neoliberal state is superior to an interventionist one cannot be resolved in general since the welfare consequences of state intervention depend on the specific institutional design as well as on the inherited economic conditions. But the neoliberal state is at best a benchmark against which to measure the quality of state intervention: given that market allocations are not efficient, disabling the state is not a reasonable goal for state reform.

Thus, having concluded, I still need to clarify two points: (1) the relation between efficiency and other criteria as the goals of state intervention in the economy and (2) the relation between this vision of state reform and the alternative projects.

I have couched the discussion in terms of efficiency since this is the only common yardstick by which the neoliberal prescription can be compared with its alternatives. Yet there are reasons other than efficiency that may lead governments to intervene in the economy.

Capitalism is a system in which most productive resources are owned privately. Yet under capitalism property is institutionally distinct from political authority: this separation is necessary for markets to exist. As a result, there are two mechanisms by which resources can be allocated to uses and distributed among households: markets and the state. Individuals are simultaneously market agents and citizens. Markets are mechanisms in which scarce resources are allocated by their owners: individuals cast votes for allocations with the resources they own, and these resources happen to be always distributed unequally. The state is also a system that allocates resources, including those it does not own, with rights distributed differently from markets.

The allocation of resources that would result from an unfettered operation of markets may differ from those resulting from a democratic process not only because markets may be inefficient but also because "the people," in its eighteenth-century singular form, may decide to pursue different goals than those that would be maximized when people act as market agents.

Preferences expressed through the political process may differ from those actualized via markets because of considerations of distributive justice. The distribution of income generated by markets depends on the initial endowments, and this distribution may be collectively deemed unjust. Security may be another reason for this divergence. Markets do not and cannot insure against all risks since some forms of insurance involve too much moral hazard. There is no private market for employment insurance because the moral hazard entailed in such insurance requires coercive monitoring (Ganssmann and Weggler 1989). Yet people may want to have more security than markets can provide.[29] Solidarity may be yet another reason: as Diamond (1994, 6) observes: "When a major earthquake strikes, many people make contributions to aid the victims. In the presence of such public attitudes and actions, it is natural for politicians to vote similar contributions from public coffers."

While justice, security, and solidarity are obvious candidates for collective goals that would not be satisfied by markets, there is no reason to restrict such goals to economic ones. Beauty is as legitimate a goal as justice: "the people" may want to preserve opera as an art form even if economic agents are not willing to pay what it takes. Opera may be an ecological good: a cultural stock people may not want to deplete out of respect for the potential tastes of future generations. Justice, security, and beauty are goals the people may decide to pursue even if markets are efficient in the standard sense and even if their pursuit is economically costly.

Clearly, this observation opens questions of rights. Popular sovereignty conflicts with individual rights. Thus, I am not claiming that all the verdicts of popular will, as expressed in the democratic process, should be implementable. Government intervention must be limited by a commitment to individual rights, including those in the economic realm. Constitutional principles are necessary to limit the realm of state intervention. The state must be not only effective and accountable but also limited. But "limited" does not mean "small."

Finally, a few words are necessary to locate this version of state reform among other political projects. We have already seen that the neoliberal project is to disable state intervention altogether, restricting its economic functions to a minimum and constraining economic policy through rules or delegating it to organs that are not representative of the political process. In this view, the state should be precommitted to a policy course so that it will be unable to yield to political temptations caused by dynamic inconsistencies. Such a precommitment imposes a hard budget constraint on private actors, who are then motivated to behave responsibly. I rejected this prescription with the argument that an economy cannot function efficiently under market discipline: the hard budget constraint does not yield the first-best allocation of resources because some forms of insurance are necessary for economic agents to be willing to take the necessary risks. And, even if insurance inevitably causes moral hazards and adverse selection, the purpose of state reform, I have argued, is to find institutional mechanisms that will allow the state to distinguish and appropriately sanction private actions that are and are not collectively desirable as well as institutions that allow citizens to punish governments that abuse their power to intervene. If such institutions are well designed, I have argued, then even if they yield only second-best allocations they can be superior to the unfettered rule of markets.

Another alternative project present on the political agenda is to enhance participation.[30] Clearly, participation matters, since it affects the mix of interests that enter into the maximand of a government that seeks to be reelected. In the extreme, if those who effectively exercise citizenship rights are coextensive with the special interests with which the state colludes, then mechanisms of accountability will be captured. Democracy is a system that grants to most individuals citizenship rights, but it does not automatically generate the social and economic conditions necessary for an effective exercise of these rights (Przeworski et al. 1995). Hence, to the extent that social and economic inequalities limit access to the political system, even well-designed accountability mechanisms may end up merely perpetuating class relations. Widespread participation, and prior to it a better distribution of assets that empower the exercise of citizenship, are thus necessary for the accountability mechanism to work. Yet participation is not enough:[31] unless participants can effectively monitor the performance of the bodies they supervise and have instruments with which to reward and punish, participation will remain impotent and thus symbolic.[32] The question of whether governments can be controlled precedes the question of who exercises the control.

Hence, in my view, the quality of state intervention in the economy depends on the quality of democracy. State reform should be guided by the goal of designing institutions that permit the society to pursue, under constitutional limitations, its collective goals by enabling government intervention in the economy and by subjecting governments to popular control.

NOTES

Several ideas concerning the economic role of the state are derived from conversations with Zhiyuan Cui, while those concerning political accountability derive from discussions with Bernard Manin and Susan Stokes. I appreciate comments by Pranab Bardhan, Samuel Bowles, José Antonio Cheibub, Hernan Cortés, Vicente Donoso, Jon Elster, James Fearon, John Ferejohn, Russell Hardin, Fernando Limongi, Bernard Manin, José Maria Maravall, and Susan Stokes.

1. For example, in a 1991 article, Rebelo declares that "[t]o isolate the effects of taxation from those of government expenditures, I assume throughout the paper that this revenue is used to finance consumption of goods that do not affect the marginal utility of private consumption or the production possibilities of the private sector" (505) only to discover that "[a]ll the models studied in this paper have the implication that the growth rate should be low in countries with high income tax rates . . ." (519). These are but prior beliefs mathematically adorned.

2. These arguments have been developed in innumerable models of "rent seeking" (Buchanan, Tollison, and Tullock 1980; Tollison 1982) and "pressure group politics" (Becker 1958, 1983).

3. The neoliberal nightmare, according to Young (1982), is of two industries lobbying government officials, one to introduce and the other not to introduce tariff protection for a particular industry, and each inviting a politician for dinner to persuade him. In this story, even if the tariff is not introduced, so that no inefficiency is in the end produced by the lobbying, the lobbying itself, the result of the fact that the state *could* have intervened, is a waste of resources.

4. Presumably, the size of the government is optimal when the marginal products of the public and the private sectors, with regard to capital stock (Barro 1990) and employment (Findlay 1990), are equal. Thus, whether the size of the government should be increased or decreased depends on the relation between its current size and the optimal level. For econometric evidence to the effect that the government is too small under this criterion in most countries, see Ram 1986 and Cheibub and Przeworski, in press.

5. How this insulation can be achieved is subject to debate. The most controversial issue is whether authoritarianism is necessary to provide this insulation. Haggard (1990, 262) argues that: "Since authoritarian political arrangements give political elites autonomy from distributionist pressures, they increase the government's ability to extract resources, provide public goods, and impose the short-term costs associated with efficient economic adjustment." Bardhan (1990, 5) takes issue with this position: "[I]t is not so much authoritarianism per se which makes a difference, but the extent of insulation (or 'relative autonomy') that the decision-makers can organize against the ravages of short-run pork-barrel politics." And: "Authoritarianism is neither necessary nor sufficient for this insulation" (1988, 137).

6. One way to think about incomplete markets is that people know that they will be making transactions in the future (Diamond 1994, 8). In turn, a good way to think about imperfect information is that agents learn from observing actions of others, including their willingness to buy and sell (Stiglitz 1994).

7. The question of rent seeking becomes ambiguous in this context: some rent-seeking activities may be a source of economically useful information, and some rents may provide desirable incentives. Hellman, Murdoch, and Stiglitz (1995) argue, for example, that governments should create rent opportunities for financial intermediaries and some productive firms. Mork (1993) argues that, in the presence of positive externalities, rent seeking, even if wasteful in itself, may still be welfare improving.

8. For a devastating critique of financial markets, see Stiglitz 1993.

9. The last point is not simple. In Stiglitz et al. 1989, Stiglitz argues that the state is a compulsory organization that can force individuals to participate in projects they do not want to, most importantly, to pay taxes, the amount of which is imposed (21). What is not clear is when the compulsory nature of the state implies that the state does not have to meet the participation constraint when dealing with private agents. Fudenberg and Tirole (1993, 245) observe that: "In some situations (mainly situations in which the principal is the government), the 'individual-rationality' or 'participation' constraints . . . are not imposed." Yet, while individuals can be compelled by the state to participate in some programs, such as insurance, enforcing compliance is costly. Moreover, under capitalism individuals can, albeit not without some restrictions, withdraw their endowments from productive uses: they can abstain from investing, leave machines idle, or stop working (Aumann and Katz 1977). In turn, incentive compatibility constraint implies that the compulsory power of a state is restricted by its incomplete information (Bos 1989, 120–21).

10. It is reassuring to learn that the World Bank (1994, 12) considers that: "Accountability is at the heart of good governance and has to do with holding governments responsible for their actions."

11. There are good commitments and bad commitments. Imagine the following situation, drawn from Calmfors and Horn 1985: early in its term, the government announces that if unions push wages up and create unemployment it will not accommodate them by expanding public employment. But come election time, the government will want to win and will employ. Thus, the initial announcement is not credible, the unions push wages up, the government accommodates, and the outcome is suboptimal. The government must precommit itself by means of rules or delegation. This is a good commitment, advocated by neoliberals as well as Elster (1995a, 1995b). But suppose that the government did not precommit, the unions have pushed wages up, and election time has arrived. Now the government wants to expand public employment. But the unions anticipate that once reelected the government will fire the new public employees. Hence, the government commits itself not to do so, say, by passing a law of "unremovability" of public employees. This is a bad precommitment.

Consider the difference in the temporal structure entailed in the two commitments by reverting to the analogy with Elster's (1979) Ulysses. In the case of good commitment, Ulysses anticipates in period 1 that he will hear the Sirens in period 2 and makes his decision *before* he hears the Sirens. In the case of bad commitment, he has *already heard* them in period 1 and makes the commitment yielding to their song. And, if governments do bind themselves early in response to the pressures from special interests, their precommitment will not be optimal. (For an exchange on this point, see Przeworski and Limongi 1993, Elster 1995a and Przeworski's comment, and Elster 1995b.)

12. Laffont and Tirole (1994) characterize both period governments as having the

same probability of being honest, and this is why they find that commitment is better if the governments are neither clearly honest nor clearly dishonest. Intuitively, their model implies that discretion is better if the first government is likely to be dishonest and the succeeding government honest; otherwise, commitment is better.

13. An "accountability mechanism," then, is a map from actions and messages of agents to sanctions by principals. Elections are a "contingent renewal" accountability mechanism in which the sanctions are either to extend or not extend the agent's tenure.

14. The consequences of citizens' rational ignorance about causal relations between policies and outcomes are emphasized by Salmon (1993).

15. In Brazil, an equally qualified person earns an income roughly 10 times higher at an equivalent position in the private sector than in the public sector. Under such conditions, it takes a lot of dedication to serve in the government and the cost of job loss must be very low. Indeed, it appears that in the United States political jobs are for many people just a ticket to the private sector. Thus, Senator Packwood reports hoping to become "a lobbyist at five or six or four hundred thousand" dollars per year (*New York Times,* September 10, 1995). Stiglitz (1993, 36) argues that such differences in resources should be taken into account when designing regulation mechanisms: "The administrative resources available to the government are decisive for the effectiveness of its performance. The limitations on salaries of government employees, as well as other budgetary restraints, put government monitors at a marked disadvantage. Is it likely that a $15,000-a-year (or even a $45,000-a-year) civil servant will be able to detect machinations of $100,000-a-year accountants? The more complex the regulatory structure, the more likely that the differences in resources will come into play." But, then, why not raise salaries of government accountants? Note that the government of President Menem of Argentina put some money into the tax collection bureaucracy and increased the revenue from 17.6 percent of GNP in 1989 to 25.0 percent in 1992.

16. The generic version of this model is this: incumbents maximize votes, $V(W,M)$, which increase in W, citizens' welfare, and M, campaign contributions, where campaign contributions are raised by selling policies that are costly to citizens' welfare, so that $W_M < 0$. At the maximum, $V_W/V_M = -W_M$, where the left-hand side identifies the highest iso-vote curve subject to the price of welfare in terms of contributions.

17. The question naturally arises: why should private contributions not be banned altogether? Laffont and Tirole (1994) argue that such a ban would be skirted by some politicians. If this is true, and if money buys votes, then there would be an adverse selection process in which dishonest politicians would be more likely to be elected.

18. We seem to know little about manipulation of public opinion. See Przeworski (in press) and Stokes (in press) for discussions of manipulation concerning economic issues.

19. Note that the press, interest groups, and voluntary associations also play this role (this is Arnold's [1993] emphasis), but the opposition parties have a unique interest in persuading voters that the government is not performing up to the best of its possibilities since their reward is to win office.

20. See Dasgupta 1993 for a model of party collusion and the argument that we should subsidize new parties.

21. In the simplest case of a two-period world, incumbents choose policies to maximize

$U = R + \delta p(R)V$, where

R are the rents in period 1,

δ is the time discount factor,

$p(R)$ is the probability of getting reelected, $p_R < 0$, and

V is the value of being reelected, which may include future rents as well as the utility of being in office per se.

22. Ferejohn's (1986) as well as Grossman's and Noh's (1990) models of accountability are implicitly based on these observability conditions.

23. This is a "shifting support scheme." See Rasmusen 1989, 149.

24. Empirical studies tend to show that prospective considerations seem to have about the same weight as retrospective judgments do in shaping voting decisions (Fiorina 1981; Kinder and Kiewit 1979; Lewis-Beck 1988).

25. For example, Fernando Henrique Cardoso's policies as the finance minister were deliberately timed to have visible effects by the time of the forthcoming presidential election. The opposition attempted to persuade voters that this was an unfair use of incumbency but these appeals fell flat: voters were ready to excuse the exploitation of partisan advantage as long as they saw the outcomes as beneficial.

26. Mechanisms of horizontal accountability not only force the executive to justify and defend its actions to other organs of the government, but it must also inform citizens. Decree powers shortcut this process and deprive citizens of the opportunity to learn about the quality of policies. By depriving the legislature of its deliberative function and the citizens of the information about the relative merits of alternative policies, decrees reduce the effectiveness of accountability mechanisms. Indeed, rule by decree should create a presumption that the government is hiding from citizens, as well as legislators, some of its reasons for choosing particular policies.

27. Their model, however, ignores the role of political parties, which can act as a mechanism of collusion between formal powers.

28. In spite of the obvious importance of the problem, I have said nothing about bureaucracies since it is yet another can of worms. Dunn and Uhr (1993, 2) suggest that we do not even seem to know how to think about principal-agent relations: "[I]t is by no means clear what place executive officials are meant to play as representatives of the people. Are they agents of the government or of the people? If of the former, are they primarily responsible to the executive which employs them, or the legislature which funds them?"

29. For example, a Polish survey conducted in 1990 showed that, while 72.2 percent of respondents supported privatization, 52.3 preferred to work for state enterprises (*Zycie Warszawy,* June 25).

30. This paragraph relies heavily on comments by Pranab Bardhan and Sam Bowles.

31. Note that I am speaking only of participation through the electoral mechanism. Yet elections alone are a blunt instrument of control over governments: problems of administrative oversight—the relation between politicians and bureaucrats—would be alleviated by direct, popular participation in bureaucratic decision making. Moreover, participation need not be limited to the political realm: there are long-standing arguments for direct popular participation in the decisions of private firms. Yet I learned from comments on an earlier version of this chapter that these topics are yet another can of worms, which I prudently have decided not to open.

32. Note that the World Bank, which does promote participation, is reserved about its effects, observing that "the extent to which participatory approaches yield better projects varies from sector to sector" (1994, 46).

REFERENCES

Arnold, Douglas. 1993. "Can Inattentive Citizens Control Their Elected Representatives." In *Congress Reconsidered,* edited by Lawrence C. Dodd and Bruce I. Oppenheimer. 5th ed. Washington, DC: CQ Press.

Arrow, Kenneth J. 1971. "Political and Economic Evaluation of Social Effects and Externalities." In *Frontiers of Quantitative Economics,* edited by M. D. Intriligator. Amsterdam: North-Holland.

Aumann, Robert J., and Mordecai Katz. 1977. "Power and Taxes." *Econometrica* 45:1137–61.

Bardhan, Pranab. 1988. "Comment on Gustav Ranis' and John C. H. Fei's 'Development Economics: What Next?'" In *The State of Development Economics: Progress and Perspectives,* edited by Gustav Ranis and T. Paul Schultz. Oxford: Basil Blackwell.

———. 1990. "Symposium on the State and Economic Development." *Journal of Economic Perspectives* 4:3–9.

Barro, Robert J. 1990. "Government Spending in a Simple Model of Endogenous Growth." *Journal of Political Economy* 98:S103–26.

Becker, Gary S. 1958. "Competition and Democracy." *Journal of Law and Economics* 1:105–9.

———. 1983. "A Theory of Competition among Pressure Groups for Political Influence." *Quarterly Journal of Economics* 98:371–400.

Bos, Dieter. 1989. "Comments 3." In *The Economic Role of the State,* by Joseph E. Stiglitz et al., edited by Arnold Heertje. Oxford: Basil Blackwell.

Breyer, Stephen. 1993. *Breaking the Vicious Circle: Toward Effective Risk Regulation.* Cambridge: Harvard University Press.

Buchanan, J. M., R. Tollison, and Gordon Tullock, eds. 1980. *Toward a Theory of the Rent-Seeking Society.* College Station: Texas A&M University Press.

Calmfors, Lars, and Henrik Horn. 1985. "Classical Unemployment, Accommodation Policies and the Adjustment of Real Wages." *Scandinavian Journal of Economics* 87:234–61.

Cheibub, José Antonio, and Adam Przeworski. In press. "An Econometric Evaluation of the Impact of Government Spending on Economic Growth." In *Democracy,* edited by Albert Breton, Pierre Salmon, and Ronald Wintrobe. Cambridge: Cambridge University Press.

Coase, R. H. 1960. "The Problem of Social Cost." *Journal of Law and Economics* 3:1–44.

Cowden, Jonathan A., and Thomas Hartley. 1992. "Complex Measures and Sociotropic Voting." *Political Analysis* 4:75–95.

Crain, Mark W. 1977. "On the Structure and Stability of Political Markets." *Journal of Political Economy* 85:829–42.

Cui, Zhiyuan. 1992. "Incomplete Markets and Constitutional Democracy." University of Chicago. Manuscript.

Cukierman, Alex. 1992. *Central Bank Strategy, Credibility, and Independence.* Cambridge: MIT Press.

Dasgupta, Partha. 1993. *An Inquiry into Well-Being and Destitution.* Oxford: Clarendon.

Destler, I. M. 1992. *American Trade Politics.* 2d ed. Washington, DC: Institute for International Economics.

Dewatripont, M., and G. Roland. 1992. "Economic Reform and Dynamic Political Constraints." *Review of Economic Studies* 59:703–30.

Diamond, Peter. 1994. "On the Political Economy of Trade: Notes of a Social Insurance Analyst." Paper prepared for a conference to celebrate Jagdish Bhagwati's sixtieth birthday, November 11–12.

Dunn, Delmer D., and John Uhr. 1993. "Accountability and Responsibility in Modern Democratic Governments." Paper presented at the annual meeting of the American Political Science Association, Washington, DC, September 2–5.

Elster, Jon. 1979. *Ulysses and the Sirens: Studies in Rationality and Irrationality.* Cambridge: Cambridge University Press.

———. 1995a. "The Impact of Constitutions on Economic Performance." In *Proceedings of the World Bank Annual Conference on Development Economics,* with comments by Adam Przeworski and Pranab Bardhan. Washington, DC: World Bank.

———. 1995b. "Ulysses Revisited." Columbia University. Manuscript.

Ferejohn, John A. 1986. "Incumbent Performance and Electoral Control." *Public Choice* 50:5–25.

Findlay, Ronald. 1990. "The New Political Economy: Its Explanatory Power for the LDCs." *Economics and Politics* 2:193–221.

Fiorina, M. P. 1981. *Retrospective Voting in American National Elections.* New Haven: Yale University Press.

Fudenberg, Drew, and Jean Tirole. 1993. *Game Theory.* Cambridge: MIT Press.

Ganssmann, Heiner, and R. Weggler, 1989. "Interests in the Welfare State." In W. Vaeth, ed. *Political Regulation in the 'Greate Crisis'.* Berlin: Sigma.

Grossman, Gene M. 1990. "Promoting New Industrial Activities: A Survey of Recent Arguments and Evidence." *OECD Economic Studies* 14:87–125.

Grossman, Herschel I., and Suk Jae Noh. 1990. "A Theory of Kleptocracy with Probabilistic Survival and Reputation." *Economics and Politics* 2:157–71.

Habermas, Jürgen. 1975. *Legitimation Crisis.* Boston: Beacon.

Haggard, Stephan. 1990. *Pathways from Periphery: The Politics of Growth in the Newly Industrializing Countries.* Ithaca: Cornell University Press.

Hellmann, Thomas, Kevin Murdock, and Joseph Stiglitz. 1995. "Financial Restraint: Towards a New Paradigm." Paper prepared for the World Bank EDI workshop Roles of Government in East Asian Economies, Stanford University, February 10–11.

Kinder, Donald R., and D. Roderick Kiewit. 1979. "Economic Discontent and Political Behavior: The Role of Personal Grievances and Collective Economic Judgements in Congressional Voting." *American Journal of Political Science* 23:495–517.

Kydland, Finn E., and Edward C. Prescott. 1977. "Rules Rather than Discretion: The Inconsistency of Optimal Plans." *Journal of Political Economy* 85:473–91.

Laffont, Jean-Jacques, and Jean Tirole. 1994. *A Theory of Incentives in Procurement and Regulation.* Cambridge: MIT Press.

Lewis-Beck, M. S. 1988. *Economic and Elections: The Major Western Democracies.* Ann Arbor: University of Michigan Press.

Manin, Bernard. 1995. *Principes du gouvernement représentatif.* Paris: Calmann-Lévy.

———, Adam Przeworski, and Susan Stokes. 1995. "Democratic Accountability via Elections." Working Paper. Chicago Center on Democracy, University of Chicago.

McCubbins, Matthew, and Thomas Schwartz. 1984. "Congressional Oversight Overlooked: Police Patrols versus Fire Alarms." *American Journal of Political Science* 28:165–79.

Miller, Gary, and Terry M. Moe. 1983. "Bureaucrats, Legislators, and the Size of Government." *American Political Science Review* 77:297–322.

Morey, E. R. 1984. "Confuser Surplus." *American Economic Review* 74:163–73.

Mork, Knut Anton. 1993. "Living with Lobbying: A Growth Policy Co-opted by Lobbyists Can Be Better Than No Growth Policy at All." In *Endogenous Growth,* edited by Torben M. Andersen and Karl O. Moene. Oxford: Basil Blackwell.

Niskanen, William A. 1971. *Bureaucracy and Representative Government.* Chicago: University of Chicago Press.

O'Donnell, Guillermo. 1991. "Delegative Democracy?" East-South System Transformations Working Paper #21, University of Chicago.

Paldam, Martin. 1991. "How Robust Is the Vote Function? A Study of Seventeen Nations over Four Decades." In *Economics and Politics: The Calculus of Support,* edited by Helmuth Northop, Michael S. Lewis-Beck, and Jean-Dominique Lafay. Ann Arbor: University of Michigan Press.

Pasquino, Gianfranco. 1994. "Shaping a Better Republic? The Italian Case in a Comparative Perspective." Working Paper 62. Madrid: Instituto Juan March de Estudios e Investigaciones.

Peltzman, Sam. 1976. "Toward a More General Theory of Regulation." *Journal of Law and Economics* 19:209–87.

Persson, Torsten, Gerard Roland, and Guido Tabellini. 1996. "Separation of Powers and Accountability: Towards a Formal Approach to Comparative Politics." Discussion Paper 1,475. London: Centre for Economic Policy Research.

Posner, Richard A. 1987. "The Constitution as an Economic Document." *George Washington Law Review* 56:4–38.

Powell, G. B., Jr. 1990. "Holding Governments Accountable: How Constitutional Arrangements and Party Systems Affect Clarity of Responsibility for Policy in Contemporary Democracies." Manuscript.

———, and Guy D. Whitten. 1993. "A Cross-National Analysis of Economic Voting: Taking Account of the Political Context." *American Journal of Political Science* 37:391–414.

Przeworski, Adam. In press. "Deliberation and Ideological Domination." In *Democratic Deliberation,* edited by Jon Elster. New York: Cambridge University Press.

———, et al. 1995. *Sustainable Democracy.* New York: Cambridge University Press.

————, and Fernando Limongi. 1993. "Political Regimes and Economic Growth." *Journal of Economic Perspectives* 7:51–69.

Ram, Rati. 1986. "Government Size and Economic Growth: A New Framework and Some Evidence from Cross-Section and Time-Series Data." *American Economic Review* 76:191–203. Comments by Jack L.Carr and V. V. Bhanoji Rao published in *American Economic Review* 79 (1989): 267–84.

Rasmusen, Eric. 1989. *Games and Information.* Oxford: Basil Blackwell.

Rebelo, Sergio. 1991. "Long-Run Policy Analysis and Long-Run Growth." *Journal of Economic Perspectives* 99:500–521.

Remmer, Karen. 1991. "The Political Impact of Economic Crisis in Latin America in the 1980s." *American Political Science Review* 85:777–800.

Salmon, Pierre. 1993. "Unpopular Policies and the Theory of Representative Democracy." In *Preferences and Democracy: Villa Colombella Papers,* edited by Albert Breton, Gianluigi Galeotti, Pierre Salmon, and Ronald Wintrobe. Dordrecht: Kluwer Academic.

Schumpeter, Joseph A. 1942. *Capitalism, Socialism, and Democracy.* New York: Harper.

Shepsle, Kenneth A. 1979. "The Private Use of the Public Interest." Working Paper 46. Center for the Study of American Business, Washington University, St. Louis.

————, and Barry R. Weingast. 1981. "Political Preferences for the Pork Barrel: A Generalization," *American Journal of Political Science* 25:96–111.

Skidelsky, Robert, ed. 1977. *The End of the Keynesian Era: Essays on the Disintegration of the Keynesian Political Economy.* New York: Holmes and Meier.

Stigler, George. 1975. *The Citizen and the State: Essays on Regulation.* Chicago: University of Chicago Press.

Stiglitz, Joseph E. 1993. "The Role of the State in Financial Markets." In *Proceedings of the World Bank Annual Conference on Development Economics.* Washington, DC: World Bank.

————. 1994. *Whither Socialism?* Cambridge: MIT Press.

————, et al. 1989. *The Economic Role of the State,* edited by Arnold Heertje. Oxford: Basil Blackwell.

Stokes, Susan C. 1995. "Democratic Accountability and Policy Change: Economic Policy in Fujimori's Peru." Working Paper 6. Chicago Center on Democracy, University of Chicago.

————. In press. "Pathologies of Deliberation." In *Democratic Deliberation,* edited by Jon Elster. New York: Cambridge University Press.

Tollison, Robert D. 1982. "Rent Seeking: A Survey." *Kyklos* 35:575–602.

Wolf, Charles, Jr. 1979. "A Theory of Nonmarket Failure: Framework for Implementation Analysis." *Journal of Law and Economics* 22:107–39.

World Bank. 1994. *Governance: The World Bank's Experience.* Washington, DC: World Bank.

Young, L. 1982. "Comment." In *Import Competition and Response,* edited by J. N. Bhagwati. Chicago: University of Chicago Press.

Contributors

Oscar Altimir
CEPAL Review
Santiago, Chile

Nancy Birdsall
Inter-American Development Bank
Washington, D.C., USA

Felipe Larraín B.
Universidad Católica de Chile
Santiago, Chile

Harvard University
Cambridge, Massachusetts, USA

Stephen A. Marglin
Harvard University
Cambridge, Massachusetts, USA

Thomas C. Pinckney
Williams College
Williamstown, Massachusetts, USA

Adam Przeworski
New York University
New York, N.Y., USA

Richard H. Sabot
Williams College
Williamstown, Massachusetts, USA

Klaus Schmidt-Hebbel
Central Bank of Chile
Santiago, Chile

Ludger Schuknecht
World Trade Organization
Geneva, Switzerland

Luis Servén
The World Bank
Washington, D.C., USA

Andrés Solimano
The World Bank
Washington, D.C., USA

Vito Tanzi
International Monetary Fund
Washington, D.C., USA

Rodrigo Vergara M.
Centro de Estudios Públicos
Santiago, Chile

Index

justice, Hayek's rejection of
    concept
"justice in acquisition," 21, 22
just society, problem of, 2, 24

Kaldor, N., 51–52, 63n. 2, 68, 96, 97,
    101
Kaleckian models, 63n. 2
Kant, Immanuel, 16
Kelley, A. C., 101
Kennedy, John F., 45
Kenya, 70, 74, 128
Kepler, Johannes, 34
Keynes, John Maynard, 32, 172, 185,
    199, 202n. 9
    as anti-Semitic, 45n. 2
    End of Laissez-Faire, The, 175
    as Eurocentric, 45n. 2
    General Theory, 43, 175
    reason for downfall of ideas of, 210
    on social change through economic
        growth, 39–43
Keynesian hypothesis (KH) of saving,
    94
Kim, S., 54
Kimuyu, Peter K., 74
Knight, John, 78
Korea, 69, 70, 75–77, 79n. 14, 124, 128,
    141, 189, 192
Kotlikoff, L., 98
Kuo, Shirley W. Y., 75
Kuznets, Simon, 6, 68, 160
Kuznets curve, 6, 52, 58–61, 63, 64n.
    11
    in stages of development, 90, 93,
        115n. 7, 121–22
Kydland, Finn E., 211

labor force in Latin America, 141–42,
    155, 156, 158, 163
    See also wage-led growth
labor theory of value, 19
Laffont, Jean-Jacques, 214–16, 226–
    27nn. 12, 17
laissez-faire, 173, 175
Latin America, 140–64
    government reform in, 200

high inequality and slow growth in,
    68–71, 78, 123–25, 136
inequality and poverty in, 144–54
Kuznets curve for, 60
lagging productivity in, 141
low educational investment in, 75–77
low investment in, 122
    by the poor, 75
macroeconomic instability in, 122
1980s crisis in, 142–44, 148–54
populism in, 124–25
redistribution in, 55, 138n. 2, 148
style of development in, 140–44
taxation of agriculture in, 75
Leibenstein, Harvey, 68
leisure, Keynes's prediction of, 40–43
Levine, R., 87, 95
Levitt, M. S., 179
Lewis, W. Arthur, 72, 96, 97, 101
liberalism
    distributive justice in, 4
    inequality reduced by state action un-
        der, 1
    Marxism distinguished from, 19
    neo-, 210–12, 222, 224, 225n. 3
    nonutilitarian, 26n. 6
    Rawls's theory of justice and, 16
libertarianism
    attitude to poverty by, 22
    distributive justice in, 4, 23
    minimal state with free market sought
        by, 1
    Rawls's social contract criticized by,
        3
life-cycle hypothesis (LCH) of saving,
    71, 94–96, 98–99
Lim, D., 102
Limongi, Fernando, 225
Lindert, P. H., 58, 59
Lipietz, A., 57
Lipton, Michael, 78
Liu, H., 54
Locke, John, 16
Lutz, Mark, 181

Maastricht Treaty, 199, 200
Maddala, G., 107